9/09

Pedal Power

Pedal Power

The Quiet Rise of the Bicycle in American Public Life

J. Harry Wray

Paradigm Publishers

Boulder • London

green press
INITIATIVE

Paradigm Publishers is committed to preserving ancient forests and natural resources. We elected to print *Pedal Power: The Quiet Rise Of The Bicycle In American Public Life* on 30% post consumer recycled paper, processed chlorine free. As a result, for this printing, we have saved:

6 Trees (40' tall and 6-8" diameter)
2,678 Gallons of Wastewater
1,077 Kilowatt Hours of Electricity
295 Pounds of Solid Waste
580 Pounds of Greenhouse Gases

Paradigm Publishers made this paper choice because our printer, Thomson-Shore, Inc., is a member of Green Press Initiative, a nonprofit program dedicated to supporting authors, publishers, and suppliers in their efforts to reduce their use of fiber obtained from endangered forests.

For more information, visit www.greenpressinitiative.org

Copyright © 2008 by Paradigm Publishers

Published in the United States by Paradigm Publishers, 3360 Mitchell Lane, Suite E, Boulder, Colorado 80301 USA.

Paradigm Publishers is the trade name of Birkenkamp & Company, LLC, Dean Birkenkamp, President and Publisher.

Library of Congress Cataloging-in-Publication Data

Wray, J. Harry.
    Pedal power : the quiet rise of the bicycle in American public life / J. Harry Wray.
        p. cm.
    Includes bibliographical references and index.
    ISBN 978-1-59451-462-3 (hardcover : alk. paper)—ISBN 978-1-59451-463-0 (pbk. : alk. paper)   1. Cycling—Political aspects—United States.   2. Urban transportation policy—United States.   3. Bicycle commuting—United States.   4. United States—Social life and customs.   I. Title.
    HE308.W73 2008
    388.3'4720973—dc22

Printed and bound in the United States of America on acid-free paper that meets the standards of the American National Standard for Permanence of Paper for Printed Library Materials.

Designed and Typeset by Straight Creek Bookmakers.

12   11   10   09   08   1   2   3   4   5

Contents

Introduction

My early experience with the bicycle was pretty typical of those in my generation. For us, the bike was first experienced as a toy. But it was not just any toy. Although bikes were ridden mostly for fun in those preadolescent days, they also foreshadowed the possibility of autonomy. Bicycles carried us beyond the orbit of parental control into a world where we were more clearly on our own. Such rides conjured images of adulthood, making us feel older and wiser than we were.

But in midcentury Southern California, bicycles were automatically eliminated as transportation options when one entered high school. They were too uncool, playthings for children. It was far better to walk than to be seen riding a bicycle. And so walk we did—at least until the day when we received our driver's licenses, which was a rite of passage difficult to exaggerate in 1950s LA culture.

For the great majority in my generation, this is the extent of their bicycle stories: interesting toys that opened up new possibilities but that in adolescence were left rusting in garages and basements across the land. This was true for me until I was thirty, when for some reason I was attracted by the possibilities the bike offered for recreation and exercise. At that time there were limited recreational options in Washington, D.C., where I lived, but I did enjoy rides along the C&O Canal tow path. And I would occasionally haul my bike out to the surrounding countryside for rides. Then I moved to Chapel Hill to complete a Ph.D. in political science at the University of North Carolina (UNC), where the opportunity for recreational rides was much greater. The country roads and undulating hills provided ideal biking terrain. Additionally, the tight housing market in Chapel Hill caused my wife Judy and me to rent a place five miles outside town. This turned out to be fortuitous, because for the first time I began to use my bike regularly for transportation.

Living out on Mann's Chapel Road was fortunate for another reason. Winston and Marilyn Harrington lived next door to us, and Winston, a fellow graduate student, also biked into Chapel Hill. Often we rode together, and eventually we began to talk about the possibility of a cross-country bike ride. At first this conversation was merely playful, but the idea lingered, grew, and eventually captured us. In 1975, we took a 3,500-mile ride that began in Chapel Hill and terminated in Los Angeles. That ride sealed the deal. Biking became a fixed part of my consciousness, and for most of my adult life I have regularly sought opportunities to ride. After finishing my degree at UNC, for example, I accepted a one-year position at Duke University. From my home, the Duke campus lay about fifteen miles down a lightly traveled road, so I regularly took the opportunity to ride there.

I left the comfortable, bucolic setting of North Carolina behind, however, when I moved to Chicago to accept a position at DePaul University. DePaul is an urban university, located in the heart of a major metropolis. The idea of living in a great city like Chicago was very appealing, and we found a place about two miles from campus. Chicago's biking environment was dramatically different from North Carolina's. Dense urban riding was difficult to escape, and it scared me. For a few years, therefore, I reverted to using the bike for recreation, mostly confining my riding to the few bike trails that existed in the area. Usually I would transport my bike to these trails by car. Over time my attitude changed, but just as important, the riding environment changed as well. I continue to use the bike for recreation, but I am increasingly aware of its utilitarian possibilities. As this has happened, distinguishing these two categories grows more difficult. A ride to the store or to campus is utilitarian, but it is also recreational— and certainly therapeutic. I also find "recreational" rides increasingly "useful" in a number of ways.

For quite a while biking and politics resided in discrete spheres of my consciousness. My professional interests centered on U.S. politics, the subject about which I wrote and taught. Meanwhile, my growing interest in the bike was something that I regarded as private and unrelated to my professional life. Then, a few years ago, DePaul revamped its liberal studies curriculum, including a spate of classes for first-year students under the general category titled "Discover Chicago." The point of these classes was to bring new students to campus prior to the beginning of the academic year for an "immersion week." These Discover classes are designed to take advantage of the fact that our campus is located in the middle of a vibrant city. During immersion week, students and instructors make various forays into the metropolitan area, the nature of which is determined by the subject matter of the classes. Then as the regular quarter begins, the classes meet in the traditional setting to consider some of the academic dimensions of the subject matter. A class on religions of Chicago, for example, spends immersion week visiting various kinds of religious centers in the city and then studies them more formally during the quarter.

It occurred to me that the Discover Chicago rubric provided an opportunity to fuse my previously separate interests, so I proposed a "Biking and Politics" class to the Discover Chicago committee. I designed an immersion week that contained daily rides of up to sixty miles, through various parts of the metropolitan area. During the quarter we connect these rides to some larger questions of politics. The course has drawn a fair amount of attention. It was featured in a story in the *Chicago Tribune* discussing the various ways Chicago universities introduce new students to the city. The class always reaches its limit of twenty-two students, a fact that has come as a surprise to some on the committee that reviewed my initial proposal. The president of DePaul, himself a bike enthusiast, joined the class on one of its South Side rides. People from within and without the university regularly ask me about the class. Whenever I discuss it with those outside the university, it is the political part that attracts the most curiosity. People see pretty easily that riding around on bikes through an interesting area such as metropolitan Chicago can be quite attractive; they do not see as easily how this activity connects to politics.

To the average person, "politics" may mean little more than unsavory activity, as in "that person got a promotion because of politics." What is it that political scientists study, when they study politics? The dirty little secret of my discipline is that political scientists are not exactly sure—or at least there is no consensus answer to this question.

But there is a basic orientation that enjoys pretty broad support among students of U.S. politics. Harold Lasswell, one of the leading architects of the "scientific" study of politics, has rather persuasively claimed that politics concerns "who gets what, when, how."[1] A few years later, David Easton offered a similar but slightly more refined description, noting that politics was "the authoritative allocation of values for society."[2] It is possible to nitpick with this definition, but Easton's formulation does draw attention to a central quality of the enterprise: Politics is integral to the distribution of things we value. Some of these things are material. Should money be spent on roads, education, the military, or distributed in the form of tax cuts, for example? Others are nonmaterial, as in rights to privacy, what may be seen on TV, and whether the Confederate flag should fly over a statehouse. By definition, values are limited and prized, with some being mutually exclusive. And so, people struggle over them. Political scientists describe the character and setting of that struggle.

There is also more to understanding politics than simply observing the process by which values are authoritatively distributed. A political system in one society may decide to spend public funds on universal health care, while the people in a neighboring society would not consider such a policy. To understand the "allocation of values" of a given society, therefore, one needs also to know how people come to care about the things that they do. Thus, political culture, political socialization, and the distribution of power also draw the attention of those who wish to understand how a given system works.

How does biking connect to the sense of politics just described? Is there any connection at all? Within the context of immediate, everyday life experience, a decision about whether to ride a bike may seem straightforward and irrelevant to politics. But of course, the context itself is crucial, as it structures the decision. Consider a familiar problem: whether one "needs" a car, and how one's sense of need is structured by the immediate context. For someone living in Houston, where substantial allocations have been devoted to an elaborate interstate system and to parking spaces and garages, and where gasoline prices are kept low by minimal taxation while rapid transit alternatives are challenged and repressed, the "need" for a car will be substantial. If one is living in Manhattan, in contrast, where traffic is dense, gasoline heavily taxed, parking expensive and a constant challenge, where a viable rapid transit system exists, and where the things one might desire are within easy reach, the "need" for a car may evaporate completely.

In the same way, a decision to ride a bike will be structured by the context of everyday life experience. This may go unnoticed, because bikes are far less intrusive than automobiles. Nevertheless, a decision to ride will be influenced by such distributional decisions as whether bike lanes are available en route, whether the rider can use public transportation for part of the journey, whether there is a safe place to leave the bicycle, and whether showers are available at the journey's end. The levels of accommodation governments have made to biking have a significant impact on the levels of biking activity. It is not surprising that there are far more riders per capita in Eugene, Oregon, than there are in Grand Rapids, Michigan, because Eugene has gone to such great lengths to make biking a viable option for its residents. And one reason Eugene has become more bike-friendly is because it has a lively bike politics. Formal and informal biking groups make claims on allocations, and the institutions of government respond. A "rational" decision to ride a bike is thus structured by the political process.

There are also important but less direct ways in which bikes connect to politics. For example, issues such as traffic congestion, levels of pollution, and physical and psychological health have drawn the attention of government. Safe Routes To School (SRTS), a federally funded program that encourages the restoration of biking and walking to school, is only one example of a bike program that connects to these broader political issues. In addition, there is much talk these days of "energy independence." Bike policy is relevant because bikes do not drain the world of finite and highly contentious energy resources. Political decisions are often interactive, causing the question of bike friendliness to seep into broader areas of concern. These implications will be explored in this book.

The definition of politics referenced earlier begs an important question: If politics is about the "allocation of values," how is it that people come to value the things that they do? Cultures contribute to consciousness, so we must consider the cultural context in which the struggle for bike friendliness occurs. But biking itself also makes an independent contribution to consciousness, just as driving a car does.

What people see, and what they think about what they see, matters politically. And what is seen depends to some degree on how one experiences the world. Put most simply, people see the world differently on a bicycle than from behind the wheel of a car, and they connect to others differently as well. I have experienced this phenomenon firsthand, and it has been corroborated numerous times in conversations with others.

Throughout the world, governments have undertaken a wide range of policy actions in response to pressure from cyclists. Political systems are more, or less, bike-friendly in their allocation decisions. Among the economically developed Western nations, the United States lags in its efforts to support riding. This situation is beginning to change, however, and the dynamics of this movement are illuminated on these pages: why support has lagged and why it is now surging. Many facets of this story deserve attention.

Like the machine inspiring it, the movement toward more bike friendliness has been a quiet one. The comparative invisibility is also connected to the fact that biking is an inherently local activity. Until quite recently, biking "news" has been almost exclusively confined to lifestyle sections of the newspaper. Occasionally there are items about someone taking a substantial journey on a bike, or some attention may be given to a local bike-a-thon, perhaps at the end of the news as a light way to cap the evening program. Although mostly invisible and largely disorganized, there is in fact a huge biking constituency. It is estimated that fifty-seven million Americans get on bikes each year. Biking organizations actively promote riding and congenial biking policies. Often they are allied with bike manufacturers, which have an obvious economic stake in expanding bike use. Many municipalities have sections in their transportation divisions that are concerned with bike policy. And coteries of elected politicians at the local, state, and national levels are sympathetic to bike use. The Bike Caucus of the U.S. Congress, for example, has more than 160 members. Many of these are nominal, but there are hard-core bike supporters in the halls of Congress.

Many bike advocates are motivated by a foundational belief in the sensibility of the enterprise. Such convictions would be irrelevant without a constituency, however. Accommodations to the bicycle do not fall out of the sky. They are the result of political struggle, and as I have sought to understand the nature of this struggle, I have discovered an interesting array of organizations, countercultural groups, and visionaries who are working to make the bike a more integral part of our experience. Each individual victory is small. Some may even be imperceptible to nonbiking citizens as they go about their business. Whether our transportation system will be transformed by the accumulation of these efforts, as many biking advocates hope, is not entirely clear. But they are undeniably having an impact. Recently, our departmental assistant noted to me, "I have never thought about this before, but I definitely am seeing more bikes on streets now than I did a few years ago." That is not an accident. And she will see more in the future. Interest in bike-friendly policies is surging, along with the growing numbers of adults who are riding more. Moreover, the movers and shakers of the biking scene are often smart, always passionate, and they believe strongly in what they are doing. Even when such groups are in the minority, they often enjoy significant political success, and they should never be discounted.

Adult bike usage is growing in all parts of the United States, but that growth is uneven. It may begin with a few folks riding bikes around town. Then a few more join them. A bike lane appears on a street. Formal and informal groups begin to form around the bike. Demands are made, followed by more accommodations. Special events are planned, and biking stories start appearing in newspapers. A Critical Mass bike ride is formed. More claims are pushed. Politicians begin to include bike policies on their agendas and to appoint bike coordinators to administrative positions. These coordinators promote further interest in biking policies, encouraging more people to ride.

This cycle does not necessarily follow the sequence described here, but the phases are familiar. A community like Davis, California, may be well along the road of bike-friendliness, while another is in a much more rudimentary stage. But things are happening so fast in so many places that parts of this book will be out of date by the time it is in print. In June 2006, the *Chicago Tribune* ran a lengthy front-page article on the just-adopted Bike Plan 2015.[3] The article stated that if fully implemented, the plan would transform the city. Two months later the *San Francisco Chronicle* ran a front-page article on that city's Bike Coalition, describing its effectiveness and even asking whether it was too powerful.[4] Such articles would have been unthinkable ten years ago; today they are windows framing the future.

This is a personal book. It is not written with the dispassion that characterizes much of the work in political science. By describing the politics of this movement, I intend to change the way we think about bicycles and to increase their use. The book is therefore itself political, and it is written from the perspective that biking deserves to be taken much more seriously and to be incorporated more fully into transportation policy. To do so will produce myriad personal, economic, and social benefits, something much of the world's most economically advanced nations already recognize. These are what might be called "pull" factors. There are also increasingly urgent "push" factors: Our monotonic, auto-centered transportation policy is discriminatory, an increasing geostrategic burden, and ultimately unsustainable.

Aside from a few entrenched economic interests that might consider biking a threat, almost everyone stands to benefit from more bicycle use. Bike riders obviously have a direct interest in more congenial biking policies, but there is a significant serendipitous aspect to biking as well, for biking benefits those who would never consider affixing their cheeks to a saddle. Many of the benefits of biking are indivisible. Drivers and pedestrians both benefit from the reduced congestion, the lowered pollution, and the greater quiet that increased biking brings. More biking, in short, will make our society better.

I think of myself as a biking centrist. I see no particular virtue in moderation. It is simply where I am. Some are so deeply committed to biking that the car is for them the unambiguous enemy. In contrast, there are things I like about the car, although I believe in our culture its utility is significantly overblown, its true cost unrecognized, and the harm it does too little understood. My centrism consists in a conviction that has deepened since working on this book: that we should move toward a genuinely multimodal transportation system and that we should do this sooner rather than later. To accomplish this, the nation must become much more *bike-friendly,* a term used throughout this book. It simply designates political decisions and public policies designed to encourage use of the bicycle.

Motivating the movement pressing for greater bike friendliness is a broadly shared affection for a simple machine. The nature of this affection is not easy to define, but in interviews and discussions with people of varied backgrounds throughout the movement, I came across the phrase "there is something about a bike ..." innumerable times. This sentiment has been evident since pedals were first attached to the velocipede in 1867. Marking that event, a writer for *Scientific American* noted that the pedal "completely changes the character of the vehicle ... it glides along as though it were alive, and with a smooth grace alike exhilarating and beautiful to behold."[5] A few years later, Mark Twain, who had elsewhere written about the bicycle with his characteristic wit and grace, penned an episode in which Connecticut Yankee Hank Morgan was rescued by "knights" he had earlier trained—on bicycles:[6] "By George, here they came, atilting—five hundred mailed and belted knights on bicycles ... the grandest sight that was ever seen! Lord how the plumes streamed, how the sun flamed and flashed from the endless procession of webby wheels!" The affection and enthusiasm evident in the earliest days of the bike's existence are still widespread among its contemporary devotees.

Chapter One

Contrasting Visions

The Bike Saddle Versus the Car Seat and Why It Matters Politically

Streetwise is a lively weekly newspaper published and sold largely by homeless Americans living in Chicago. This interesting entrepreneurial idea provides employment to needy citizens while creating a product that invites public consideration of issues that often concern the homeless and are often overlooked by the commercial media. Tyrone Moore is a *Streetwise* vendor who works a busy intersection near DePaul. As my office is near this corner, I regularly run into him. To my mind, he is amiable, hardworking, and a pretty crafty businessman. Others agree. In fact, the DePaul student newspaper once ran a sympathetic story featuring Tyrone. But it is also clear that others see him differently. As he plies his wares, a few people are openly hostile. I once heard a well dressed twenty-something mutter "Get a job" as he passed Tyrone, who ironically was busily working at the time. Most people merely seem uncomfortable and mildly annoyed by his presence. Usually people do not return his cheery greetings, and many try to avoid eye contact altogether.

It would soon be obvious to anyone spending a few minutes observing these encounters that people "see" different things when they see Tyrone. Although the varied responses must be perplexing, as far as I have been able to observe, Tyrone accepts them with equanimity. If asked, "Who are you?" I'm pretty sure Tyrone would respond with something like "Well, I'm me." But who Tyrone is to others depends as much on whom these others "are" as it does on Tyrone's essential qualities. There is an additional complication. Tyrone's "essential" qualities can change, depending on the perceptions others have of him. He becomes more or less loving, more or less angry, more or less despairing. And so it is with all of us. We may not think of ourselves as ambiguous, but we are nevertheless mired in varying perceptions others have of us.

The subjectivity of perception is commonly recognized in academic circles, and it has taken numerous forms. I remember coming across one compelling version of this idea in Norbert Hanson's book *Patterns of Discovery*. "Seeing," Hanson argues, is routinely thought to be simply a retinal reaction to some external stimulus. A person sees something "out there," and the eye transmits this sensation in an unfiltered way to the brain. Hanson's insight (think of in-sight) is that vision is as much internal as it is external. What one "sees," in short, crucially depends on who one is. To illustrate his point, Hanson asks the reader to imagine astronomers, juxtaposed in time, gazing at the sun hovering low on the horizon. One comes from an age dominated by Ptolemy; the second from the age where the ideas of Copernicus dominated star gazing. Both are confident in what they see, but both see very different things. If asked, the Ptolemaic astronomer would say that he is observing the sun moving in its orbit around Earth. In contrast, the Copernican would say that at this moment her point on Earth is rotating away from the sun.

Thus, "vision" is incorporated into a broader worldview that serves to organize daily life and to assign meaning to a complex world that resists understanding. It is tempting, these days, to regard the Ptolemaic astronomer with disdain because the Copernican view is so widely accepted. But from the "perspective" of perspective, this does not matter. In earlier days people organized their lives around the "truths" of Ptolemy, and who is to say that we will not one day refine our ideas further about what we see when we gaze at the sun on the horizon?

To Hanson's observations, one could add that what we see is also obviously affected by the equipment that is used in the process of seeing. Obviously many of us see differently, and better, when we wear glasses. Similarly, what we see differs if viewed through a magnifying lens or a microscope. Television offers the illusion of "being there," yet the imperatives of that medium dramatically affect our sense of the world. One study, for example, has shown that heavy TV users are significantly more likely than those who watch little TV to think they will encounter violence when they go out into their neighborhood.[1] These differences hold even when controls are instituted for social class and education. Or, consider the oxymoron "reality TV," in which viewers are encouraged to think that these highly stylized media creations are simply slices of reality.

So we live not according to what is actually out there, but in reference to what we perceive is out there. We simplify reality, perceive it through particular lenses, and bend it to our experience. Although this is not a difficult idea to grasp, in everyday life, we tend not to think about it. Rather, perceived reality tends to overwhelm reality itself. When we encounter someone like Tyrone, for example, usually we do not think, "This is my subjective perception of Tyrone." While our perceptions of him can be altered by further experience, at the point of encounter each of us think we know him. It is possible, and probably wise, to keep a certain amount of fluidity and openness in our interpretations of what we see, but it is impossible to imagine living sanely without having settled on the meaning of large swaths of daily experience.

People develop their perceptions of the world through their own experiences. In this chapter, I call attention to two questions. First, how does the bicycle affect our perceptual world? Second, how do these perceptions connect to politics?

I chose American politics as my major field of study in political science because of a lifelong interest in the United States. One manifestation of this interest is extensive travel in this country. I have crossed the United States via automobile many times. While working for the Department of Education in Washington, D.C., I visited housing projects throughout the country. After Judy and I were married, we spent six months traveling around the country while living out of a pickup truck. By the time my friend Winston Harrington and I decided to take that cross-country bike ride mentioned in the introduction, I had seen lots of the country in lots of ways, and I have seen more since. But in the months leading up to that ride, I was never quite able to put to rest a question bobbing around the fringes of my consciousness: What would we see, really? We knew that the ride would be a test of physical endurance, but would it be anything more than that? Would we see anything more than our front tires for the 3,500-mile duration? As it turned out, I was astonished by what we saw, in part because I had "seen" so much of the country before. My perceptions of the country were altered, and altered significantly, by that ride.

The decisions about the best ways to move people vary from society to society. They depend on a number of things, including cultural predispositions, topography, resources, climate, size, and the distribution of power. In addressing the problem of people movement, no other society has responded with such a single-minded resolution as ours: We are an autocentric society. Far more than in any other country, when people move in the United States, they move via the automobile. The implications of this point are sprinkled through the remainder of this book; at present, it is only important to note that as we move through the world, we also experience it.

As we move about via automobile, the automobile frames our perceptions. The environment presents itself to us in a particular kind of way, and this presentation is not without significance. Like an encounter with Tyrone, we do not usually think about this. On the contrary, we tend to think that our contact with the world is simply an objective experience, not dependent on the kinds of subjectivity we have been discussing. So it is useful to consider how the bike contrasts with the car as a mode of seeing. How is the world different if one experiences it from a car seat or from a bicycle saddle?

The evolutionary trajectory of the car is unambiguous in one respect: It is toward making the environment outside the car subservient—and less relevant—to the primary mission of moving persons inside the vehicle from one point to another. Factors such as the increasing power of the vehicle, the improvement of roads, the uniformity and predictability of interstates, the reconfiguration of the landscape, the increasingly enclosed nature of this modular capsule—necessitated by the requirements of air conditioning, optimal sound systems, as well as seatbelts and the proliferation of tinted windows—are widely considered to be useful innovations. From a certain perspective they clearly are. But, whatever their utility, the innovations also separate the driver from the surroundings.

This trajectory can be seen in the way automotive marketing strategies have changed through the years. In its earliest days, the car was considered a plaything enhancing one's recreational life. Most references to the automobile in the *New York Times* in the early twentieth century were found on the society pages, in giddy reports of this or that socially prominent couple gaily motoring through Central Park.[2] A hit song of the day, "Come Along with Me, Lucille, in My Merry Oldsmobile," caught this sentiment precisely. Even in midcentury, the most commanding sales slogan was to "See the USA in your Chevrolet."

As the car system evolved and further separated the driver from the environment, marketing strategies adapted as well. Today the car is largely marketed through TV ads showing drivers bringing the environment to heel. In these ads, the world outside the vehicular pod increasingly assumes the characteristics of an obstacle course, something to be negotiated as efficiently as possible. Often there is but a single car in the ad, racing through the desert, up some national monument, or trampling restraints in a parking lot. Speed and efficiency of movement are the name of the game. Drivers do not subsist in the environment so much as they triumph over it. The arcade games that prepare youngsters for driving are apt.

In contrast, consider the characteristics of the bicycle. The cross-country bike ride placed these into stark relief, and so I will draw upon that experience to illustrate them. The characteristics are obvious, but their consequences may be less so. First, the rider is the complete source of power for her bike. Her legs are the engine. Nothing is achieved without her effort. Far from obliterating the environment around her, the rider immediately becomes sensitive to the nuances of the terrain. No hill forgives her. On our cross-country ride we regularly asked people we encountered about the terrain along our path ahead. We quickly learned not to rely on the responses, however, because they were so often wrong. Hilly terrain would often be described as flat, for example. At first we thought folks were having little jokes at our expense, but we came to understand that they simply did not know the terrain. It had been made irrelevant to their experience and hence to their perceptions.

Second, in contrast to the driver, the biker is placed more emphatically into the natural or built environment. When it rains, the rider gets wet. He feels the heat, the cold, and the wind. No roof constricts his view. He smells the smells, which can be a mixed blessing. On more than one occasion we nearly succumbed to the distinctive aroma of road kill baking in the noonday sun. This is a special olfactory delight when climbing a mountain, during which time the rider is ingesting oxygen through every orifice of his body. On the other hand, a ride through Gary, Indiana, offers the urban variation of olfactory distress, as sagging oil refineries and steel mills still manage to emit their noxious gases. For better and for worse, the environment is immediately and continuously relevant to the rider in a way that it is not to the driver.

In this open environment, the bike rider is not going very fast. A typical road speed is about fifteen miles an hour, and at this rate things do not pass by very quickly. Rather, they linger and thus become embedded in one's consciousness. Important but small things may be noticed that motorists would not likely see at all. Moreover, stopping a bike is so simple that riders can do it whenever it strikes their fancy. It is not necessary to wait for a roadside turnout, to slow down from seventy-five miles per hour, to worry about trailing traffic, or to unbuckle and get out of and back into a car. Thus, vistas are more firmly planted in consciousness.

Furthermore, bikes are very quiet machines. This quality also directs the attention of the rider toward the environment. She hears things that might otherwise be drowned by the persistent roar of an engine. This unobtrusiveness, this softer passage through the environment, means that others are more likely to be encountered as people instead of objects and that animals are not so quickly frightened away.

One day during our cross-country ride, we casually waved at someone working in his yard in western Kentucky. Two days later, as we pulled onto the campus of Southern Illinois University, this person flagged us down and opened the conversation by stating that he had waved at us a couple of days earlier. He had come to Carbondale to witness his daughter's graduation. We felt a special connection, and a friendly conversation ensued.

Even the domestic animals one normally sees in a rural environment assume new character. On our second day out of Chapel Hill, we came upon a magnificent stallion in a big pasture. He started and then began to lope along beside us. He seemed prepared to run with us all the way to California had not a fence intervened. Cows were unfailingly interested in our meandering. They were so attentive that we eventually began conversing with them. (They are quite good listeners.) Along our way we saw several deer and beaver. We saw a porcupine and a coyote, loping through a gorge in southern Utah. We saw flocks of geese flying north, filling the air with their doleful cries. We saw a skunk but, unfortunately, not soon enough. In a car, many such encounters never would happen, and if they do, the most likely response is worry about not hitting the creatures or getting rear-ended in the course of speeding along the way.

Nature springs to life when one is on a bike. One hears and occasionally feels the rushing mountain stream. Plant life is much more apparent; small bunches of flowers are noticed. Crossing the Mojave Desert in a car invites the perception that it is pretty lifeless, but on a bike the desert floor assumes a new dimension and reveals its rich harvest of improbable life.

Similarly, driving through the Rocky Mountains in Colorado had not prepared me for the sensory experience, and the attendant altered perspectives, of biking through them. I had seen the Rockies from my car, stopping occasionally, but mostly stealing glances at them while making sure I remained on the road. I knew they were beautiful, even inspiring. But in the miles approaching Denver they loomed in turn majestically and ominously in the foreground, and we could not help but think of them as primarily an ordeal. Our goal was to survive them. As it turned out, both of us consider the Rockies the most exhilarating part of our ride. And the exhilaration was experienced in the moment. It was not because we had accomplished the physical feat of riding through them. Their awesome character was enhanced every time we peered down a mountainside and saw a small ribbon of highway where we had been riding an hour or two before. Their unremitting beauty was framed by the fact that we were thrust more directly into the environment and also because it was so easy to stop and soak it up. We drank from cold, clear mountain streams because we had to, and we were reminded of the precious gifts the mountains provided. We gorged ourselves on the pristine air. To this day, when I fly over the Rockies and gaze down at them, they evoke special feelings, and I am bemused that they seem so little noticed by the other passengers.

Of course we had three or four truly awful days on the trip as well. The ride from Glendale, Arizona, to Las Vegas into high-desert winds and without water for forty-seven miles is seared into my brain. Such things are also inherent in the nature of riding. The point is not to idealize bike riding but simply to indicate how perceptions differ on a bike in comparison with a car. That ride, now thirty years in my past, still influences the way I think about the world.

I kept a diary during this journey, and in it I describe a day that came late in our experience. By that time we were grizzled veterans of the road, and the entry conveys a sense of how the bike affects one's perceptions of the environment. This entry is titled "Day Thirty-seven—108 Miles." From Bryce Canyon, we planned to ride to Kanab, Utah, on our way up to the north rim of the Grand Canyon. The seventy-five miles came very easily, however, and as we rode we enjoyed the warmth of the high-desert sun. After hanging around town for a couple of hours, we decided to ride on to the smaller hamlet of Fredonia, an additional seven miles just inside the Arizona border.

Fredonia is a small town, but it had a surprisingly good Mexican restaurant owned and operated by a very friendly couple. There was not a lot in the town, and after the meal we discovered that there was no place to camp. Although we felt sure we could have obtained accommodations in a moment had we asked, we decided to push on. Fredonia sits at an altitude of 4,500 feet. To reach the north rim, still a hundred miles away, we would have to climb to 9,000 feet. Getting in a couple of hours of climbing in the early evening made sense to us.

As we climbed on this warm summer evening, the flora changed, first from sagebrush to juniper and piñon trees, then to ponderosa pine. Struggling up the mountain, the smell of the pine was unmistakable and exhilarating. At about 7,500 feet, twenty-five miles or so outside Fredonia, we decided to call it a day. It was dusk, and we had arrived at a "scenic overlook" turnout. Camping at such places was illegal, but we had long since realized the ease with which bikers can vanish into the topography. Pitching our tent just off the overlook was no problem.

We sat on the edge of the overlook, taking in the view and watching the shadows lengthen before us. Gradually the lights of Fredonia and, in the distance, of Kanab, began to wink on. Periodically we would see a pair of headlights leave Fredonia, moving toward us on the only road out of town. For a while, they followed the curve of the desert road and then would disappear beneath us. In a few minutes they would rush by our camp, hurrying on to the north rim. As they sped by, we felt a strange kind of connection to them. We knew where they had been, and we knew where they were going.

When dusk gave way to darkness, we realized there would be only a sliver of a moon that evening. In the thin atmosphere, with no moon or artificial light, stars filled the sky in astonishing profusion. We lay on our backs for about an hour, talking little and watching the sky. During that time dozens of shooting stars danced across the sky. In the stillness of that summer evening, my mind wandered back over the past few hours. I thought about how peaceful and harmonious, how majestically rhythmic they had been. Prior to our trip, Winston and I would often joke about "becoming one with the universe" during our ride. At that moment it did not seem so funny.

A 3,500-mile ride across land that has been frequently traversed in other ways underscores how the bike influences perception. It also provides time to think about such things. It would be a mistake to conclude, however, that these effects are a function of the length of the ride. They are inherent in the bike riding itself. A person considering whether to drive or ride the three miles to work is more than likely comparing the utilities of the choices, rather than their perceptual consequences. Nevertheless, perceptions will be affected by the decision. Because the world is experienced in a different way on a bike than it is in a car, the rider inevitably thinks of that world differently than does the driver. And as we shall see, these varied perceptions have political consequences.

The issue of perception is central to a course that I teach titled "American Culture and Politics." As part of this class, students engage in various excursions and consider the cultural implications of these. If the course is offered in the winter, we often go to the auto show at McCormick Place. It is the largest exhibition hall in the world, and the auto show is by far its largest annual event. It provides a mother lode of culturally relevant experience. In January 2003, I went with a class to that year's auto show. This was two months prior to the U.S. invasion of Iraq, and the incipient war was a preoccupying national concern. There was much opposition to the invasion and, particularly in urban and university communities, people wearing antiwar buttons were common. One of the challenges of this class is to get students to see the connections between everyday cultural experiences—activities not normally considered political—and politics. As our bus pulled up in front of McCormick Place, I told the class that I would give $20 to any student who saw someone at the show wearing an antiwar button. No one collected.

Now, of the several hundred thousand people who visited the show that year, there were doubtless a fair number of people who opposed going to war. (National polls at this time indicated about 40 percent of the nation had such reservations.) And I would not have been stunned to see, in this throng, a few people who so strongly opposed the war that they were wearing buttons. But I also knew that the odds were pretty heavily against this possibility. Among those who are excited enough about cars to find an auto show appealing, we were not likely to find many who so strongly opposed the war that they would wear a button. The auto show itself cultivated and exploited many feelings, such as envy, desire, competition, and sexual inadequacy that were relevant to the international political context of the day. Think of George Bush strutting on that aircraft carrier a few months later, his manliness accented by his flight suit, proclaiming "mission accomplished." Can one imagine him in anything other than a Humvee?

In contrast, during the 2004 political campaign the following year, I came upon a bike rider at a stop light who had a "Barack Obama for Senate" button on her backpack. I commented that Obama and a bike just seemed to go together. She smiled, but it was clear she was not completely sure what I meant. But there is a relationship here as well. When I took my "Biking and Politics" class on a Critical Mass bike ride several weeks before the 2004 presidential election, the pro-Kerry, anti-Bush sentiment was palpable. Critical Mass rides (discussed in chapter 6) draw a high proportion of biking enthusiasts and are the antithesis of the auto show. The tenor of the crowd prompted one of my students, a staunch supporter of President Bush, to remark wryly that he felt as if he were in the belly of the beast.

The auto show/Critical Mass duality is complex and can be over-blown. Moreover, to say that the bike is used by people who have certain political perceptions is not to say that the bike caused those political perceptions. Indeed, an avid cyclist may well be completely apolitical; others may segment their lives such that connections between biking and other parts of their lives are never made. It is also likely that someone who decides to ride a bike regularly already has norms that are consistent with the perceptions generated on a bike. The relationship between bike riding and values is doubtless reciprocal. A person who considers bike riding as a serious recreational activity may already be concerned about the impact of toxic waste on the environment, but bike riding can deepen that sympathy and elevate its significance in one's thinking. Biking through the world leads one to see the world differently, which may in turn influence how one thinks about politics. Such political effects of biking are impossible to measure precisely because at their borders they are quite diffuse. But I have no doubt that the effects are there.

Trends in modern society are away from general (unwanted) human contact and toward more privatized lives. We rush out of gated communities, embedded in cars, on roads designed to speed us hither and thither. The convenience of ATMs, home delivery services, Internet shopping, and the like, come at the cost of human contact. When we do enter the public arena, to shop or dine, we are sped through lines designed to get us someplace else as rapidly as possible. Increasingly we encounter public space with cell phones glued to our ears or with iPods extending our private spheres. This process encourages us to think of those we encounter along the way as inconvenient, perhaps even unwanted, "others"—as objects. The notion that public space is nothing more than a multiple of miniature private spaces nurtures such attitudes, as well as the idea that others are impediments to our private concerns. This is certainly the case when driving. When we drive, other people, whether pedestrians or drivers, annoy us, and they annoy us all the time. Moreover, safely encased in two or three tons of steel, we feel free to express our anger, which in turn makes others angry.

Mark Cloud lives in metropolitan Atlanta, a region noted for its vast urban sprawl and the traffic snarls this sprawl generates. He has had his fill of inching along Atlanta's concrete ribbons, and in a recent

newspaper column he draws a bead on the source of his discontent—
the polite motorist:[3]

> Hey nicest guy in the world! I think it's just great how you're letting
> everybody cut in front of you. And I mean ev-er-y-bo-dy. Cars … trucks
> … vans … no problem for them, because you stop and let 'em all come
> on in. Man, are you nice.… I sure thank my lucky stars that I'm stuck
> right behind you. Otherwise, I wouldn't get to see such selflessness
> in action. You're like a traffic cop and Mohandas "Mahatma" Gandhi
> rolled into one, unilaterally deciding who shall proceed while sacrific-
> ing your own forward progress for the benefit of others. It's nothing
> short of inspirational to bear witness to your morning rush-hour altru-
> ism.… And dear (Martin Luther) King of the Road, pay no attention to
> those rabble-rousers behind me who keep honking. They are impatient
> fools who are so blinded by their perceived need to "get to work on
> time" that they fail to see the magnificence of your charity to others.
> I'm sure they're all back there pounding on their steering wheels and
> screaming to themselves something along the lines of, "Why doesn't
> that idiot just let one car in and then go? Why does he have to stop
> for every friggin' car? Moron." I'm just guessing that's what they're
> saying … your benevolence serves as a lesson in driving civility to us
> less enlightened motorists who do not allow every other vehicle on the
> road to get in front of us. Please forgive us, for we are selfish. We can
> only dream of a world in which we are as nice as you.… But until that
> driving utopia is achieved, I sure hope I don't ever get behind you …
> again. Because contrary to what Baseball Hall of Famer Leo Durocher
> says, nice guys don't always finish last. The poor saps stuck behind
> them in traffic do.

When people read this column over a cup of morning coffee, it
likely evoked considerable sympathy. Although cast a bit stronger than
many might prefer, who among us has not experienced the feelings
conveyed in this essay when driving? On the other hand, it is worth
noting the particular perspective from which Cloud writes. There is
no sense of outrage expressed over situations in which he has been
the beneficiary of some motorist's Gandhian excesses. He claims an
interest in fairness, but this view is belied by his contemptuous tone.
He tries to shift this contempt from himself to the others behind
him. But he can only surmise that this is how they feel because it is
how he feels.

The point is not to belittle the road-weary Mark Cloud. Part of his attitude is no doubt connected to his personality, but some of it is also related to his situation, which is why so many of us recognize it. He writes as if drivers who let "ev-er-y-bo-dy" into line are rather common. There would be no reason to write if it were otherwise. But is this the case, or is this what some motorists perceive when they are, day after day, stuck in traffic? The context of motorized traffic urges us toward the boiling point that bubbles in Cloud's overheated perceptual engine. Cars isolate us and nurture an alienated, me-against-the-world perspective, and simultaneously cars are the main impediments we face. This is a volatile mix. Like Cloud, our attention is constantly being directed toward those we consider lousy drivers.

The anger and anxiety of motorists are more evident from the saddle of a bicycle, possibly because the presentation of self on a bike is very different from one who is in a car. Consider the bike as it influences the nature of general human contact. Unlike the driver embedded in tons of steel and often obscured by tinted windows, the rider is thrust out into the community and made more prominent by being on a bike. One's humanness is more apparent, as is the humanness of others. There is, as a consequence, a greater tendency for recognition, contact, even conversation. This happens with other riders, of course, but also with pedestrians and drivers. People are less likely to be regarded as objects or impediments, not simply because of their evident humanness but because they are much less likely to impede.

This point also first occurred to me on the cross-country ride. In the weeks before we left, our friends had varied reactions to the idea of a long-distance ride. Most were intrigued and supportive; a few were dismayed. In this latter group, there was an undercurrent of concern about safety issues. This was not just concern about the dangers oblivious drivers pose to bikers on highways. It also extended to a worry about encountering people who wished us ill. We were, after all, going to ride 3,500 miles through areas that were largely unknown to us, and we would be fairly unprotected. Friends worried about our vulnerability on bicycles.

On the fourth day of our ride, I was reminded of these fears. We were riding through the Appalachian Mountains in eastern Kentucky when two guys on motorcycles pulled along beside us. After a minute or two, they motioned for us to pull over, which we did. My thoughts scanned unpleasant scenes in films such as *Easy Rider* and *Deliverance*. As it turned out, they were quite friendly and were merely curious about what we were doing, as our bikes were laden with gear. We exchanged pleasantries for a few minutes, after which they wished us well and motored off. This encounter typified much of what was to come, and we discovered an irony of long-distance riding. We had expected to be somewhat more vulnerable on our bikes, yet as the trip unfolded we felt less so. People went out of their way to be friendly and to help us. They sometimes showed remarkable trust in us as we pedaled into their lives. I think part of the reason for this was, by encountering them in this simple and unprotected way, it was first evident that we trusted them.

While this idea first occurred to me on the cross-country ride, it is also more generally applicable. Like most large urban centers in America, Chicago is quite segregated. Large swaths of the city are known to white folks only by rumor. And for this reason, the thirty-five-mile South and West side ride taken by the "Biking and Politics" class is one of my favorites. Although DePaul works harder than most universities to diversify its student body, the majority of its students are white. About 85 percent of the students who have taken the "Biking and Politics" class have been white, and the great majority of these have never been to the South or West sides of the city. The more adventurous may have driven to the West Side for a Bulls basketball game, parked in a gated lot, and dashed back out to the suburbs immediately after the game. Even though many of these students chose DePaul because they like the idea of a diverse, urban educational experience, the thought of riding through areas that they know largely through rumor and unfavorable TV news stories is daunting.

Students in the class are unprepared for what they encounter: diverse neighborhoods with intriguing, non-Wal-Mart commerce, interesting and rich street life, curiosity, and a great deal of friendliness. They also notice the diversity within the diversity. On these rides there has never been an unsafe incident or a time when I wished we had taken another turn. Undoubtedly, the group nature of the ride has helped evoke these positive responses. Twenty-five riders in a group are novel and invite interest. Kids will sometimes ride with us for a while or ask if we are some sort of "bike-a-thon." But I have

The Biking and Politics class gives students a distinctive view of Chicago's neighborhoods.

ridden through these neighborhoods many times, often by myself, sometimes with one or two others, without serious incident. Once or twice someone may have yelled something unfriendly, and occasionally I have chosen to make a turn before encountering a group of guys hanging out on a street corner, but such instances pale against the overwhelming friendliness I have experienced.

It would be naive in the extreme to think that nothing could happen to someone on a bike in these neighborhoods, or in Appalachian east Tennessee, or in my little yuppie enclave on the North Side of Chicago. But I am absolutely serious about feeling less vulnerable to some violent act on a bike than in a car. To see another as a fellow human being is to recognize commonality. The bike promotes such recognition. And this recognition is reciprocal.

The philosopher of science Abraham Kaplan, postulating the Law of the Instrument, famously noted, "Give a small boy a hammer and he will soon find that everything he encounters needs pounding."[4] Kaplan was reminding academic investigators that the tools they used to observe the world can easily distort what they see. With apologies to Kaplan, we can adapt his law to the matters we are considering here: Give a young man an automobile, and he will soon find that everyone else is a jackass. An exaggeration perhaps, but any reader who has driven a car will understand the point. Mark Cloud is not an oddity. Of course, there are angelic drivers and satanic bikers. Bikers are capable of "road rage," and some drivers serenely go about their tasks. But the central tendencies, the structures, of the two modes of transportation differ, and it is counterintuitive, even unscientific, to assume that such differences are irrelevant to our sense of connection to others.

Assumptions about what others are like have obvious social significance, but they are also politically relevant as they often motivate political action. As noted in the introduction, the substance of politics is the "allocation of values." The manner in which decisions are framed and considered, and the kinds of political policies one supports, will to some degree be influenced by how we think about others. Is this a world in which everyone struggles on their own in a survival of the fittest, dog-eat-dog reality, or is this a world that can be made better by recognizing our common and shared humanity? Many things will influence how such a question is answered, including the perceptions gleaned from how one actually experiences others in the world. Our mode of transportation is relevant to the perceptions we have.

Riding a bike not only influences our perceptions of other people in ways that are politically relevant; it also changes the way one "sees" the environment. Air and noise pollution are more evident on a bike, and common areas like parks more obvious and precious. Polls show that most Americans are concerned about the erosion in the quality of the environment, but this concern does not rank very high on the electorate's "to do" list. While no national surveys isolating bike riders exist, it is plausible to assume their increased exposure stimulates a heightened interest in a toxic-free environment.

Chicago is well known as the "Windy City." What most do not realize is that this nickname was born more than a hundred years ago because of the reputation local politicians had for bragging about their city. There are significant winds here, but Chicago is well down the list of the nation's windiest cities. As I rode my bike through the spring of 2006, however, I noticed that the winds seemed more powerful than normal. Fighting these winds every day called them to my attention.

This might have been a misperception; perhaps I had repressed the memory of past windy springs. Perhaps it was simply connected to the fact that as I get older, everything gets more difficult.

So I wrote the office of Tom Skilling, the legendary Chicago meteorologist and weatherman, and asked how the wind speeds of this spring compared with others. As it turns out, 2006 was the windiest Chicago spring in fifteen years. One of the effects of global warming is that weather patterns become more volatile. It is impossible to say global warming "caused" that windy Chicago spring, but that is not the point. I had asked a number of nonbiking friends if they had noticed the winds, and none had. But I had, and it raised questions in my mind about global warming. Riding a bike caused me to think about the fact that we were having a pretty windy spring and to wonder what, if anything, that might mean.

It is worth noting, finally, that biking not only changes one's perceptions of others and of the environment in ways that are politically relevant, but it also alters one's perception of the self. Political scientists have long noted that a "sense of political efficacy" is an important factor in determining whether one participates in politics. This sense of efficacy is derived in part from one's perception of the external political world and in part from one's perception of oneself. A person is unlikely to be active in politics if she believes her actions will be thwarted by a "power elite" that really controls politics. Low self-esteem can lead to demobilization as well, and it can be generated by a number of things, including whether one feels in control of one's life or whether one feels dominated by factors beyond one's control.

The bike and car affect self-esteem differently. In an age of technological complexity, the bike remains a simple machine and one that is easily mastered. Virtually anyone can learn to repair a flat tire in a few minutes, which is by far the most common mechanical problem bikers encounter. The fact that bike repair and maintenance classes are widely offered by biking organizations, civic groups, municipal governments, and even by bike shops, at little or no cost, also suggests that the underlying norms of the biking community promote a sense of efficacy.

Compare this with the experience of the automobile, which typically confronts its owner as one more technological gizmo mechanically beyond comprehension. As such, it assaults our sense of efficacy. A trip to an auto shop is usually a harrowing experience. We are completely dependent on a mechanic's ability to diagnose the problem as well as his sense of integrity in not overcharging us. He could tell us anything. And often we learn that our "full warranty" somehow did not prevent us from incurring hundreds of dollars in repair costs. Thus, the automobile is simply one more part of our lives that we do not control.

David Herlihy's definitive history of the bicycle shows that its earliest proponents were aware of its influence on perception. He cites a British writer from 1906. Although written in the argot of the day, this entry makes the point:[5]

> The bicycle exerts "a good influence on the youth and manhood of the nation." Outwardly, he asserted, the cyclist becomes, "more generous and more social" and even acquires a greater "love of nature and attachment to his native land." Inwardly, the sport "teaches [the cyclist] caution and gives him presence of mind in emergencies," and even reveals hidden "mechanical or inventive genius." Moreover, the practice makes a person more "self-reliant" and teaches "temperance and self-control."

Writing eleven years earlier, another enthusiast proclaimed: "The bicycle has done more to foster love of out-of-door life than any other invention."[6]

Allen LaFan, a former police officer and current city inspector for Aurora, Illinois, is someone who knows how the bike can transform perception. I first heard of LaFan through a story on a public radio station about a program that put Aurora building inspectors on bicycles to do their work. The story led me to interview LaFan, who was mainly responsible for the implementation of the program. A father of two in his midthirties, he had not ridden his bike since he was sixteen years old. But it occurred to him that he was spending a lot of his time driving around in a car, pretty much "like a lump." He began to bike to work, then to ride his bike on inspections, and ultimately to design and implement a program that put other city workers on bicycles. Now, LaFan's biggest problem is expanding the program fast enough to accommodate the growing interest in the program.

It was actually getting on the bike and riding to work that stimulated LaFan's interest in a broader program. As a rider, the world

immediately seemed different to him. He reported with some embarrassment ("I know this is going to sound hokey!") the positive feelings
about actively being in the environment, smelling smells, hearing
birds, and so forth. On his first day on the bike, he said that he spoke
to more people than he normally would speak to in a month. And
he also reported that people saw him differently as well. "My job," he
says, "is to enforce city codes." This means that he often has to tell
people things they do no want to hear. Often tempers are strained.
But he says much less animosity is directed at him now. He is not sure
why this is the case. But he believes, "People are a lot less likely to yell
at you if you are on a bike."

The altered interpersonal dynamics generated by the bike is something Enrique Penalosa understands clearly. Penalosa served as the
mayor of Bogotá, Colombia, between 1998 and 2001. At the time, Bogotá
was choking in automobile traffic, and on entry to office he was handed
a traffic study that called for building an elevated highway at the cost
of $600 million. Penalosa went the other way. He greatly expanded the
bus system for half the cost and created hundreds of pedestrians-only
and bicycle-only streets, including the longest pedestrians-only street in
the world. He experimented with a car-free weekday policy that banned
the use of automobiles entirely, excepting emergency vehicles. A poll
was taken of an initially skeptical public, and 70 percent asked for more
car-free days, which they have gotten.

Penalosa's motives for these innovations bear upon the argument
of this chapter. Although he cares about environmental issues, that
was not his primary concern. Rather, he wanted to make Bogotá a
more civil society. He was concerned that spending large amounts
of money to support the automobile transportation system pulled
public money away from more important kinds of social spending,
such as education. And he wanted to change the character of human
interactions, making these more personal. He understood that the
nature of daily human contact had direct bearing on the civility of
the city. His efforts were quite successful. Although a one-term limit
prevented his reelection, Penalosa has continued this work and has
become a world-famous poster child for making urban space more
livable and humane.

I have found, to my surprise, that as I have gotten older I am riding
more. This is certainly not a choice made out of economic necessity. I

do it because I like it. The bike seems appropriate to the scale of the problem: how to move one person relatively quickly from one point to another. I like the bike's efficiency in moving me through traffic, plus the fact that I am usually in a good frame of mind on arriving at my destination and almost never angry. I notice those in oversized vehicles honking and screaming at each other in frustration, as three-hundred-horsepower engines inch them along. I like the way the bike works against the sedentary trends in our culture and the serendipity of exercising while traveling. I enjoy almost all the moments of contact with others along my route: waving to motorists, recognizing pedestrians, and chatting with other bikers about the weather. I like the fact that I am reducing congestion and pollution, and that I am helping preserve the world's finite resources. Looked at from a social perspective, the acts of a solitary individual seem ridiculously small. Looking outward, however, the acts connect one to the larger world and to generations yet to come.

Chapter Two

Biking in Amsterdam

The Politics of the Possible

The London Olympic Games of 1948 were particularly notable. Coming in the aftermath of a war that had devastated much of the continent, the games cast a different light on the international arena. They served as a badly needed venue of hope and, in contrast to the tragedy of war, as a celebration of human excellence. The heroine of those games was Fanny Blankers-Koen of the Netherlands. As a comparatively small country, Holland tends not to rank among the leading medal-winning nations of the games. The year 1948 was a very good one for the Dutch, however, as they won a total of five gold medals. Three of these were captured by Blankers-Koen, whose blazing speed catapulted her to victory in the one-hundred- and two-hundred-meter sprints and the eighty-meter hurdles. She instantly became an international celebrity and a national hero.

The "Flying Dutchwoman," as she was known, returned from London to a tumultuous celebration in Amsterdam. At a ceremony in her honor, government authorities presented her with an appropriate gift, in recognition of her distinctive accomplishment. The gift was a bicycle, and its presentation elicited a rhapsodic cheer from the adoring throng.

This gift had political and cultural significance. The people of the Netherlands have always had great affection for the bicycle. Bicycle production ceased during the war, and the occupying German army confiscated many of the existing bikes for use. This provoked a bitter reaction from Dutch citizens. A subsequent German military report noted, "The Dutchman, who is practically born on a bicycle, views the seizing of his bicycle to be nearly the worst thing that could ever happen to him ... no other German enactment has called up such bitterness in all ranks of society as this one."[1]

So the gift to Blankers-Koen was not only something that would be very useful to her; it touched her compatriots as well, since it symbolized the nation returning to its traditions and culture. Berend Jan Mulder, a Dutch professor who introduced me to the Olympics story, still proudly rides a 1947 bicycle handed down to him from his great-uncle. By any standards, the bike is a clunker: a single-speed, pedal-braking behemoth. But because of the personal history of this bike, and also because it was one of the first bikes produced after the war, it carries special meaning for him. More important—and this point seems to be a standard throughout the country—it does the job. It gets Jan Mulder where he wants to go.

I visited Amsterdam in the summer of 2005 to study and experience its biking system. Several things prompted this desire. Most obviously, Amsterdam is internationally recognized as one of the world's leading biking cities. It is, moreover, located in a country that Americans tend to admire greatly. When people travel to countries, they almost always do so as a matter of choice. Those visiting the Netherlands are therefore a mostly self-selected group and predisposed to think kindly about the country. Even so, it is impressive how many visitors have such warm feelings for it. Americans tend to believe Holland has gotten most things right, and, by virtue of this view, their biking system is worth pondering. Additionally, the fact that English is so commonly spoken there was also an advantage. I might have gone to Bogotá, which has quite an interesting biking story, but the "third world" aura of Latin America might have made this story less compelling to some ("Of course they ride bikes—they're poor!"), and my faltering Spanish would also have made the Bogotá story less accessible.

The train ride from the Amsterdam airport to the main terminus in the heart of the city places the Dutch transportation system into immediate relief. In the first place, most who need to go to the city do so by train. This is in obvious contrast to the American style of people movement. Looking out the train window, an American will also notice the cars that are on the highway. By our standards, they seem so small. Finally, the number of bike riders pedaling their way to work is also striking. It was raining on the morning we arrived, but the weather did not seem to be much of a deterrent to cyclists. Undaunted, they pedaled on—some holding open umbrellas aloft, others accepting the brunt of the rain, all apparently resolute in the task before them. As we entered the city, bikes and bikers were everywhere. According to Amsterdam's Department of Transport and Transportation, bikes are used in 40 percent of all trips taken in the city, public transportation accounts for another 40 percent, while the remaining 20 percent are auto trips.

Visitors are invited to experience this aspect of Dutch culture. Bike rental agencies are common and quite easy to use. Rental bikes are well maintained and cheap, and the longer one keeps a bike, the lower the rate. I decided to wait a couple of days before renting a bike. I wanted to get my bearings in the city (a failed effort, as the winding roads and seamlessly shifting street names are difficult to master) and to fight off the jet lag. After getting situated in our hotel, we wandered out into the city partly on foot and partly using the extensive public transportation system. Excellent public transportation, typical in so much of the industrial and postindustrial world, also expands bicycle usage. The most obvious limitation of a public transportation system is that it cannot take everyone exactly where they wish to go. (Of course, the more extensive the transit system, the closer it can come to such a goal.) Inevitably, people relying on a rapid transit system, even an extensive one, end up walking quite a bit.

Using bikes in tandem with a public transit system sharply reduces what some see as the main virtue of cars. When we arrived at the train terminal on that first day, we were stunned by the vastness of the bike parking facility there. It was like a multideck parking facility at an American shopping mall, except that it was exclusively for bikes. And it held them by the thousands. People commuting by train to the heart of the city have additional public transportation options at that point, but many jump on bikes and ride to their final destinations.

This combination of public transport and private bicycle makes an automobile superfluous for many residents of the region. The bike is used to accomplish most short- and medium-range tasks; public transit is more commonly used for lengthier trips or in severe weather. And trains and bikes are often used together. Most people in Amsterdam do have cars, but the combination of public transportation in a city that is also widely receptive to bikes makes car ownership much less important. Having more than one car in a family does not make much sense at all. Such options make it possible to squeeze cars. Gasoline is heavily taxed, parking spaces limited and expensive, speed limits modest. In consequence, those who do own cars use them much less than in the United States. As they are much less important to their lives, Dutch citizens are far less likely to think of a car as a "need."

I will not go into the series of fortunate events that put me into contact with Berend Jan Mulder and Ria Oudejans, biking enthusiasts who live in north Amsterdam with their small daughter Mian. Ria got wind of my project and went out of her way to help me by arranging meetings with appropriate officials in Amsterdam. Initially, I had sent an e-mail to Berend introducing myself, explaining the purpose of my impending visit and asking if he could help me. Berend was in the middle of an examination period at his university and so asked his wife Ria to respond to my inquiry. She described Berend as a "passive" member of the Dutch Fietsersbond (Bikers' Union), adding, "My husband is active in the sense that he bikes all over the place, but then again so am I, since our car went up in flames, so I am as good a source as he is, though he would say I am not since I disrespect all the rules made for bikers. But who doesn't in Amsterdam?" It was the chirpiness of this statement that intrigued me. A car goes up in flames. No biggie. She would just ride her bike, toting, I was later to learn, three-year-old Mian wherever she went.

Everyone seems to bike in Amsterdam. There are more bikes than people in the Netherlands. In Amsterdam alone, 75 percent of the city's eight hundred thousand inhabitants own bikes, with many owning more than one. In contrast to cars, it does make sense for households to own more than one bike, as they are used for varying purposes. I rode quite a bit in the city, but I also spent a fair amount of time observing the biking practices of the population. Kids ride bikes to school. Teens and young adults ride bikes on dates. Riding them to work is quite common. Seniors ride them everywhere. People ride in suits and formal attire. One popular vacation is the family bike-camping trip in which parents and children load up their bikes with camping gear and other necessities and strike out for various parts of Europe. In contrast to the United States, women are extensive bike users. In fact, 55 percent of all bike trips are taken by women. Bikes are ridden without respect to social class.

The last statement is something of an exaggeration. There is a social class distinction in biking, but it is not what one might think. In Holland, middle- and upper-class people ride bikes for transportation more than do those who are less well off. While there, we went to an evening of music at the Concertgebouw, the famous Dutch concert hall. We decided to bike to the event and discovered that we were far from alone. When chatting about this with the managers of our hotel, they told us about a special event at the Concertgebouw the previous winter, one attended by the queen. It was a formal affair, with many high-status types in attendance. At the concert's conclusion, everyone waited for the queen to leave, as is the tradition. Our hotel managers attended this concert, and they noted that after the queen's departure, many of the luminaries rode away on bikes. This included the chief executive of Phillips Electronics—one of the most important corporations in Holland—who pedaled off into the night resplendent in his formal attire.

Everyone I talked with in Amsterdam mentioned this phenomenon, with many adding the proviso that the less well off did not ride as frequently as the rest of the population. In part, this was attributed to the fact that many of these are recent immigrants to the country. They tend to come from places where the rich drive cars while the poor walk. The car is thus seen as a status symbol for these folks, in a way that it is not for the middle and upper classes. For these latter groups, the prevailing ethic is against ostentation. Ria Hilhorst, a sociologist who heads the biking policy unit in the Amsterdam Department of Transport and Transportation, noted that transportation planners throughout the Netherlands are concerned about the fact that bike usage drops off among poorer citizens, and they are working on culturally sensitive ways to combat the trend.

On our second day in Amsterdam, Berend and Ria invited us to their home for dinner. Our conversation eventually turned to culturally distinctive attitudes about biking. When I mentioned to Ria that many people in the United States think of biking—especially biking for utilitarian purposes—as retrogressive, she was startled. Her eyes flashed, and although her words were reasonably accepting, I sensed she was caught between desires to be polite to a visitor while also wishing to communicate that an attitude held by his countrymen was stupid in the extreme.

The bicycles that people ride in Amsterdam bespeak their place in the culture. Unlike the bikes characteristically ridden by Americans, Amsterdam bikes are highly utilitarian. They are solidly built and heavy, resting on tires designed to resist punctures. Usually they have a rack on the back, which is also much sturdier than its American counterpart. Dutch racks are strong enough to support an adult riding sidesaddle behind the bike's operator—something that regularly happens there. Oversized saddlebags, fully rainproof and capable of carrying a surprisingly large load, are common. Characteristically, the bikes have few gears. Many are one-speed; three speeds define the outer limits. Those who belong to bike clubs and tour on weekends will have higher-end road bikes, but many others commonly tour on lower-end bikes.

The bikes are typically geared low, which means pumping is very easy and bike speed comparatively slow. Often braking is part of the cranking system, which means that riders stop by "pedaling backward," instead of using hand brakes. This feature frees the hands for other uses, such as carrying packages and umbrellas. Virtually all of the bikes have fenders, which slightly adds to the weight and clunkiness of the bike but also keeps riders from getting muddy stripes down their backs as rotating tires pick up water from wet streets. And bikes are characteristically outfitted for the kinds of carrying needs their owners have.

One style of bike deserves special mention. It is a two-wheeler, but quite a bit longer than the typical bike. The frame is extended to accommodate a carrying bin (similar to the body of a wheelbarrow) between the front fork of the bike and its front wheel. At a bike store, I saw one young couple shopping for such a bike. The woman wanted to carry her child and the family dog along with her, and she was testing different styles in the parking lot. Dutifully, the child and dog would climb into a bin, and the mom would ride around the lot with them. The possibilities of such a bike clearly excited this young couple. I saw this style of bike fairly frequently in Amsterdam. Once, I came upon two women who I surmised were taking their children home from school. One had three small kids in the carrying bin; the second had three kids in the bin and an older child riding sidesaddle on the back of the bike. That made nine people being transported by two bikes. And the most interesting part of this scene was that the women were chattering away as they rode along apparently as happy as chipmunks. The matter-of-factness of this episode made it particularly compelling.

People in Amsterdam often have custom-built bikes designed for special needs. Ria Oudejans, for example, is a fairly tall woman of around six feet. To accommodate Mian, she wanted a bike with a front child's seat and a windshield. Because of this, she preferred the extra room a "woman's frame" provides when she gets down from her saddle. On the day that she, Berend, and I explored northern Amsterdam and beyond, young Mian rode along as well. In her large rear saddlebags, Ria brought along various child care necessities as well as food. She clearly loved this bike, as it was well suited to her needs. Such custom-made bikes are of course expensive, but considering the integral role that bikes play in Holland, they are not extravagant. Obviously, they are far less expensive than cars.

It is worth considering why bikes have come to have such an integral role in the Netherlands. One immediately thinks of politics and particularly the bike-friendly policies that have been adopted by the Dutch political system. Politics has obviously played a huge role here, and we will turn to this topic momentarily. But any consideration of politics begs a prior question: What underlying values lead Dutch citizens to believe that it makes political sense to build a bike-friendly environment and continue to encourage bike usage? Politics does not occur in a vacuum; it is conducted in a larger context of social values that makes some ideas sensible and others not.

I asked the "Why Holland?" question frequently during my visit there. Some answers were more persuasive than others. Some people noted, for example, that Holland is flat and biking therefore easier; others that the weather is relatively nice. But flat terrain is not necessarily more conducive to biking than hilly terrain. Hills, after all, have their compensations. Every upward struggle has its corresponding

Utilitarian bikes like these are common in Amsterdam (Photos courtesy Huub Derksen)

descent. And flat lands tend to be subject to higher winds, which many bikers consider more problematic than hills. Dutch weather is not bad for biking, but it is also not ideal. Frequent rains must be tolerated, and in the winter, snowfall is not unusual. Many parts of the world with more appropriate weather use bikes far less.

Other responses were more persuasive. The Protestant Calvinist heritage that is a fundamental cultural strut of Dutch society was commonly referenced. Of course, anything as prominent as an important religious tradition is capable of generating diverse social outcomes. The United States, also greatly influenced by Calvinism, is not so sympathetic to biking. Those in Holland who connect biking to Calvinism overwhelmingly refer to the idea that life was not meant to be easy. It is a struggle requiring effort, and this inevitable fact should be accepted as a part of living and therefore with a measure of grace. Biking is like that. One does not get something for nothing. Ria Oudejans recalled a moment when she began to bike after her car was destroyed. She complained about the winds, and on separate occasions her husband and her cousin Huub responded identically. Basically, they chastised her for complaining about something she could not avoid and told her the wind was something she simply had to accept. Though neither was particularly religious, their admonishments were classically Calvinist.

Policy analyst Hilhorst also mentioned Calvinism when describing the tendency of so many to ride in Holland throughout the year, including the times when there is rain and snow. "The citizens of our country expect a measure of adversity in their lives," she said. She also connected the Dutch preference for avoiding ostentation to Calvinism. There is a sense of humility in Calvinism, owing to the recognition that one never fully deserves God's grace. Calvinists believe in modesty, including modesty in the presentation of self. Bikes are modest machines. They do not impose, and so they serve this preference quite nicely.

Professor Berend Jan Mulder also noted the importance of the "polder model" in Dutch culture. (A *polder* is a piece of land that exists below normal water levels and consequently is surrounded by dikes.) The polder model refers to a style of decision making that has received considerable attention from scholars in other European nations. This idea runs deep in Dutch history. It involves decision making that relies on consensus, because it recognizes the common stakes that everyone has in the outcome. In the Middle Ages, farmers, noblemen, urban and rural dwellers, merchants, and serfs needed to cooperate to build and to maintain the dikes because, in Berend's phrase, "the waters are coming." Without unanimous agreement and shared responsibility, the polders would have flooded, to the detriment of all. The model is pragmatic. It stays at the surface of things, inviting those concerned with the particular issue to the table to talk, not about deeper differences that may exist but how best to resolve an immediate problem.

Biking suits the polder model well because of the common stakes that can be seen in the generation of this activity. Biking will not solve the deeper problems of global warming, for example. On the other hand, biking benefits everyone, riders and nonriders alike. As such, everyone has an interest in it. Having what the Dutch would consider a rational transportation policy is generally beneficial. Those active in the biking movement in Holland tend to be political leftists, and they probably have many differences with the CEO of Phillips Electronics, for example. This does not mean they cannot work with him to solve immediate problems or that he cannot see the importance of solving such problems as well.

So there are cultural norms that are relevant to biking, but it is also important not to overemphasize this point. The current biking system in Amsterdam was not merely culturally "natural" for the Netherlands. It emerged as the result of political struggle. After World War II, the trends were clearly away from the bicycle. Automobile usage grew significantly and at a rate that confounded Dutch authorities. In 1946, the Transportation Department issued a Directorate for a National Plan. This plan projected that 300,000 cars would be in use in the Netherlands in 1960 and 450,000 by 1975. The actual numbers were 522,000 and 3.4 million, respectively.[2]

For a while, it seemed that the car would push the bicycle into history's dustbin, just as it did in other countries. But as car usage grew, many Dutch citizens became increasingly cognizant of its less desirable side effects—especially pollution, congestion, and the usurpation of public space, which is always a concern in this densely populated country. People increasingly worried that the car was crowding out other traditional uses of the street—for biking, for pedestrians, and for children at play. The sharp increase in fatalities and serious injuries directly attributable to the automobile was a stimulus to this concern. Between 1950 and 1972, traffic fatalities tripled and injuries increased almost fourfold.[3] Almost a third of these casualties were cyclists.

While the usefulness of the car was recognized and was mostly responsible for its expanded use, these important side effects were much more clearly noted by the population than they are in places like the United States. Social realities of limited space and ecological imbalances mattering immediately undoubtedly contributed to Dutch prescience. Thus, while each individual purchase of a car seemed to make sense, there was growing recognition that the car was crowding out a useful and much more benign mode of transport. The Dutch understood, moreover, that it was not simply the car's inherent attractiveness that led to its increased usage. Americans tend to think of the triumph of the automobile as something that was fairly won in the marketplace. In contrast, the Dutch recognized that the rise of the car was not simply a "free market choice"; it also was connected to the postwar enactment of policies favoring the automobile. The Dutch Bicycle Master Plan (BMP) published by the national Ministry of Transport, Public Works, and Water Management notes this fact:[4]

> The significant rise in prosperity has not only contributed to cars becoming more affordable, but also actively promoted their use, including for those distances for which the bicycle was used in the past ... attention to bicycle traffic was minimal. The prosperity expectations were such that within the foreseeable future bicycle traffic would decrease, certainly for commuting, to a negligible share compared to car traffic ... between 1960 and 1975, the construction of bicycle facilities lost much ground due to the increase in car traffic [that] left little room over for the cyclist.... As a result utilitarian bicycle traffic was pushed into a tight corner.

This quote is contained in the BMP of 1999, but it was lifted from a Transport Report issued in 1983, after the tide had begun to shift back to more favorable biking policies. It is interesting that the report identifies 1975 as the low-water mark of biking policy. For in that year, and in response to these concerns, the Dutch Cyclists' Union was formed, with its largest branch located in Amsterdam. The purpose of this organization was to prod the government toward the adoption of an integrated transportation policy, one that had the bike as a central component.

The Union engaged in direct confrontation, blocking streets in protest and staging cycle demonstrations. The pithy phrase used by the cochair of the Cyclists' Union to describe its birth was that people finally said, "Enough is enough." The technical core of the Union is the "bottleneck group" that issued its first report in 1976 identifying more that three hundred stretches of road that were problematic for cyclists. By 1978, public sentiment had galvanized to the extent that a city council was elected that began to respond to cyclists' concerns.

Today the Cyclists' Union is located in central Amsterdam. Its offices are on the grounds of a former hospital complex. In the seventies, this complex was closed, as the hospital moved to a more modern site in another part of the city. Seeing an opportunity in a city where housing is always in great demand, squatters moved into the abandoned buildings. Mostly the squatters were artists and immigrants, and the government eventually sought to eject them. A confrontation ensued, precipitating a minor social crisis. Eventually the dispute was resolved in classic polder model fashion. There was widespread recognition of the various stakes involved, and the solution took these into account. Housing in the complex was made available to the squatters. They had to pay, but at greatly reduced rates. And the residents accepted significant maintenance responsibilities, including cooperative gardening and cleaning. In addition, parts of the complex were to be used for public purposes. The Cyclists' Union, though not part of the government, was allowed space there to conduct its business.

Natascha van Bennekom is the codirector of the Cyclists' Union. At the time of our interview she was thirty-two years old and the mother of two children. She does not fit the stereotype of an avid cyclist (she was a Russian language and literature major in college who seemed to fall into this position), but she is clearly committed to ensuring that biking remains integral to the transportation system of Amsterdam. She does not own a car and in fact has no driver's license. She says that between the public transit system and her bike, her transportation needs are satisfied.

There are about five thousand members of the Cyclists' Union in Amsterdam, thirty-five thousand members nationally. The number of active members is much smaller than this, with activity partly determined by whether a biking issue has emerged in a councilmanic district in which the member resides. A voluntary activist core is crucial to the Union. These volunteers deliver the Union bulletin thrice yearly and serve as representatives of the organization at district meetings and in deliberations with various civil servants. Their on-the-ground expertise makes them valuable sources of information for the Union. The biggest stimulus for membership is parental concern for ensuring that biking is safe for children.

The thirty- to forty-euro annual membership fee is used to support the activities of the organization. The Union is also subsidized by the government. The codirectors' salaries are paid by the government, and the office space is subsidized by the government as well. To an American, this system seems odd—the government subsidizing an organization whose purpose is to prod the government in a particular policy direction—but in Holland this is not unusual. Van Bennekom rejected the idea that the government was co-opting the Union by subsidizing it. Similarly, those in city administration positions did not think of government support for the Union as anything like "giving aid and comfort to the enemy." On the contrary, they saw the Union as performing a useful service. This relationship seems like one more iteration of the polder model.

Administratively, Amsterdam is divided into a number of districts—much like councilmanic districts in many American cities. Changes in biking policy are, therefore, often district-specific. One of the jobs of the Union is to oversee these changes so as to provide greater integration and coordination. The Union also serves an informational purpose. It publishes a magazine for its members, informing its readers of recreational opportunities, current political struggles, and ongoing safety and health issues.

According to van Bennekom, a utopian streak runs through some cycling enthusiasts, and occasionally the Union comes under pressure to support bike-specific policies that are quite expensive. But the dominant sentiment in the organization is pragmatic and integrative. Biking is seen as an important part of the answer to the problem of population movement. The support for a multimodal transportation system, one that provides a range of transport options for citizens, enjoys broad social acceptance. Given this fact, and given the specific advantages of the bike (i.e., its soft environmental imprint), biking advocates deserve to have a prominent place at the transportation policy table.

Ria Hilhorst, the head of the biking policy unit in the Directorate of Infrastructure Traffic and Transport (DITT), agrees. Hilhorst is the government counterpart to van Bennekom. The DITT has a sweeping and integrated view of the problem of people movement. Its intent is to keep the city accessible, safe, and attractive. Keeping the transport infrastructure from being overburdened during peak traffic hours is the primary concern. Thought is given to smooth auto traffic flow, but the DITT does not automatically turn to the construction of new roads to achieve this end.

The DITT explicitly recognizes the importance of keeping Amsterdam aesthetically attractive. This objective is part of the mission statement of the organization, and the DITT calls an attractive city "an important factor in the well-being of its residents." Highway construction often conflicts with this goal, though it need not always. Trains, rapid transit, buses, trams, taxis, bikes, roads, and parking all come under the purview of the DITT. The bike is integral to the organization. Here is its overarching statement about this mode of transportation: "The bicycle is the ideal means of transport in *a* city: fast and environmentally friendly. Cycle routes must be well laid out and safe. DITT policy is geared toward encouraging bicycle use by providing a distinctive, high-quality network of cycle paths" (emphasis added).[5]

It is instructive that this statement is not taken from a bike advocacy unit but from the agency responsible for transport and transportation. To an American, such words read like bike favoritism. If it is, it is a favoritism that makes sense to most Dutch citizens. Though bike riding takes more personal effort, the collective advantages that bikes offer in urban areas are obvious and substantial, so it is worth taking steps that encourage as many as possible to saddle up. The extent of this sense of common interest is revealed by a response to a question on bike safety that I put to Ria Hilhorst. Her unit is very concerned with bike safety, yet almost nobody in Amsterdam wears bike helmets. In the United States helmets are strongly advocated as a means to reduce the likelihood of serious injury. It seemed odd to me that Amsterdam would not have similar programs. One of the reasons she cited was a general ethic that drivers have an obligation to take care of riders, and many bikers believe that wearing a helmet suggests otherwise!

Beginning with the assumption that "freedom of movement is one of our fundamental rights," the bike policy unit of the DITT actively seeks to expand the use of the bike, especially for such instrumental purposes as riding to work, to school, and to market. The group argues that a unimodal transportation system contracts this freedom, and they see expanded bike use as key to reducing congestion, traffic jams, serious accidents to pedestrians, and parking problems that also inhibit this "fundamental right." The idea is to make all areas of the city easily and safely reachable by bike.

Houses in Amsterdam typically have little or no yard space. To compensate for this, the city is dotted with a number of great parks, which give to its residents a sense of the pastoral. Through all of these parks run substantial bike trails. These trails are the safest place to bike in the city, and they are heavily used—for recreation certainly, but mainly as connectors to various parts of the city. Although they are used constantly throughout the day, it is particularly interesting to sit in a park during morning or evening "rush hours" and observe the bike traffic.

On their utilitarian bikes, people ride at a leisurely pace. There seems to be little sense of competition during these rides. People are going to work, after all, and are appropriately attired for their work lives. Young and old, male and female, riders glide past one another without provoking any competitive impulses in those being passed. Yet this riding is quite efficient, as the kilometers seem to melt away under the steady rotation of the pedals. And it is also worth considering, while sitting in a lovely park, that biking makes this ambience possible. These extensive bike routes do not disrupt the park itself, nor do they detract from its quiet. If all the people riding bikes drove cars instead, the additional requirements for pavement and parking would be such that the park system would be seriously eroded, if not completely eliminated.

A couple of automobile freeways exist in Amsterdam. On such highways, bikes are banned, but off-trail bike paths paralleling these highways for bike commuters are universally available. The roads of the city are of two basic types. First, there are fairly broad, 50-kph (about 31-mph) roads that gird the city. These are supplemented by a network of smaller, 30-kph roads. The stated ideal is to have separated bike paths along all 50-kph roads and bike lanes along all 30-kph roads.

Bike paths are riding spaces that clearly separate riders from most motorized traffic. (Small mopeds are allowed to use them as well, and there is a helmet law for moped users.) Typically there is a sidewalk for pedestrian traffic abutting the bike path. Although the separation of the sidewalk and the bike path is obvious to the trained eye—characteristically, they are at slightly different elevations and composed of different materials—a pedestrian not familiar with this system can easily wander into bike traffic. This is an important reason why bikes in Amsterdam almost always come equipped with warning bells. At 50-kph highway intersections requiring traffic signals, there are special signals for riders on the bike paths. These give preference to bikes, allowing them to proceed before motor traffic. This is done for reasons of efficiency and safety, as it is better to get bikes through intersections to avoid problems with turning vehicles.

Bike lanes are found on many 30-kph roads and will be familiar to urban riders in the United States. These are painted lanes on the roads that are exclusively for bikes. The lanes rest between the moving car traffic and the space designated for car parking. On these roads, bike traffic is obligated to obey the same rules and signals as the motorized traffic. In the spirit of the universal biking code, however, this obligation is not deeply felt.

The stated ideal for bike paths and lanes has not been achieved. Smaller and more lightly traveled residential streets typically have no separated areas for bike traffic. This setup is not a big deal, and it is probably not worth the expense to install them. A more significant problem is that the installation of bike paths along the 50-kph roads has not been universal. On some stretches of these roads, riders have only bike lanes to use. The installation of bike paths is of course more expensive and, because they typically are achieved through the usurpation of parking space, more contested. Cyclists' Union head van Bennekom told me that the expansion of bike paths continues, but at an incremental pace. For example, a road in need of repair and that is therefore partially closed for a period of time might be reopened with additional meters of cycle path.

Increasing riding safety is the most important ongoing effort of the biking community in Amsterdam and indeed throughout the Netherlands. These efforts have been successful. Between 1975 and 1998, the total number of bike fatalities fell by 57 percent in the Netherlands, compared with a 24 percent decline in the United States over the same period.[6] The contrast is actually starker than the numbers suggest, because Dutch riders report that about 60 percent of their trips are utilitarian—riding to work, to school, or to shop—while 40 percent are recreational. In the United States, 70 percent of all rides are recreational. Since utilitarian rides are far more likely to occur within cities, the chances of collisions with cars are much greater. The fatality rate for bikers in the United States is now about twenty times greater than that of the Netherlands, despite the fact that so much riding here is recreational.

Traffic calming has also been an important element in making biking and pedestrian trips safer. The 30-kph speed limit in most residential areas is augmented with traffic circles and speed bumps. This comes out of the general sense that the car should not be privileged in the transportation network. Driver education is much more extensive in the Netherlands than in the United States, and people must be at least eighteen years of age to obtain a license. This education includes assimilation to the notion that roads are multipurpose passageways. Drivers are trained to anticipate unexpected moves of bikers. This ability is tested in the driving portion of the license exam, and a driver will not receive a license if he or she fails this portion of the exam. One of the things assisting the education, of course, is the fact that so many drivers are also bikers. As such, they come to driving with a keen sense of the dangers cars pose to bikers.

Shortly after returning to the United States, I interviewed Randy Neufeld of the Chicagoland Bicycle Federation. He is currently active in the Complete Streets movement, an effort to make all significant streets open for pedestrians and bikers as well as motorists. Extensive driver reeducation would obviously be necessary to implement this concept. I mentioned to him my time in Amsterdam and how drivers there, partly because of extensive education, reflected a distinctive sensitivity to bikes. Neufeld, who has also spent time in Amsterdam, told me of a day when he sat for two hours watching traffic flow at a busy intersection in central Amsterdam, "because that's the kind of guy I am." There was a bike lane along this avenue—not a bike path—and many drivers made right turns at this intersection across the lane. He described what he saw as a "ballet of users," in which "every single motorist making a right turn"—and he was emphatic on this point—looked back to check for approaching bikes and waited for them to clear before making the turn. It should be noted that safety issues are connected to the broader reality in diffuse ways as well. A driver is more likely to look out for bikers if that driver is a biker, has been a biker, or has friends who are bikers. And since so many people ride in Amsterdam, drivers expect bikers to be using the lanes. The pervasiveness of biking, in other words, provides its own momentum for bike safety.

Safety is not the only concern in Amsterdam. Bike theft has become a major issue in the city. It is difficult to know how many bikes are actually stolen in Amsterdam, because many thefts are never reported. But everyone I talked with agreed that it was a serious problem. Ria Hilhorst suggested that this issue shaded into safety concerns as well, because one of the ways people combat theft is by riding bikes that are old and in advanced stages of disrepair. Such bikes are less likely to be stolen, but they are also more dangerous to ride.

The government has taken steps to combat bike theft, including an extensive public education campaign, reminding people to lock their bikes and publicizing the consequences of theft. These consequences in fact have increased, as this crime is now being more severely punished than in the past. Additionally, locking systems have become more sophisticated. A permanent lock for the back wheel is now a common feature on many bike models. It is easily activated and, along with the traditional chain locks, conveniently allows for more complete securing of the bike.

Secure bike parking facilities are also springing up in Amsterdam. As these facilities are subsidized by the government, they are available to bike owners for a small user fee. These multileveled facilities serve a dual purpose. They provide a safe place for bikes, and they also help to get bikes off the streets. So many people in Amsterdam ride bikes that finding a place to park them is something of a problem. There is a concern that a surfeit of parked bikes not only impedes pedestrian traffic but also works against the general aesthetics of the city.

My visit to Amsterdam came shortly after the Dutch vote against further commitment to the European Union. Most of the people I talked with were disappointed in the vote and hoped that it would eventually be reversed. The reasons for this rejection were complicated. Further integration was opposed by segments of the Dutch left as well as by segments of the Dutch right. Concern over immigration motivated many. Some in this historically tolerant society were bothered by the admission of groups whose internal norms were hierarchical and not especially tolerant. Several people mentioned to me the irony of this as well. How tolerant can one be of those who are perceived to be intolerant? Will the admission of large numbers of those who are perceived to be intolerant change the character of the society? Can a genuinely tolerant society be intolerant toward the intolerant? It is causing the Dutch to think about themselves as well as others.

What is relevant to the purposes of this book is that this question also connects to biking and politics in the Netherlands. Muslim immigrants, for example, are far less likely to ride bicycles than are others in Holland. Some claimed that this tendency is because in the immigrants' home countries, the car is a standard of success, so auto ownership is a sign of struggling upward. Others claim that the bike gives more freedom to Muslim women than traditional Muslim males are willing to accept. There is concern that such norms will upset the character of the country, and the government is trying to figure out culturally sensitive ways to introduce immigrants to the virtues of biking. It is indicative of the importance of biking in the Netherlands that the large and complex issue of immigrant integration had a clear biking dimension.

Michael de Jong,[7] a millionaire real estate developer, is on a worldwide crusade to get Industrialized Man out of his car and onto a bicycle. He sponsors promotional bike races in Africa and other parts of the world, and he himself travels extensively all over the world by bike. He has become essentially a Dutch bicycle ambassador to the rest of the world. He caught the attention of the *New York Times* with his latest interest: finding the best ways to bike out of the major airports of the world to the centers of the cities that they serve. He then posts these routes on the Internet. The *Times* caught up with him at LaGuardia. De Jong gave up cars when one he was driving in Barbados was struck by a bus in a head-on collision. Now he uses fold-up bikes that he can carry with him in a suitcase as he travels the world. He has customized accessories to carry suitcases when necessary.

In most cases, the routes he finds get him to the city cores faster than other means of travel, but this result is not his purpose. He is not trying to save time. "Imagine how much better the world would be if more people rode bicycles," he told the *Times*. Clearly, Michael de Jong is a man on a mission. He was born and raised in what the *Times* called "bike-happy Holland," and in high school he regularly rode ten miles each way to high school. As I read this story, I clearly recognized his sensibility, to which his native land had contributed greatly. And I liked the phrase "bike-happy Holland." It can be aptly juxtaposed with "car-stressed America."

On my last Sunday in Amsterdam, I decided to bike to Zandvoort, an attractive beach community thirty-five kilometers from Amsterdam. It is the most popular access point to the North Sea in the region. As it turned out, this mid-July day was full of warm sunshine—perfect for beach going—and the beaches of Zandvoort understandably were packed with people.

For me, the ride to Zandvoort was fully as enjoyable as the time at the beach. A bike trail links Amsterdam and Zandvoort, of course. It basically follows the main highway between the two cities, although it does meander through the countryside a bit. The ride was leisurely, sprinkled with personal encounters. Most of these were quite brief, a few more lingering. The heavily used trail served solo riders like me, although most rode along in gaggles of various sorts. Many families were trekking to the beach with older kids riding their own bikes, while the younger ones were transported by their parents.

The ride was fun. On this day we rode into a headwind going to the beach. No one seemed to mind. Perhaps the famous Dutch Calvinism kicked in; perhaps the riders were thinking of the pleasure of a wind-assisted return ride. In any case, the labor involved in working our way to the shore was compensated by the increasing ingestion of fresh sea air.

Of course, most people access the beach by taking the highly efficient train that regularly runs between the two cities. The combination of bikes and trains meant that there was a relative lack of cars on the main highway. In considering the problem of moving people to the beaches, the Dutch have decided that bikes and public transport would provide the major part of the answer.

It is just this manner in which biking is integrated into the consciousness of the Dutch people that is ultimately most impressive. And the actions of the government suggest that their intent is to maintain biking's prominence. At the time of my visit, the Nescio Bridge was under construction, but Berend still wanted me to see it, so we rode to the construction site. Spanning the Rhine Canal and connecting the central city to newer housing developments in the north, the project is regarded as crucial to the continuing integration of the city. Completed in 2006, at a cost of thirteen million euros, the bridge is for the exclusive use of walkers and bikers and is structured so that these two modes of traffic will not conflict.

It is a project in which the residents of the city have taken great pride, because it extends the notion, so important to Hollanders, that a city should be a source of aesthetic pleasure. A London architectural firm won the right to design and construct the bridge, and it took advantage of the unique opportunities the project presented. One hundred sixty-three meters of this 790-meter bridge are freely suspended, making it Holland's first suspension bridge. The award-winning design shows what is possible with modern structural technique. Cyclists and pedestrians follow fluent, curving alignments, supported by a minimal system of cables and masts. The cycleway is 3.5 meters wide, while the walkway is 2 meters wide.

Nescio Bridge underscores important aesthetic differences between biking and driving. When engineers construct bridges for automotive traffic, their overriding concern is to get vehicles over the bridge safely. This imposes constraints on design. It is important for bridges to be as straight as possible and for motorists not to be distracted by the unique views bridges almost always afford. Typically, the sightlines of motorists are shielded from the hazard the potential aesthetic pleasure poses. Instead, the environment confronts the motorist as a problem, so the motorist must be separated from it, the better to focus on the task at hand. A bike and pedestrian bridge offers broader opportunity, and the designers of Nescio responded. The minimal system of cables and masts increases visibility and opens travelers to the environment, as does the bridge's meandering path. Its users are invited to enjoy the river traffic passing below, the wetlands along the shore and the architecture of Amsterdam beyond. The undulating curves of the bridge are aesthetically pleasing in their own right, and local citizens have already given it a popular nickname: the Eel.

Thinking privately and without regard to public consequence, driving a car can appear to be an obvious choice for someone deciding to move from point A to point B. Driving a car is, after all, physically—if not psychologically—effortless. But a decision to drive a car is always made in a social context, as we are inherently social beings. This means that the decision to drive or not will be structured by social contingency. It will be structured by whether alternatives are abundantly and safely available. And it will be structured by how clearly people understand the comparative social efficiencies of various modes of transport. Such contingencies are a matter of politics.

The Dutch understand that the personal benefits the car brings to people means that it will always be an important part of the transportation puzzle, but they have a much clearer sense of the social inefficiencies of the car than do most Americans. The bike brings substantial personal benefits such as improved physical and psychological health, but it also exacts personal costs such as effort and less convenience. The bike, however, excels in the collective benefits its use brings, which is the primary reason that its use is actively promoted in the Netherlands.

Whether Amsterdam can serve as a model for American cities is an interesting question. Dutch culture is much more communitarian than the highly individualist culture of the United States. The Dutch people's unique place on the planet makes them distinctively aware of the fact that "the waters are coming." Their disinterest in the ostentatious display of wealth also sets them apart from citizens of the United States. But cultures are peculiar things. They necessarily have structure, and they therefore persist through time. But cultures are constructed by people to help them live at a given place and time. They are never frozen. As the nature of that existence changes, cultures are forced to respond. It may be the case, for example, that we, along with the rest of the world, come to see that the waters, indeed, are coming. The question of American culture will be addressed in the next chapter, but the immediate political question is not whether we can become just like the Netherlands but what we can learn from them that would be useful to us. It is interesting, in this regard, that in 2006, the city of Portland, Oregon—already one of the leading biking cities in the United States—sent a nine-person bike delegation to Amsterdam to pick up ideas that they might be able to use in their city.

As I pedaled to the beaches of Zandvoort on that beautiful Sunday in the Netherlands, I thought back to my teenage years in Southern California and the trek people in our part of the region made to the fabulous beaches of Huntington, Newport, and Laguna. We would go down Highway 39, known as Beach Boulevard today. I thought about what a warm Sunday in July would mean—and of course still means—to beach traffic flow in Southern California. The highways are bigger now and more numerous. Concrete and asphalt are more invasive, now lathering the entire LA basin and splashing onto the surrounding desert. But traffic flows have not been eased by this dominating tide. If anything, the roads are more jammed than ever, bearing angry or resigned people in snarled traffic that inches them to and from their precious Moments in the Sun. Can't we do better than this? Of course we can. But as the Dutch know, doing better requires political will.

Chapter Three

Culture Storm

Cultures are so endemic that noted anthropologist Clifford Geertz believes humans are genetically programmed to create them. Our brain is not so large that it allows us to see perfectly, but it is large enough so that we can recognize the limits of our perception. Some things are eternally hidden from view; others are obscured and subject to various interpretations. The strengths and limits of our brains would not be especially problematic were it not for the fact that humans enjoy and require the company of others. The resistance of the world to our gaze and our propensity for association combine to require culture, making it necessary for survival.

In a world fraught with ambiguity, cultures provide a way of "seeing-that" and hence a way to live together. These shared meaning systems provide a common frame to interpret reality. To paraphrase Geertz, humans are animals suspended in webs of significance that they themselves have spun. Culture *is* that webbing.[1] Consider the most common of shared symbol systems: language. Being able to converse and to represent ideas and the phenomenal world to others is essential to feeling integral to the group. The symbols on this page have meaning to those sharing the system, representing something beyond the ink stains they literally are. This recognition enables conversation about them.

Cultures grow out of the experience of the group, helping members make sense of that experience. And cultures persist, which allows group life to endure. We need to know that meaning is relatively durable, that a chair one day will not be a religious object the next. This durability facilitates routine social interaction, one of the more important forms of which is politics. The dynamics of biking and politics in the United States cannot be understood without consideration of relevant aspects of our culture. The previous chapter noted that the reality of life in the Netherlands, the sense that "the waters are coming," shaped powerful cultural norms in that country that are congenial to bike-friendly policies.

People grow into their cultures, which makes them particularly seductive. This process of assimilation begins at the moment of birth and continues through what Jessica Mitford has called "the American way of death."[2] Most of this assimilation occurs, not through reading books or rational deliberation, but through everyday life experience, so most of the assimilation is subconscious. This distinguishes culture from ideology. When Americans look at the world, they do not think, "This is the American version of reality"; they think they see reality itself. This holds for those in other cultures as well. Cultures therefore serve to limit political possibility. People will not do things that do not occur to them or that do not make sense to them.

Even the most powerful cultural characteristics will not be all-encompassing, however. In complex societies, cultural integration is always less than total. Inevitably, they contain vibrant and self-sustaining multi-, sub-, and even anticultural strains. In this era of recognized multiculturalism, some question whether it is even useful to think of a national culture. I believe it is, but in any case, it makes sense to consider distinctively powerful cultural currents. Although humans may be genetically wired to create culture, not all participate equally in the act of creation. Some cultural myths are sustained because of the power enjoyed by those who push them, and they therefore may be particularly widespread and compelling. The stories that we tell each other are not equally heard, and in this way a dominant national culture may be said to emerge. But even the most pervasive cultural struts are subject to change. Cultures may be durable, but they are not static.

For example, anyone living in the United States faces serious disadvantages if they do not speak English, yet in particular locales some are able to manage reasonably well. Others create amalgamations like "Spanglish" to get along. Some groups bend the language to accommodate regional needs, while others such as teens, hipsters, or political scientists adapt the dominant language to build subgroup exclusivity. A person not in one of these language-specific subgroups feels marginalized by this incomplete access to the symbol system. There are guardians to the "official" language, and those who learn to use it "correctly" enjoy social advantages. Language is a key to stability; at the same time, however, language evolves because it must. Even the dominant language grows and adapts—sometimes to the chagrin of language purists who are nonetheless helpless as neologisms constantly emerge: nouns morph into verbs, slang is made legitimate by its pervasiveness, words from "foreign" languages creep into English, and new words emerge to describe new realities.

The example of language persistence, accommodation, and adaptation illustrates a process inherent in culture. To understand the state of bike friendliness in the United States, we must consider the culturally hostile environment in which advocates of those policies have struggled. In this chapter, we shall explore the problems posed by two powerful and venerated struts of that culture. Later, we shall argue that these are beginning to erode. As the historic basis for these values gives way to new realities, the culture is inching fitfully toward reformulation, as cultures do. This process opens new possibilities for bike policies.

Individualism and Materialism

The cultural struts of *individualism* and *materialism* are worth considering because they are distinctively American and because they shed light on why bike friendliness has lagged in the United States. Evidence of these values can be found in most cultures, but in no other country are they as celebrated and as important in shaping assumptions about the nature of reality and the purpose of life.

Individualism is the abiding conviction that people are personally responsible for their fates. Achievement in the world is largely seen as a matter of individual choice. We are reluctant to recognize social structures that impede, enhance, or otherwise affect the character of our lives, and notions of interconnection and shared fates are downplayed. There is much to admire in individualism, and throughout our history it has probably been as close to a constitutive myth as ideas get. We are admired for it; immigrants are attracted by it. But as important as individualism is, it serves awkwardly as a cultural foundation for the society. The need for human association is universal, yet this fundamental myth of the culture implies the opposite, suggesting that people come together in order to be apart.

Materialism as it is used here identifies the pattern of beliefs that privileges the generation, possession, accumulation, and consumption of things. This pattern is animated by the conviction that well-being is largely a function of the quality and quantity of one's consumption. Materialism reaches beyond the recognition that goods can produce pleasure. Pleasure itself is commodified, becoming something that is purchased in market exchanges. Everyone recognizes that goods and acquisition produce pleasure, and everyone recognizes that other, nonmarket exchanges—such as a jog in a park—do so as well. What is culturally distinctive about the United States is the *weight* given to market exchanges, as the pleasures of a jog in the park are subsumed by the "need" first to have the right running shoes and outfit. An actual jog may become less important than, through one's consumption choices, being thought of as a person who "just might" jog in the park.

Just as no culture is purely communitarian or completely antimaterialist, it is also obvious that many Americans eschew the dominant cultural values of individualism and materialism. Many see themselves as connected to others and choose careers or volunteer time based on this sense of social connection. And many consciously reject the pull of accumulation as an end in itself. While such caveats are useful, these alternative norms are relatively minor cultural countercurrents. They should not detract from the recognition that materialism and individualism are extraordinarily and uniquely powerful in this country. That power is reflected in numerous distinctive public policies.

Consider some policy consequences of the broadly shared individualist ethic. The United States is the only Western industrialized nation that employs capital punishment. In contrast, a nation seeking entry into the European Union must abolish capital punishment as a condition of entry.[3] The United States also has the greatest economic inequality of advanced industrial nations, and it is the only one not to guarantee health care to all of its citizens. Outside of education, the social welfare provisions are quite meager by the standards of other economically developed nations. Within the public education system, huge disparities exist. In some metropolitan areas, per-pupil expenditures are three times as great for the most favored children as they are for other children living a few miles away.

Each of these matters is complicated and influenced by a number of factors. Capitalism cannot explain the differences, however, as all the advanced economic nations are capitalist. The relevant consideration is why, among capitalist nations, the United States is so smitten with market solutions to problems. That consideration connects to culture. Moreover, whether U.S. policy is right or wrong in any of the areas just described is beside the point. Perhaps health care should be a market decision, not a mutual guarantee. That is another conversation. Right or wrong, an important reason these policies are in place is because of the powerful role that individualism plays as Americans seek to make "sense" of the world.

Materialism also impacts policy. Because it is so imposingly physical, our commitment to materialism is immediately obvious. Representing less than 5 percent of the world's population, Americans consume about a quarter of the world's primary resources. Consider some of the results: the ubiquitous, oversized vehicles (fully loaded) gliding past endless billboards and beseeching store signs, even as the radio informs of still more purchasing possibilities; the vast supermarkets, where something as simple as buying chips is turned into a lengthy chain of decisions; the endless iteration of shopping malls, featuring total environments calibrated to the rhythms of consumption, capped by the crown jewel, Mall of America, now an awe-inspiring vacation destination for many; the oversized homes, crammed to the rafters with the latest delights of the consumer society, including multiple TV systems whose raison d'être is promoting greater acquisition, even as trash bins are filled and refilled to make way for the absorption of new things. There is a popular button, "I shop; therefore I am," that is usually worn with the tongue at least partly in cheek. But it is clear that many take this responsibility quite seriously.

Economist Jared Bernstein[4] describes the way policymakers have framed economic issues over the last thirty years as "You're on Your Own," or YOYO. The major economic policy initiatives of this period—tax cuts for the wealthy, cutbacks in social programs, the attempt to eliminate Social Security, and so forth—flow out of this larger vision. The resulting YOYO economy represents a marriage of the values of materialism and individualism. It seeks to cut programs of social insurance in order to maximize the money available for material consumption. Bernstein's attention is not focused on the culture, but he does note that "hyperindividualism" resides at the core of the YOYO value system.

Like people everywhere, Americans generate cultural norms that make sense to them, given their circumstances. Both individualism and materialism are deeply rooted in our history. The first person to use the word *individualism* in a serious social treatise was Alexis de Tocqueville. He used it in his epic work *Democracy in America,* which he wrote after visiting our young country in 1831.[5] In effect, the term was coined to describe us. And colonial historian Gordon Wood[6] has observed that, by the time of our Revolutionary War, Americans were notably materialistic. It is worth considering, therefore, why the values of individualism and materialism have been so compelling and have had such staying power.

The American Experience

Our historic and continuing deep religious tradition is well known,[7] and because the United States was the world's first Protestant nation, important strains of that orientation have influenced the culture. With respect to individualism, Martin Luther's assault on hierarchy and his assertion of the priesthood of the believers certainly were important. Additionally, the human condition, as it tended to be interpreted by various Protestant groups, contributed to an individualist ethos. John Bunyan's *Pilgrim's Progress,* the most widely read book in eighteenth-century America besides the Bible, lays bare the human predicament: People are born in sin. All will one day be judged by God, according to their own merit. Most will be condemned to eternal damnation, but a few struggling Christians will, through a life of demonstrated devotion and resistance to the pulls of a sinful world, escape the wrath of God and enter the kingdom of heaven.

These ideas evolved into a secularized individualism in the broader culture and as such reached a very broad audience. It is instructive that Horatio Alger, a minister's son, delivers the secularized story to a significant nineteenth-century audience confronting the distinctive hardships of an industrializing society. Alger's moral fables, such as *Ragged Dick* and *Mark the Matchboy,* confirmed the relevance of individualism at a time when the new order seemed to be moving lives beyond personal control. His stories invariably tell of a few individuals with the right stuff, struggling upward, overcoming the obstacles in the world by personal effort, wit, and a capacity to keep one's nose to the grindstone. Lesser individuals, those without the right stuff, are the ones who never make it out of the street. Bunyan would have understood.

Our materialism also connects to this religious tradition, but in a more subtle way. Max Weber is the most prominent of several scholars to unravel the paradox of the Protestant tradition fostering an immersion in the material world, even as it formally called for a withdrawal from that world. Seeking respite from the trauma resulting from unworthy sinners being judged by an inscrutable God, many came to believe that God would likely smile on the chosen few. In this way, success in the outside world became a sign of a righteous inner life. To this, Jackson Lears adds what he calls the "other Protestant Ethic."[8] He notes that the point of conversion, of being born again, is an ecstatic experience often involving whoops, shouts, and jubilant convulsions among converts. This loss of self-control is the visible evidence that God is working in one's life. And so "letting go" in a frenzy of acquisition is less alien to this tradition, more widely recognized for its austerity, than it might seem.

Religions are notoriously subject to diverse interpretations, and there is much in the Protestant tradition that would justify a concern for others over the concern for the self, just as one can find a biblical basis for rejecting materialism. We noted in the last chapter that the Dutch have drawn very different lessons from Calvinism than have Americans. The particular cultural gloss we placed on the Protestant tradition was no doubt connected to other aspects of the American experience. Wood notes, for example, that the sharp hierarchies existing in European countries during the colonial period limited materialist aspirations. In Europe, only aristocracies could legitimately desire the baubles being generated by developing capitalism. A class system existed in the colonies, but with new communities opening almost daily and immigrants regularly streaming to the "New World," the gentry here had a less certain grip on cultural development. A fluid class system obviously elevates individualism, but it also influenced consumption patterns. By the time of the revolution, many in the upper class were upset at the ease with which nonelites were able to buy things that were "inappropriate" for their social rank. As the nineteenth century dawned, America was the most commercial nation on Earth.[9]

The long frontier history of the United States also contributed significantly to the development of individualism and materialism. The national march westward was relentless, hampered only by "inconvenient" indigenous cultures and weak political systems that were easily conquered, eliminated, or marginalized. In contrast to Europe, where land issues had long been settled within (but not between) countries, the main problem in America was getting the right Europeans to settle and develop newly acquired land. Into the twentieth century, land was either given away by the government or sold at rock-bottom prices. With such ease of access, the idea of being responsible for one's fate was certainly more plausible than in "old Europe," as were the possibilities for material success.

Much has been written about the significance of the frontier in shaping American consciousness, and the stories we now tell ourselves about it are instructive. Frontier life required a substantial amount of cooperation. People survived and prospered by helping one another. Our individualism is fed, however, by the dominant synecdoche of nineteenth-century America, the solitary Western Hero. As Americans know him, that Hero does not build a society that allows him to live cooperatively with his neighbor; he stands against society. Societies are corrupting, made for weaklings who cannot stand on their own two feet. Authentic people, like the Hero, are autonomous. Usually they are men of few, and awkward, words, their inarticulateness symbolizing their social detachment. Often they "save" the society, but when they do they prefer riding into the sunset to joining it. And although the Hero may have turned in his six-shooter for an AK-47, he is still with us. As befits an individualist culture, the antisocial hero continues to enjoy an exalted place in our story telling. The essential shape of the narrative remains.

The Industrial Revolution came late to America, but when it did, it represented a serious threat to the developing culture. Doubts about industrialization are older than the Republic. The Boston Tea Party was not simply a revolt against taxes. It also reflected anger toward the East India Tea Company, to which the crown had granted substantial favors against individuals and small businesses in the colonies. Thomas Jefferson considered the yeoman farmer the foundation of a democratic society, believing that life generated the independence and civic virtue democracy required. He purchased the Louisiana Territory partly in hope of keeping the United States a rural society indefinitely. Later, social critics wrote about the demeaning effects that "wage slavery" had on workers in the industrializing North, arguing that, although the workers were paid, they were still enslaved by the industrial system.

One need not romanticize the hardscrabble, difficult life in rural America to recognize that it did have its compensations. People had a measure of control over their lives, organizing work routines themselves. What was sowed, weather permitting, was also reaped. Work relations in the new, sharply hierarchical industrial order were markedly different, and the sense of vulnerability greatly increased. People lost control over their lives, threatening the very individuality that was so important. For many men, the new work life was experienced as a form of emasculation.

The individualist tradition also contributed to the weakness of the U.S. labor movement, which might have fought more forcefully to maintain a sense of human dignity in the emerging order. In the end, the industrial system offered its own solution to the problem of emasculation by marrying individualism to materialism. To emotionally damaged people, it offered the balm of consumption. Individualism was now to be expressed by making personal product choices. Living an autonomous life might no longer be possible, but one could still be somebody by having lots of nice things. The source of people's angst was reinvented as its solution.

The American television system has emerged both to sustain the values of materialism and individualism and to keep them wired together. We are a TV nation, and uniquely so. The best estimates indicate that the average American spends about thirty hours a week watching TV, making television watching easily our greatest leisure-time activity. Some suggest that TV encourages social connectedness— even a sense of community—because large numbers of people can share a common experience like the last episode of a popular sitcom.

Whatever its community-building effects, TV elevates individualism at a more basic level.

As an electronic, visual, and very intimate medium, TV is personality oriented. Television is about getting to know people, "up close and personal." It does not do issues well. Issues require pause, reflection, reformulation, and so forth. Whatever the level of attention, TV washes over the viewer, relentless in its march. On the other hand, TV loves the intimacy of "personality." The national mania for personality information is driven by television.

Finally, television pulls us out of face-to-face communities, placing individual viewers at the center of the TV universe where, at the flick of a finger, they can move from one ersatz reality to another. Like no other invention, TV brings us home. And in today's multiple TV households, TV is increasingly watched alone. As we watch, we become subject to American television's distinctive and single-minded devotion to selling goods. That is, in fact, its point. It is not an accident that the more people watch TV (controlling for social class), the more they consume.[10] American television reinforces and extends mass consumption—ironically, often by appeals to individualism. "You deserve a break today." "Treat yourself. You're worth it." "You can, yes, you can, have it all."

American Dreamers

Our species' capacity for symbolic representation gives rise to imaginative thought. Just as we can impose meaning on things that are, we can imagine things that are not. We are dreamers, and utopian dreams have an esteemed lineage. In the long tradition of utopian thought, the locus of the ideal life has been the community. Since we are destined to spend our lives in a community, utopian thinkers ask, What kind of community is best? The American Dream, in homage to the cultural norms we have been considering, exists in stark contrast to that tradition. It is silent about the qualities of a shared social life. This is quite odd when one thinks about it, but since it is generated by our own cultural norms, we tend not to think about it. Driven by individualism and materialism, it is intensely private and thoroughly egocentric, a dream of individual struggle toward a life of personal ease, control, security, and comfort. Accumulation is central to the goals toward which we privately struggle. One pinnacle of achievement, acquiring a "dream house," has led an observer to note, "For the first time in history, a civilization created a utopian ideal based on the house rather than on the city or the nation."[11] One might add that usually the house has a fence around it, for the American Dream is indifferent to the plight of one's neighbors, one's community, and one's nation. It is in fact an aggregation of millions of private dreams that seemingly bear no relationship to each other.

But the house, though the subject of dreams, remains outside the ability of many in our society to obtain. The automobile plays a more immediate and extensive role in our symbolic lives. Cars, also, are the stuff of dreams. Some argue that our devotion to the automobile is the result of a conspiracy of car manufacturers and oil companies to suppress alternative forms of transportation. While these interests have never been reluctant to exercise their considerable political clout in pursuit of profits, the story has another important dimension: This political power has always been exercised in a very congenial cultural context.

If one had to pick a metaphor that best represents American culture, one might easily select the car. Its central role in American life has been noted. No other nation in the world answers the question "How should people move about?" with the monotonic ferocity of the United States. Except for the home, cars are likely to be the most expensive things Americans buy, and they are purchased many times throughout one's life. Each year, hundreds of billions more are spent to operate them—on highways, parking, parts, gas, insurance, licenses, tolls, highway patrols, fines, and the like.

Things other than cost also suggest the importance of automobility to Americans. Car magazines proliferate. People wait for the annual fall display of new vehicle models with eager anticipation and flock to auto shows throughout the country. Many spend countless hours working on their cars—souping up engines and customizing them, drawing inspiration from MTV's *Pimp My Ride.* Various types of car clubs draw people together. Acquiring a driver's license is a major rite of passage. The gift of a car frequently symbolizes the occurrence of a major life event, such as graduation or an important anniversary. People often impute emotions to their cars, a habit Freudians call *cathexis.* The animated film *Cars,* a nostalgic ode to the emergence

Expanding highways has not relieved congestion.

of the car culture of the 1950s featuring cars as anthropomorphic beings, was a major box office hit in 2006.

The car serves materialist inclinations well. A new purchase is a major status symbol and often an indication of one's social place. It is central to the materialist experience, as cars come with a dazzling array of possible options. Many of these have actual functions, but all serve as additional merit badges on the status sash. General Motors, Ford, and Chrysler are in the top five corporations in advertising expenditures, and in these ads the promise of status, power, and control dominates.[12]

The automobile is also an apt expression of individualism, as its very name implies autonomous movement. If the cowboy, loping over the range in search of freedom and adventure, remains a central mythic figure, the car is promoted as the logical heir to the horse. John Wayne would never take the bus. The car allows for highly flexible private movement. It caters to individual whim, taking drivers precisely where they wish to go. Driving a car reinforces privacy and separation. Automobility expresses the desire for loose social bonds. It also contours social reality, creating what some have called the "drive-thru" culture.

It thus increases individualist isolation even as it expresses it. The endless iteration of styles and features allows consumers to feel that they have acquired a special car built just for them.

The central place of the car is underscored by the recognition that it is integral to the American Dream. Not only is it a major marker along the road to that dream, it literally takes us to the dream house, now characteristically located in suburban enclaves. Eliminating the necessity of locating suburbs along railroad spurs, cars have been a powerful stimulus to suburban proliferation and sprawl. In turn, suburbanites have more room to gather stuff, allowing for more complete accommodation to materialism and individualism. Moreover, the major impetus to suburban homes was to withdraw from the social messiness created by the Industrial Revolution, to be a "haven in a heartless world." The architecture of suburbia reflects the push for withdrawal. Garages, once located along alleys at the back of lots, have moved to the front of the property; they are frequently connected to the house and are the most prominent part of the structure. Internal garage and house passageways reduce opportunities for social contact. Front porches, which in older cities pulled people out of their homes and into a community street life, no longer exist in most suburban locations. Instead, when people wish to be outdoors, they use backyard patios that maintain privacy and reinforce disconnection.[13]

Those desiring a more bike-friendly nation struggle against powerful and uncongenial cultural norms. The bike is a sturdy agent of individualism, but it is an individualism built on a deeper sense of community and environmental connection. The car is more representative of the American tradition of individualism—that is, individualism as separation and isolation. And while the bike can also be a focus of the drive for acquisition, it is not hot-wired into that process the way the automobile is. There is no getting around it: The bike speaks to different cultural values than does the car, and that has posed a problem for bike advocates.

The Gathering Cultural Storm

Every culture contains norms that express the "right" way to live. One culture suggests that ultimate happiness is obtained in a life of contemplation; another has it that happiness is a function of material accumulation and individualism. So long as the people living in the two cultures are happy pursuing the proffered paths, why does it matter what those values are? Any culture limits possibility; why worry about a culture that has evidently served us reasonably well, even if it does consign bike friendliness to political and social backwaters?

The picture sketched to this point does not adequately describe the present conditions, however. There is cultural unrest, out of which a storm is brewing. This storm grows partly because the internal contradictions of materialism and individualism grow increasingly obvious, partly because newer social circumstances make these values less compelling, and partly because those benefiting from the current norms seek to sustain them with increasing intensity. Cultural norms work best when people grow into them as part of everyday life experience. This reduces consciousness of the norms, imparting to them the sense of reality itself. A shrill articulation of the norms elevates consciousness of them, suggesting they are merely ideological. These various forces stimulate a gathering storm, one that is not recognized explicitly by most people but is nevertheless felt. People know something is happening, but, lacking a cultural frame, they don't know what it is. They don't know how to name it. To paraphrase Italian social theorist Antonio Gramsci, the old is dying, but it is not yet clear that the new can be born.

There is much to be admired in the value of individualism, and, given the American experience, it is impossible to imagine it not always being an important aspect of American self-identification. An indomitable spirit, a willingness to struggle against odds, an enthusiastic optimism can lead to exceptional accomplishment. In our society, riding a bike to work may be an expression of individualism, and, as we will see in the next chapter, the bike movement itself contains many eccentric individuals. But it is important to understand the limits of individualism. It cannot ultimately be satisfying as a root value of a culture because it does not supply a solid foundation.

Humans are social beings, driven together because we need each other to fulfill our greatest selves. A culture that suggests people gather together in order to be left alone borders on incoherence. Yet individualism does reside close to the core of our culture, even as its inability to account for everyday experience grows. It is incessantly propagated in commercial and political rhetoric. Often it is described as freedom, by which most Americans mean nothing more than an absence of constraint—the ability to do one's thing, to "light out for the territories" of Huck Finn's dreams.

This is an impoverished view of freedom, best obtained on a deserted island. But what kind of freedom is that? One is free to dine out, but where to go? One is free to read books, but who will have written them? One is free to hear music, but who will sing? Even the most fervent proponents of freedom are not looking for such places to live. A deeper sense of freedom is nurtured by mutuality and cooperation and thus, ironically, by constraint. A culture may value individualism, but it also must recognize that individualism inevitably must emanate from shared lives and shared fates. What mutual guarantees provide the best soil for individualism?

Materialist accumulation also has its appeals. The desire for things may be part of human nature. As a source of identification and ultimate happiness, however, it is similarly flawed. This is especially the case as this value has been made foundational by profit-making economic interests of the society. If accumulation "delivered the goods," if it made us happy, that would be one thing. But when one recognizes the differing motives involved in commercial exchange, one can see why happiness built on materialism is problematic. The buyer may pursue an object out of an interest in happiness and identity, and the products may momentarily provide these. But the seller is interested in moving goods, which requires the subversion of happiness and identity.

In the modern economy, happiness and identity are the true enemies of commercial exchange, even as they are represented as its goals. Despite ephemeral nods toward identity, it must in fact be assaulted. Consumers are constantly told that recent purchases are not enough, that they are still not OK, that their lives are yet incomplete, that they "need" the additional or new things being marketed. The more certain one's sense of self, the less susceptible one is to the blandishments of the American world of consumption. That is why adolescents, for whom issues of personal identity are on the front burner of psychosocial development, are such rapacious consumers. Consumers chase identity and community up a down escalator. New promises of identity and happiness constantly emerge underfoot, but as soon as they are engaged, another step appears that also quickly vanishes. The consumer must purchase simply to keep pace. Today's promise of happiness and fulfillment must become tomorrow's outmoded iPod. If momentary happiness is not replaced by resurrected angst, the system would fall apart.

As the central artifact of the culture, the car not only embodies the values of materialism and individualism but also reveals their contradictions. To increase sales, cars are marketed, not simply as utilitarian machines but to enhance our fantasies. Indeed, fantasy itself is enhanced. As regularly as clockwork, cars are purchased to satisfy materialist dreams, to make us feel as if we "are somebody" or are sexually adequate. Once they are purchased, however, cars are almost always a source of great anxiety. The possibility of purchasing a lemon is a continuing concern. We fear being swindled by hustling sellers, and we worry that the warranty, despite its promise, is worthless. The first dent often induces melancholy in the owner. Even if such fears ultimately prove groundless, the car's status is reduced the moment new models roll off the assembly line. Inevitably, the ticket to happiness and fulfillment becomes simply a "used car."

The car also works against primary human urges for community and fellowship. It has a major impact on patterns of social interaction, a fact noted by numerous social critics.[14] In preautomotive days, streets were public meeting places—centers of play, commerce, and public discourse. They were, in short, the generators of community. Merchants would ply their wares from carts parked in the streets, neighbors would meet and linger while strolling through them or beckon from their porches, and children would play in them. Because they had such general utility, when the Better Roads Movement sought to transform streets into more efficient systems of mobility, it was met with active resistance, and even violence.

The development of highways was premised on the idea, now commonplace but once controversial, that mobility is the point of roads. The other functions of the roads receded and eventually disappeared. In the earliest days of automobility, low-powered, open cars traveling on relatively primitive roads that followed the contours of the landscape provided some source of social connection. Early drives through Central Park in New York were not too different from strolls down Fifth Avenue. Such auto-inspired connection is a thing of the past. Now interstates cut huge concrete swaths through urban spaces, simultaneously obliterating neighborhoods and obscuring what remains. The vast interstate system of Los Angeles, for example, is disconnected from its environs. At any point in this system, one could be anywhere. Only the uniform highway signs provide orientation. There is no sense of Watts on the Harbor Freeway, of East Los Angeles on the San Gabriel Freeway, or of Hollywood on the Hollywood Freeway. Even these older names for the various arteries of the interstate system have been replaced by numbers, as place names no longer serve a purpose. On this system, one of the most diverse metropolises in the world seems completely uniform.

These days, people are less in the world than they are driving through it. Increasingly, drivers are disconnected from each other as well. Today's high-powered, hermetically sealed pods are agents of social isolation. Tinted windows, themselves augmenting the sense of separation, are perpetually closed to take advantage of air conditioning and music sound systems—and to shield us from the noise generated by other traffic. A recent Nissan Sentra ad presents the car as a virtual home, giving the driver no reason to leave its total environment. As the car embodies materialist and individualist conceits of the culture, it also lays bare their contradictions. Purchased with the idea that they will set us free (notice how car ads typically show the solitary motorist, in control, zipping along a lonely road through sparsely populated lands), they in fact imprison us. Americans now spend more time in cars than any people ever have, and to achieve this dubious distinction, they have extinguished much of the open space celebrated in auto ads.

A recent study shows that the sense of social isolation is growing in the United States. In 2005, "one quarter of Americans say they have no one with whom they can discuss personal troubles, more than double the number who were similarly isolated in 1985. Overall, the number of people Americans have in their closest circle of confidants has dropped from around three to about two."[15] Many things are no doubt at work to increase this growing sense of isolation. Our growing reliance on increasingly private automobiles has at minimum reinforced that trend. It is ironic that, when interviewed about the study, Duke sociologist Lynn Smith-Lovin noted, "That image of people on roofs after Katrina resonates with me, because those people *did not know someone with a car*" (emphasis added).[16] Smith-Lovin was commenting on a simple fact about car owner-ship, but cars are an expression of the YOYO economy.

In his study of Los Angeles, David Rieff ponders the fact that motor-ists spend so much time idling in their cars. He concludes:[17]

> All the fabled California cults ... were really far less radical, when you stopped to think about it, than one ordinary resident of the Los Angeles basin, driving alone on the freeway, unencumbered by spouse, children, or relations, through spaces that, unless he has lived or worked there, are more like empty spaces than real places to him. All around him are other, similarly occupied people.... [N]obody could have imagined that it would have been possible to so completely decontextualize people, or that the internal combustion engine would have made this atomization seem like a gift.

Something else about the car is relevant to the consideration of the values of materialism and individualism. One can concede that cars yield certain efficiencies from a private perspective. A car, for example, might make me feel good about myself at least temporarily, and it might quickly get me to the exact place I wish to go in comfort and with little effort. Even though, as previously noted, cars are enormously expensive to own, operate, insure, and maintain, one can conclude that, by private choices exercised in the market, they are what consum-ers prefer. Such sentiments are understandable in a culture having materialism and individualism as root values. Given the problems inherent in these norms as root values, however, it is appropriate to raise additional questions about the efficacy of automobiles. When one thinks beyond the self and considers autos from the perspective of social efficiency, the American car system is a disaster.

As ownership grows, more land is given over to concrete—for wider, more elaborate highways and for parking. Highway analysts reveal that, because parking facilities must be designed for periods of maximum use, each vehicle in operation requires six parking spaces.[18] Studies show that highway construction does little to relieve congestion. It simply expands the number of automobiles in use. As their use grows, other transportation options are crowded out, thus discriminating against those who cannot drive, including the young, many elderly, as well as people with physical challenges. Those who can drive therefore face increasing demands to transport those who cannot. Partly in response to this, in many families today, the number of cars is equivalent to the number of people in that family eligible to drive. Three- and four-car families do not think of themselves as extravagant. Rather, their car purchases are made to satisfy basic "needs" required in today's autocentric society.

Cars pose serious ecological and health problems as well. Automobility is the most dangerous form of population movement. Each year more than forty thousand people die in auto accidents, while several hundred thousand more are injured. Carbon dioxide emissions generated in the operation and manufacture of cars contaminate the air we breathe and are a major source of global warming. Heavy salting of streets during winter in northern cities threatens water supplies. Cars drain the world of finite resources. Our dependence on foreign oil causes us to support repressive political regimes in the belief that this support will ensure a continuing flow of oil. Disposing of used cars is a continuing problem. Whatever the personal efficiencies of the car, these must be balanced against the social inefficiencies evident at every phase of the car's existence.

The problems of autocentrism are placed in bold relief by one of the most freeway-happy cities in America: Houston.[19] During the 1990s, the Houston region built more roads than any other *state* except California and of course Texas. Yet during this time congestion almost doubled, roughly reflecting national trends and maintaining Houston's position as one of the most traffic-snarled regions in the country.[20] The response has been to expand road construction further, obliterating homes and parks that once stood in the way. The Katy Freeway, once a four-lane road, is being remade into a sixteen-lane superhighway. The project is already $1 billion over budget. In 2005, the regional Transportation Policy Council enacted a $77 billion 2025 transportation plan that promotes the biggest road-building bonanza the area has ever seen. It equates to 117 Katy Freeway projects, enough lane miles to stretch from San Francisco to South Africa.

For years, the "More Cars, More Highways" gestalt has totally dominated the Houston region's culture and politics. The power of Texas oil interests is exerted in a state that is also the epicenter of individualism. It is hardly surprising that the car plays such a central role there. Even in Texas, however, there have been countercurrents to the dominant culture, and the latest transportation proposal plan has increased their force. Questions about where this is all supposed to lead are being asked. Scientists, academics, doctors, and transportation critics have rallied with ordinary people whose homes are in the way of this project to summarize the huge inefficiencies being generated simply to keep people in cars. The internal logic of the automobile, like the internal logic of materialism, is not self-limiting, so it eventually evolves into conditions so absurd that the logic itself crumbles.

The power of materialism and individualism to bind us, to convey a convincing picture of reality, is diminishing. And it will continue to diminish as their contradictions with everyday life experience grow. Material goods are finite. Access to them drains scarce resources and exacts a toll on other things we desire as well, such as open space, forests, even a planet that can sustain life. A norm that posits limitless accumulation ill suits a twenty-first-century society. And as our society grows more complex, our lives are also more obviously interdependent. Consider the "simple" act of driving a car. It certainly seems like a solitary act, and cultural illusions reinforced by ads may sustain that impression. In fact, however, our ability to drive is totally dependent on others. Someone needs to build cars, others to ensure that they are built to certain standards, still others to maintain them. Someone teaches us to drive, and to drive according to rules that are commonly agreed to, on roads that are safely constructed and regularly inspected. Others enforce the rules, issuing licenses and traffic tickets. Our culture is notable for generating road rage, yet even here driving would be impossible without a more powerful sentiment of driver cooperation. And so it is in almost every phase of our lives. Consider the network of dependencies involved in eating a meal or attending a college class. This is not to imply that individualism must go by the wayside. Indeed, in some sense the possibilities for individualism are greater than ever. But it cannot be a root value. It must rest on a foundation of common interests and a sense of shared fates that will allow it to flower.

The interdependence that has grown with the Industrial Revolution has required government response despite a culture that works against it doing so. Social Security, Medicare, environmental protection, student financial aid, and other social welfare programs have come about because people have demanded them. But they exist awkwardly, in uneasy relation to the larger culture. We tend to be defensive about such programs, and they are notable for their tepidness. On the other hand, there are full-throated roars against programs that allegedly stifle initiative and cater to the "undeserving."

If the old is dying, however, why cannot the new be born? For one thing, shifting toward the shared ideas that bind us is particularly problematic in a culture that works against the very idea of community. The values of individualism and materialism discourage collective resolution to social problems, thereby preserving the status quo. If individual effort and capacity are the legitimate determinants of success, there is little for the government to do except to get out of the way. Materialism is similarly egocentric, regarding happiness as a private pursuit, a function of personal market choice. Government tends to get in the way of these choices by taxing our hard-earned money, leaving us with a smaller pool of resources with which to optimize happiness. There is not, as yet, a reliable vocabulary of opposition.

There is an additional drag on the emergence of new cultural norms. Since the current norms ratify the status quo, those who currently benefit disproportionately from them defend them mightily. Some people get fabulously wealthy because material desire is promoted, even as individualism sustains their exalted social positions. This includes the leaders of the mass media system through which much information is transmitted. Clearly the purveyors of the current culture have been ratcheting up the propaganda on its behalf, perhaps most powerfully through the American advertising system.

That system, now manically imperialistic, seeks to turn every phase of daily life into opportunities to consume, leading to what one social critic has called, "the advertised life."[21] Consider the cultural life of the Super Bowl, how and why it has been hyped into a national religious experience dominated by the promotion of consumption. Then, expand such thinking to include the trend of sports in general. From there, consider what has happened in other areas, with recreation and leisure, with holidays, with education. Leaf through a magazine, walk into a supermarket, or go to a movie, and think about how such experiences are increasingly larded with imperatives to consume. It is ironic that the goal of mass consumption is represented as a way to express individuality.

Tarnished Dreams

Social critic Jeremy Rifkin[22] notes that the American Dream has been changing in recent decades. The traditional Horatio Alger formulation holds that, through denial, self-improvement, and hard work, the individual rises to achieve material affluence and success. In short, a man earns his castle. In this formulation, there is no basis for complaint, because both winners and losers deserve their fates. Rifkin summarizes an impressive array of data to show that while there is still substantial interest in affluence, the beliefs about how best to attain it are changing. People are losing faith in the American Dream, believing success is now a matter of luck. One recent survey showed a stunning 34 percent of Americans reported no longer believing in the traditional formulation. Doubts are particularly strong among younger and less affluent citizens, and they erode confidence in the cultural myths that are supposed to bind us. If people doubt that they can make it through their own good effort, they are also unlikely to believe that those holding favored positions have attained them because of merit.

Major events can also effect cultural change by causing people to reinterpret reality and meaning in their daily lives. Nearly all of us can recall where we were on September 11, 2001. Our quarter was just beginning, and I was teaching an American government class at 8:30 that morning as the events were breaking. For this course, I always meet with students in small groups outside class to help us become acquainted. The discussions are not necessarily political, but 9/11 obviously dominated the conversations that quarter. Everyone was stunned—by the events themselves, by their own ignorance and previous indifference, by how the events personally affected them, by their grieving sense of connection to those who perished that day. There was also considerable but largely unfocused anger toward whomever or whatever was responsible. At the corners of these conversations was an additional sort of anger—unarticulated and diffuse, but nevertheless palpable. It was the anger of people who had been immersed in routines of happy indifference suddenly having to think about matters larger than themselves.

It was a privilege to be a part of those conversations because the attitudes and emotions expressed in them were, I believe, pretty much a microcosm of those of the nation. The search for meaning and understanding came at a time when the old rules did not seem to apply. The security generated by our unprecedented military might simply increased the sense of shock at what a few people with box cutters could do. We felt a strong sense of connection to people we did not know: to those who lost loved ones in that tragedy, to the many heroes who risked and lost their lives in selfless efforts to help others, to strangers we encountered on the street. The damage that was done was not limited to the World Trade Center and the Pentagon; it rippled throughout our society. Lives were disrupted. People stopped traveling, and when they resumed, it did not feel the same. There was a serious economic downturn. The swirl of events and emotions precipitated by that occurrence also offered a rare "teachable moment," a time when people were drawn out of daily routines in search of larger meaning. Such a moment might have been an impetus for cultural transformation toward a new set of shared values that more realistically reflected the nature of daily experience.

The story of 9/11 illustrates the interconnection of our lives. We all felt the subsequent economic impact, including the drain from resources that have been devoted to getting those who were responsible. But we also felt a spiritual and emotional connection. There was a sense that everyone mattered and that they mattered in surprisingly equal ways. The business executive who lost her life on that day mattered no more than the janitor who cleaned her office; Americans in the tower mattered no more than foreigners. People were ready for common sacrifice. Millions contributed to relieve the pain of those who most immediately suffered from 9/11. A somewhat amorphous but broadly felt sense of community and shared fates emerged, mainly needing a storyteller to place it in bold relief.

But the nation's Chief Storyteller was ill suited for this task. President Bush often noted, subsequently, that "everything changed" as a result 9/11. Culturally, however, the president sought to ensure that nothing changed. The individualist strut of our culture was not reconsidered. As FDNY T-shirts faded, firefighters returned to their traditional positions of social invisibility and paltry remuneration. The collapse of the Cold War had already increased the sense that the world was our oyster, but now our policy became more unilateral. An international variant of individualism became more pronounced, built on the hubris that we could control the course of world events. The president declared a "War on Terror," but this war evoked no sacrifice. In the past, declarations of war had been accompanied by tax increases to finance them. This time, a tax cut primarily benefiting the wealthy and causing huge deficits to be paid off by later generations came along with the war. For an administration that had never been able to conceive a situation not justifying tax cuts, this was politics as usual. This "me-first" lack of consideration for future generations is yet another elaboration of the individualist ethos. There was no Kennedyesque call for Americans to ask what they could do for their country. Instead, the president simply advised Americans to go shopping. The duties of the American Consumer were exalted over the duties of the American Citizen. We were not asked to engage in any common effort beyond the common obedience to authority.

As the War on Terror morphed into the war on Iraq, that adventure was also presented in culturally familiar terms. Once we got rid of Saddam Hussein, we were told, everything would be fine. When his statue was pulled down by an American tank, we were led to believe our mission was accomplished, except for rounding up a few more bad guys whose faces were displayed on a deck of cards. Experts had long noted that the complexities and divisions in Iraq made overthrowing the government there a very complicated and possibly catastrophic enterprise, but individualist simple-mindedness carried the day. Once the war began, every effort was made to conceal any sense of sacrifice. Our "volunteer" army was represented as people making rational choices about their futures. For years the mass media was cajoled into presenting only the most sanitized version of the effects of the war. The Pentagon forbade pictures of flag-draped coffins of returning soldiers. When *Nightline* devoted a Memorial Day evening to showing photographs, without comment, of American soldiers who had been killed in Iraq, the show was roundly criticized by supporters of the president's policy and accused of giving aid and comfort to the enemy. These representations of reality, based on familiar cultural struts, wobbled as our descent into the mire deepened.

Hurricane Katrina is another event that rattled dominant cultural norms. In collective consciousness, cities often are viewed as embodying different aspects of the nation. When one thinks of Washington, D.C., New York City, Chicago, or San Francisco, different images spring to mind. For many, the horror of Katrina was exacerbated by the fact that it happened in a place that many regard as embodying America's soul.

What was revealed there was not pretty. Those who were left behind on the city's rooftops, those whose homes were most severely damaged, those who were shipped off to the Houston Astrodome were not a random selection of the population. Mainly they came from the ranks that are routinely ignored, even hidden from view—the black, urban poor, the unseen underbelly of the American Dream, a "third world" society within our borders. After continuing government inaction, an enraged Kanye West was moved to comment that the president "doesn't care about black people." He might well have referenced those supporting the dominant norms of the culture, for which the revelation of desperate lives is at least an inconvenience. Katrina also served as a more broadly ominous portent. Unlimited consumption is leading to global warming. It is impossible to prove that Katrina, specifically, was the result of global warming, but it is certain that, unless global warming is arrested, a profusion of Katrina-like events is in our future.

Cultures normally promote quiet. They relax us, telling us to "see-that" things are orderly and clear. Events like 9/11, Hurricane Katrina, and the Iraq war have combined with the everyday experience of lives that are intricately connected to generate a culture storm. There have always been those who have opposed the preeminence of the values of materialism and individualism. Sometimes these have generated subcultures reflecting very different value structures, but they have never been ascendant. The current storm presents an interesting cultural moment because there is a growing sense that things are not as they are supposed to be.

For years, the Gallup Organization has asked Americans how they feel about the direction of the country. It is a general question, and one that is therefore subject to multiple interpretations. Responses may reflect surface events, or they may reflect something deeper. But from 9/11 into 2007, the number of people saying this country is on the "wrong track" far exceeded those who reported the country was headed in the "right direction." A chilly wind, from a habitually optimistic people. And popular disdain of people in authority—politicians, business leaders, newscasters, and religious leaders—has soared as well.

Despite the increased pressures to consume discussed earlier, many people are making occupational decisions that indicate there are things on their minds besides maximizing incomes. Others are rethinking past decisions they have made. Sociologist Juliet Schor, one of the keenest observers of this newest phase of materialism in the United States, also notes that about one-fifth of the population has chosen to step off the consumer escalator. This group, whom she labels "voluntary downshifters," has recognized and valued the things that materialism could *not* achieve in their lives and so made lifestyle changes that have entailed making less money.[23]

After a long dormant period, student activism is increasing, and it is being driven by values that contradict the cultural strains we have been discussing. Many student activists today are motivated by a sense of shared fates and interconnectedness. They confront corporate and political leaders on issues of globalization, workplace conditions and worker exploitation, and environmental decay and global warming. The student boycott movement is especially strong, and it is also culturally interesting as it suggests the power that can be exercised by not consuming.[24]

Social critics are beginning to write in ways that are relevant to cultural reformulation. Jared Bernstein's review of the problems of our current economic system ultimately notes that the YOYO values of economists, the assumptions that they bring to their analyses, are causing much social harm. In his concluding chapter, he makes a strong case for using a different set of norms to make economic assessments, which he calls We're In This Together (WITT). Jeremy Rifkin discusses the crisis of the American Dream as a way to introduce an interesting cultural development in the European community. He chronicles the emergence of a very different way of thinking there. He writes, "The European Dream, with its emphasis on inclusivity, diversity, quality of life, sustainability, deep play, universal human rights and the rights of nature, and peace is increasingly attractive to a generation anxious to be globally connected and at the same time locally embedded."[25] Rifkin, who for twenty years has divided his time between Europe and the United States, knows full well that cultural transference is unlikely, but he also knows that norms are adaptable and that norms similar to the ones Europe is moving toward are also increasingly urgent for the world, including the United States.

The bike is caught up in this culture storm. In some ways the dominant culture seeks to domesticate the bike by turning it into one more variant of commodity fetishism, but most of those in the bike movement see it differently. A decision to ride a bike is a very individualistic decision in our culture. But the bike deepens one's sense of connection to others. It is also a statement about limits and sustainability. As it assimilates the bike, the culture also accommodates to it. Cultural change is necessary in order for the bike to be widely adopted as a transportation alternative. At the same time, however, increased use of the bike stimulates cultural change. The old cultural story that is losing its grip on the nation at large is on life support among a significant segment of the bike community. In this vanguard, creating culture from the ground up, are "bike eccentrics," to whom we now turn.

Chapter Four

Biking Eccentrics

Who Are These Folks, Anyway?

The cultural terrain may be shifting, but most people still think that those who ride bikes for purposes other than recreation are not quite with it. Two recent popular films epitomize the place that "biking for mobility" occupies in popular culture. In the first film, *Napoleon Dynamite,* the estranged stranger of his high school class, poignantly reaches out to Pedro, who is also lost but in another dimension. Nonetheless, they are able to build what seems less a friendship than an alliance. Pedro reveals his nerdishness by showing Napoleon the "Sledgehammer" bike that he regularly rides to school. In bathetic solidarity, Napoleon expresses envy instead of disdain. "Dang! You got shocks, pegs. Lucky! You ever take it off any sweet jumps?" The next scene shows Napoleon impaling himself on Pedro's bike as he attempts a ridiculously small jump off a ridiculously built ramp.

In the second film, *The 40-Year-Old Virgin,* the hero is perhaps the adult version of Napoleon. His nerdishness is underscored early in the film as he haplessly pedals his bicycle through a world that is quite literally passing him by. Later on, the woman with whom he has a budding relationship buys him a "cool" bike and helmet. In the ensuing scene the energized hero is seen confidently racing through the city streets on his new bike. The joke here is that the hero is still a nerd; he simply thinks he is not.

These two films capture a sentiment that remains strong in the popular culture. To many Americans, postadolescent bike riding (of a nonrecreational nature) signifies either childishness, a lack of social and economic success, or possibly a combination of the two. In the mainstream culture, a bike comes attached with social stigma. Unlike in Amsterdam, using a bike for something other than recreation implies "loser." This American view is less a matter of the inherent inadequacies of the bike than it is a function of how vigorously the car is embedded in our consciousness as a benchmark of success.

This investigation inevitably connected me to people who were seriously into a biking gestalt. I realized that a group I have called, for want of a better term, "biking eccentrics," comprised an interesting and important chapter of the story. Biking eccentrics are people for whom the bike has become an important way to frame experience; they are, therefore, eccentric from the perspective of the dominant culture. They do not simply ride bikes. They think about the world largely in terms of the bike.

By definition, most of us do not resist the authority of the dominant culture. Rather, we're good citizens. We don't ask questions. People wander about, in Thoreau's classic phrase, "buying and selling, and spending their lives like serfs"—a characterization that is more apt today than it was in the nineteenth century. We dutifully attend auto shows, ingest our allotment of car advertisements on commercial TV, and regularly seek to upgrade our lives by upgrading our cars. Thus is normalcy defined in America. To ask questions, as biking eccentrics have done, is to be weird or an outsider—possibly even subversive. Asking questions about dominant modes of existence does not necessarily make one right, but it often makes one interesting.

A dominant worldview, on the other hand, is not "right" simply by virtue of its dominance. One of the things that can make eccentrics interesting is that they may have a worldview that offers a more compelling story for social cohesion than the one with which we are more familiar. Or, they could be full of beans and therefore destined to remain in cultural backwaters. Historical change is inscrutable that way. What I do know is that there is often more to people who are seriously into biking than is commonly assumed, and it is worth considering how they frame the world. Although the eccentrics profiled all reside in the Chicago area, they are without question a national, if minor, phenomenon.

Randy Neufeld: The Pioneer

Randy Neufeld is a tall, fit-looking man in his late forties. He is very thoughtful, with a soft-spoken demeanor that initially masks a resolute commitment. Although he would be reluctant to say this about himself, he is one of the most important figures in the national biking advocacy scene. Neufeld began working in the Chicagoland Bicycle Federation (CBF) in 1987. At the time, it was a fledgling organization that had no money and was dependent on an idealistic volunteer staff fitfully advocating bicycle-friendly policies. Under Neufeld's leadership, this inchoate group grew into the largest local bicycle advocacy organization in America. Neufeld no longer heads the CBF, but he is still a key member of the organization.

Much in Neufeld's background would have projected a life of political work—even a life of political work in bicycle policy. He was born in Allentown, Pennsylvania, and raised in a devout Mennonite family. His father, grandfather, and great-grandfather were all Mennonite ministers. Mennonites are traditionally ascetic "plain people" noted for their pacifism and their worldwide commitment to helping people recover from natural disasters. Following his family tradition, Neufeld majored in religion at Bethel College in Kansas, and although he no longer thinks of himself as conventionally religious, he acknowledges the huge impact that his Mennonite upbringing has had on his consciousness. He argues that, although it is not uncommon for people to leave the Mennonite church, it is rare to leave that tradition altogether, and he still considers himself a "cultural Mennonite," as does his wife, Susan Geil.

One of the continuing legacies of that tradition in Neufeld's life, for example, is his attraction to the notion of "simple living." This is a lifestyle that is wary of the attractions of material goods and the encumbrances engendered by thoughtless consumption. A complementary sentiment is an appreciation of the natural world—a world often ravaged by the drive for material accumulation. This discon-nection from the acquisitive impulses extends his sense of personal freedom, and it also sets him apart from the main currents of our culture. Although he makes a decent salary at the CBF, comparable to that of other nonprofits, money has never been especially important to him, nor is it a source of motivation. He told me, "No matter what our income, Susan and I have always believed that we are the wealthi-est people in our income bracket." Because their needs are not great, they always have more than enough money to satisfy.

Another characteristic that connects to his Mennonite upbringing is that he has led a purpose-driven life. In his early adult years, he was a political organizer and activist for progressive causes and politicians. He loved the political work but eventually began to look for a "saner lifestyle." The episodic nature of the political work he was doing—periods of frantic, eighteen-hour days followed by periods of relative dormancy—began to wear on him. He started to look for political work that was more constant but also a little less frenetic. In 1987, he joined the CBF. After interviews with the board of that organization, it was clear that they wanted him, but they had no money for a salary. He told them, "Hire me, and I will raise the money." They did, and so did he.

The specific decision to move into bicycle advocacy might also have been foretold by his background. The bicycle is inherently attractive to someone philosophically committed to simple living. He attended high school in Phoenix, and when a wreck totaled his car, he simply started riding his bike to school. Characteristic of many newer western cities, Phoenix sprawls into its desert environment with very limited public transportation. In consequence, Neufeld began riding his bike to destinations other than school. This was not very typical for a teen-ager in the 1970s. Moreover, adolescence is not usually a time when distinctive life trajectories are sought. Typically, teens find comfort in peer conformity. (This is what makes the joke about Pedro's bike possible.) I asked him whether riding to high school and possibly be-ing considered an "odd duck" was unnerving. He replied that being an odd duck was "kind of a source of identity for me." I assume his Mennonite heritage prepared him for this perspective as well.

When Neufeld came to Chicago and got involved in political work, he still had a bike but never thought about it seriously. But in 1985 he and Susan made a fateful decision. They took off on a six-thousand-mile,

Randy Neufeld and Mayor Richard Daley are a powerful biking tandem in Chicago (Photo courtesy Eliot Wineberg).

six-month bike trip, riding in a big loop around the western two-thirds of the United States. They thought of it as "a before kids fling." It was a transforming experience, opening previously unimagined vistas and causing him to think of the bike's untapped potential. When he decided to look for new work in 1987, he thought of bicycle advocacy.

Since that time, the Neufelds have been a car-free family, but they are not totally opposed to the car. They occasionally rent one for extended trips. And they will sometimes use taxicabs. They also accept rides from friends. But they depend overwhelmingly on bikes and public transport for their mobility. They are fortunate to live in Chicago, which by American standards has an extensive public transportation system.

At the time of our interview, Randy and Susan had two high school–aged kids, Jonah, sixteen, and Hannah, fourteen. I was curious about how being carless in Chicago was for them. Once again my thoughts turned to social ostracism. Neufeld pondered the question, wanting to avoid projecting his own values onto his children. Jonah takes public transportation to school. Whitney Young, an excellent Chicago high school that draws students from all over the city, is several miles from the Neufelds' North Side home. "But I think he chooses public transportation, not so much because he rejects the bike but because the rides to school are very social occasions. Whitney Young students hook up with each other along the rapid transit routes. He often wears bike advocacy T-shirts to school, so I don't think being carless bothers him very much." Hannah attends another excellent public high school and was in her first year. This one is closer to home, and she does bike to school. Neufeld said that she was concerned about having a bike that "looked cool" but not about biking itself. On the contrary, she seems to like being thought of as the kid who bikes to school. And Neufeld says that he thinks both of them take a little pride in being "almost famous." It turns out that being carless in Chicago has a certain amount of cachet—at least some of their peers think it's cool.

Recently the family took an extended trip to Europe. (No, they did no bike touring.) True to his Mennonite heritage, Neufeld did not miss the opportunity the trip provided for moral instruction. He wanted to underscore to his children how not owning a car freed up significant piles of cash. "We're going to Europe," he told them, "because we don't drive to the store. We bike, or we wait for the bus." It was a trade-off that made sense to the Neufeld-Geil family.

Alex Wilson: The Saint

I met Alex Wilson during the summer that I was planning for my first "Biking and Politics" class. At the time, he was the Student Marketing Coordinator for the CBF. In his late twenties, his job was to work with area college student groups to promote biking. He was intimately involved in the Chicago biking movement and was a storehouse of knowledge of that scene. As I got to know him, I came to understand the totality of his commitment to biking and the thoughtfulness that structures this connection to the world.

Many of us can articulate a philosophy of life that reflects ideals we hold important. But life is complex, and as we confront the complications of daily experience, our ideals are frequently compromised. For some, these compromises are so big that it is doubtful the professed values are actually believed. Wilson is not like that. In his case, the space between the values he holds important and the way he lives is about as small as it can get. He once said to me, "I want to do my work; I don't want a job." And again, "I don't identify my work with how I make money," by which he means that if he can do his work, money is not important to him. For him, work is a way of life. He does manage to wring enough money from his work for a modest existence, but it is far below the level most would accept if they had a choice in the matter, as Wilson does. Nevertheless, he is content with the choices he has made. When the idea of writing the chapter on "biking eccentrics" occurred to me, he was the first person who came to mind.

Wilson was born and raised in Lincoln, Nebraska, the fourth of six children in a devout Mormon family. His dad worked in a Goodyear tire factory, and his mom was a music teacher. He attended church several times a week for most of his young life, but he began to question his faith around the age of sixteen and is now an atheist. Like Neufeld, he also feels that the religious environment in which he was raised contributed to his current worldview. It has always been important to him to have strong beliefs and to act on them. Additionally, Wilson believes the Mormon tradition contributed to his strong work ethic, a commitment enhanced by a larger sense of mission.

In high school, class visits to Chicago greatly stimulated his interest, and he began to think about how he might eventually move to that more cosmopolitan environment. He reports that in high school he was even wary of developing ties and commitments that might prevent him from leaving Lincoln. The Wilson children were all interested in the arts, an interest fostered by their parents despite the economic burdens it entailed. Wilson was attracted both to the violin and to painting. In his senior year he was admitted to the Art Institute of Chicago for study as a painter/print maker. He had no funds for college, and his parents could not afford to help him.

To gain the funds necessary, he joined the Army Reserves upon graduation and deferred his Art Institute admission until the spring quarter. The six months of active duty required by the Army Reserves at that time were important to Wilson's development. The military placed him in a social context that differed dramatically from life in Nebraska. Of the sixty men in his platoon, only a dozen were Caucasian, so for the first time, he had the experience of being a minority. Beyond this, he became acquainted with substantial numbers of blacks and Latinos for the first time. Outside the military, the places where he was stationed in South Carolina and Georgia seemed dramatically segregated to him, and he felt this more deeply because it affected his friends. The social experience of the army influenced him significantly and contributed to decisions he would later make.

Wilson became interested in bikes in early adolescence. An older brother built and raced bikes, and when he moved on, he left behind an array of bikes and bike parts in the family garage. For Wilson, the bike became a source of liberation, spiriting him to the far reaches of the city. In contrast, the family car (the Wilson family never owned more than one car at a time) was always a source of embarrassment. Invariably, they were "beaters," and since his father regularly worked overtime at the plant, they were mostly unavailable anyway. While the kids could have cars, buying and maintaining them were their responsibility. Early on, Wilson figured out that cars suck money, and so, even through high school, he used a bike to get around. His interest in art and classical music tabbed him as something of a "weirdo" anyway; biking did not add significantly to social stress. In fact, he has never owned a car, so his weirdo status remains intact.

When Wilson eventually came to the Art Institute, his life was soon beset with various instabilities. He describes this period as a time when "there was just a lot of craziness." The army would not support a veteran attending a private institution—a fact that was not made clear to him before he signed on. So he struggled financially, never able to find full-time work and living in difficult neighborhoods. He moved several times over the next couple of years and eventually dropped out of school. His financial problems contributed to some emotional instability and a split with his girlfriend, Lauren Salmi. Shortly thereafter, he moved back, defeated, to Lincoln. Life was not turning out as he had imagined. He was very unhappy in Lincoln and spent most of his time carousing and in other ways "offending" his family. But he bought a Trek touring bike and began to ride again. Riding was like a balm to his wounded spirit. Even today, he speaks of his Trek wistfully, almost apologetically, because he normally is not particularly attached to the machines he rides. He is always changing them anyway—adding and removing components—never abandoning the interest nurtured in his family garage. But about the Trek, he says, "I really loved that bike."

Eventually Wilson and Salmi reunited, and in the spring of 1993, she rented a van, drove to Lincoln, and brought him back to Chicago. He brought his bike with him, and for the first time began biking in the city. Things were better economically also. Salmi worked in a bank, and Wilson got a job with a design company and later in commercial printing. He rode his bike to work and discovered how much he liked doing so. Particularly on the way home, he would alter his routes as a way of exploring the city. Salmi was a biker, too, and they enjoyed recreational riding, including several century rides in the region.

In 1997, something happened that dramatically changed the lives of these two twenty-six-year-olds: Salmi contracted a rare form of cancer. She spent much of the next four years undergoing chemotherapy and radiation treatments, as the cancer came back a second, and then a third time. (As of this writing, she has since been cancer-free.) Throughout, Wilson served as the primary caregiver. It was a very poignant time for them. The treatment would often leave Salmi debilitated. But there were good days as well. Through it all, they grew much closer. They came to appreciate the good days, to understand the significance of the life given us and the importance of living whatever life one has in a satisfactory way. On Salmi's good days, days when Wilson felt he could get away, he began to take some exploratory rides with his neighbor. The neighbor loved using the bike to access various nooks and crannies of the city. These rides expanded Wilson's sense of discovery, and he became much more reflective about the gestalt of the bike. The rides nurtured a budding awareness that, "there is no bad in biking. It is entirely good." He began to believe seriously that the city would be a much better place if everyone rode bikes. In September 1998, he went on his first Critical Mass ride, and it captured his imagination.

He became actively involved with Chicago Critical Mass. While it has no formal leadership structure, a core group causes the monthly masses to happen. Since nothing like a formal charter or a statement of purpose exists, there are inevitably competing ideas about what Critical Mass actually is. Wilson saw the rides as inclusive celebrations, and he used his expertise and scavenging skill to push this vision. First, he created and distributed hundreds of Critical Mass flags that may be attached to bicycles. Then, he located a source for "seconds" T-shirts, designed a logo for the fronts of the shirts, and printed large slogans like "One Less Car" and "Bikes Are Fun" on the backs. He then gave these away by the hundreds at random mass rides. He also created, designed, and published the pocket-sized *Derailleur,* the monthly "Unofficial Zine of Chicago Critical Mass." (He has not been the sole publisher, but he has been by far the most frequent.) Each issue is devoted to a theme and contains much useful information. Through the years, he has given away more than fifty thousand copies of the *Derailleur.* These things were accomplished with little monetary support, and he likes it that way. Over the years, Wilson has spent thousands of dollars of his own money promoting biking, always with an eye toward maximizing the impact of the expenditure. He is a very creative scrounger.

In 2001, Wilson found the pulls of full-time bike advocacy irresistible, and he went to work for the CBF. He first worked in the college liaison position, but later he developed a biking program for inner-city youth, an idea that continues to captivate him. To work on this idea more consistently, he cut back on his association with the CBF and now works with them on a project-by-project basis. In a conversation with the head of the CBF about his plans, the director told him, "Hell, Alex. You just want to give bicycles away!" Wilson smiles at the thought of that conversation, thinking that the guy had pretty much nailed it. He does want to get bikes into the hands of poor kids, but he believes he has a better idea than just giving them away. The program has gone through several iterations and has been variously funded by governmental and independent not-for-profit institutions, but its basic outlines have been fairly constant.

Wilson now operates West Town Bikes, a shop that has become an epicenter of grassroots training and empowerment. Classes are regularly held there that teach enrollees, for example, how to repair and maintain their bikes. There is no charge for these classes, although "donations" are encouraged from any who can afford to pay. Located in Humboldt Park, a neighborhood with significant numbers of economically struggling people, the shop also serves as the location for Wilson's youth program. Each year, he recruits teens from the neighborhood into the program. There is never a shortage; in fact the demand always exceeds capacity. The program provides participants with bikes, but they have to build or refurbish them. This they do with old bikes and bike parts that Wilson has collected from a variety of sources. Then the participants undergo extensive instruction about urban bike riding. All the while, they are learning how to maintain and improve their bikes. Wilson leads weekly rides as the course unfolds. Since the kids are in the process of building their own bikes, they ride extra bikes that he keeps around the shop for this purpose. They ride first in the neighborhood, then in adjacent neighborhoods, and finally to more distant parts of the city, including the Loop—the heart of downtown Chicago.

This simple concept has broad ramifications. To understand these, one must begin with the lives of poor urban kids. For many middle-class Americans, being poor simply means not having enough money. The broader and more insidious effects of poverty are often missed. For example, Wilson notes the violence that is such a regular part of his students' lives. They all know someone who has been shot or killed or who is in jail. Some young people in his program are literally raising themselves. Some are hungry. And almost none of them have ever been anywhere outside their neighborhood. One might think that the prospects for such kids are bleak, even hopeless. Yet in discussing the students in his program, Wilson paused while groping for words to describe how they were able to deal with such dire circumstances. "They're resilient?" I offered. "Resilient, certainly," he replied, "but more than resilient. It is astonishing how many can and do shine."

The circumstances of the students cause Wilson to begin his class not with a ride but with a four-mile walk. He wants to test the kids for stamina; to see the group dynamics; to show them that if they have no money, they can still get places by walking; and to experience neighborhood change. The program is empowering. It imparts to the young people a skill, along with an augmented sense of self-worth and confidence. It teaches them that they can enrich their lives without

Alex Wilson and students in his youth bike program (Photo courtesy Kevin Lyons).

spending large sums of money. It gives them a sense of wonder and of possibility. Wilson particularly likes riding into the Loop with his classes. It worries him a bit, however. They are not skilled riders, and they are not always "model" children. A ride into the Loop therefore involves some risk. But it also has a huge upside. Although they live only a couple of miles from the Loop, many of these kids have never been there. They marvel both at the adventure of getting downtown and at sights they have previously seen only on television.

Many parts of Wilson's life have come together in his current work. It is certainly work in his sense of the term—that is, work as a mission. And his work is informed by an ethic that is obvious. Other parts of his past also bear on his present life: his early tinkering with bikes in his family garage in Nebraska; the powerful multicultural experience of army life; learning to scramble for things and to make do with little in his early adult life; learning from the CBF about the system of foundation grants; and perhaps most important, coming to understand the significance of a meaningful life, richly lived, through Salmi's battle with cancer.

Wilson and Salmi live on the edge. After her cancer treatment, Salmi quit her bank job, went to massage therapy school, and is now a therapist. This has meant that, like so many Americans these days, they have no health insurance—a fact of greater significance to them than it is to more typical thirty-somethings. They are very conscious of this, but they also believe that too many people are kept from doing things that they believe are worthwhile by such insecurities. And Wilson truly believes in the value of his work. "I feel like I'm raising an army of bike freaks," he says. And for him, an army of bike freaks certainly portends a better world.

Gin Kilgore and Michael Burton: Love Me, Love My Bike

At the time of their marriage in 2002, Gin Kilgore and Michael Burton were thirty-one and thirty-eight, respectively. An outsider witnessing their wedding would have recognized their biking eccentricities. They were ridden to and from their public park wedding in a friend's pedicab. Those attending the wedding, however, were not surprised. After all, a friend had ridden more than three hundred miles from his Michigan home to attend the wedding. And like the bride and groom, many of the guests were part of the bike advocacy movement in Chicago, and to them this mode of transportation was both natural and an affirmation of important values. More than a hundred attendees of the wedding joined the newlyweds in a bike parade winding through two miles of Chicago streets from the ceremony to the reception. According to witnesses, it was a festive and eye-catching event, and it reveals the essence of how Kilgore and Burton connect to the biking movement. For them, the bicycle is integral to the process of community building and cultural renewal.

Prior to beginning research for this book, I had never heard of Burton or Kilgore. But in interviews with other people in the biking movement, and at various Internet biking sites, their names kept popping up. Among other things, I noticed that Burton was leading an effort to "depave Lake Shore Drive," a major highway running along Chicago's lakefront. This struck me as overly ambitious—ridiculous, really—but it also deepened my curiosity about its author. Kilgore also was associated with various biking causes, and in addition, while employed by the Chicago Area Transportation Study, she had posted an intriguing narrative. It said, in part, "[Critical Mass] helped me realize what a transportation nerd I really am. I take as much, if not more, pleasure in commutes than destinations. I write odes to the el [the train component of Chicago's mass transit system] and preach the good word of the bike to anyone who will listen or can't find a tactful way to excuse themselves.... And, of course, I can't help but spin my wheels about the environmental, land use, equity, health, and overall quality of life problems caused by our culture's over-reliance on the private automobile." When I learned that Kilgore and Burton were married, they seemed like natural candidates to profile in this chapter.

I wrote to Kilgore explaining the project—particularly the chapter on "Biking Eccentrics"—and asking for an interview. She responded warmly but sharply. "I don't reckon we think of ourselves as eccentrics—our transportation choices and overall lifestyles seem so logical to us—and as most of our friends also live car-free lives, it's easy to forget that we might be a bit unconventional. I do imagine a day when using a two-ton machine to cart individuals around for short distances seems eccentric."

I was invited to join them in a Sunday brunch at their home, a three-flat in a working-class section of the city. They live on the top floor and rent out the other two apartments in the building. As one ascends the stairs, there are numerous signs—pictures, odd pieces of bike paraphernalia—indicating one is in "bike country," and my first question to them was whether the other residents of the building are also bikers. They are, in part because Burton and Kilgore are reluctant to have cars parked on their property, wasting precious urban space that might be better used. They intend to demolish a concrete slab behind the building that is currently given to this purpose.

Burton is a graduate of the University of Michigan, where he majored in economics and English. He was a politically active leftist there, and when he moved to Chicago, he sought work that was consistent with those values. He first worked for a large food co-op in Hyde Park near the University of Chicago. He is now employed by Bickerdike Redevelopment Corporation, a nonprofit community development organization that seeks to enhance neighborhoods while maintaining their ethnic and economic identities.

Several things have contributed to Burton's gravitation toward the bike advocacy movement. He has ridden a bike throughout his life. When he arrived in Hyde Park, he bought a car for "almost nothing" but used it rarely. Even in those days, he says, the bike was a much more central mode of transportation than the car. He also walked a lot, as the Hyde Park neighborhood is reasonably self-sustaining. In 1995, he spent some time biking around Europe. Typically he would train to a city, then use his bike to move about. He found this both exhilarating and consciousness expanding. He marveled at the "ordinariness" of bike transportation in so much of Europe. A later stint as a bike messenger in Chicago further increased his sense of the possibilities of the bike. Still later, he got an office job in the Loop, and it dawned on him how easy it was to bike through the winter in Chicago, something he had not previously imagined. When it turned out that biking was not only relatively easy but also great fun, he began to think seriously of the bike as an outlet for his activism.

Kilgore's bike trajectory differs from Burton's. As she grew up in Hyde Park, a bike was not an important part of her youth. Mostly, she walked around that part of the city. She admits to a deeply engrained hostility toward the automobile, something that she traces to her

Gin Kilgore and Michael Burton on their wedding day.

early life as a pedestrian. Additionally, as a teen driver she almost hit a pedestrian—an incident she still recalls vividly and with some anguish. She attended Brown University, studying English and urban policy. While there, she hoofed all over Providence with a small group of friends—unlike most students, who either relied on cars or stayed on campus.

After graduation from Brown, Kilgore returned to Chicago and began to prepare for a teaching career. She enrolled at the University of Illinois in Chicago for graduate work in education, and she found employment in Head Start programs. Her new life often required mobility during "off-peak" transit times, when public transportation is more sporadic, and she became frustrated with her total reliance on this means of transport. Her friends, including her boyfriend at the time, encouraged her to buy a bike.

Kilgore is an ebullient person with many enthusiasms as well as a keen sense of the distasteful. She vividly remembers buying her bike, even the date of purchase (September 11, 1997). She recalls riding it that day from the bike shop to her boyfriend's apartment some miles away. It was a beautiful fall day. As she reached the top of a small incline, she saw, through the Chicago skyline, the sun hanging low on the horizon. She knew nothing of the bike, not even how to shift the gears. No matter. She was exhilarated, and she wondered why she had not been doing this all along. She has never looked back. Most people taking their first ride on a busy urban avenue during rush hour might have been too preoccupied to enjoy the dramatic scene of that day, but from that point, Kilgore was hooked on the bicycle.

Kilgore had a few friends who were seasoned urban bikers, and she stresses how important these people were in encouraging her and helping her to become a competent rider. Increasingly, these folks were using their bikes to get around. Many would ride to work. But they also started riding to social affairs. Often they would ride to these in groups, which increased the fun. This may well have been the source of her recognition, cited earlier, that she takes as much pleasure in the journey as she does the destination. These developing associations stimulated a change of consciousness that was perhaps foretold by the rush of that first ride. The first years of her return to Chicago were years of lassitude and drift. Now she recognized a nascent "community of concern"—people who were thinking about their lives and how they wanted to live. She wanted to be active in this community, to contribute to its developing ethos.

Meanwhile, Burton was one of three or four people who decided to try to bring Critical Mass to Chicago on a systematic basis. There had been an occasional mass ride in Chicago prior to 1997, but the events were sporadic and started from different locations. Burton

wanted to make them year-round, monthly affairs and to begin each
ride at the seat of municipal government—the Daley Center in the
heart of the Loop. Pulling off that first Critical Mass was a scramble.
Information was spread by word of mouth and through leafleting, but
no one knew how many would turn out. Burton's experience as an
activist had taught him that there is often a large gap between those
who say they will do something and those who actually do. He hoped
that fifteen or twenty folks might participate, and was elated to have
more than a hundred on that inaugural ride.

At the suggestion of a San Francisco friend, Kilgore started attending the Chicago Critical Mass in its first year of operation. If Critical
Mass is not quite the anarchist activity that some suggest, it is still a
very open group. Anyone who wants to work in it is welcome. Kilgore
soon became part of this activist circle, which is how she and Burton
met. This group found comradeship both in promoting biking and
in having fun. One part merry prankster, one part agent provocateur,
one part activist, the group spun off a number of interesting ideas
and activities. They leafleted; they disrupted the annual auto show;
they tweaked official functions such as "Bike to Work Week." (Biking
throughout the year was preferable.) They gave things away to help
people bike. In response to San Francisco's staging of bike summer,
Burton came up with the idea of "Bike Winter" to promote winter
riding in Chicago. This has become an elaborate operation, with a
Web site, a series of workshops focusing on winter riding, and a regular schedule of winter events—including the February "Frozen Snot
Century" to Milwaukee and back. Kilgore became one of the founders of Cycling Sisters, an organization that is concerned with getting
women into biking by overcoming the "false barriers" generated by
the dominant culture.

Since cultures are shared ways of looking at the world that provide
meaning to the members of a group and help them interpret experience, it is fair to say that Burton and Kilgore are actively engaged in
creating an alternative culture. How far this culture can be extended
is an open question. Kilgore is the more pessimistic of the two. She
despairs that more people have not, in the face of rather compelling
evidence, awakened to the huge toll an autocentric culture exacts.
In the face of the growing energy and ecological crisis, for example,
she regards the response of progressive environmentalists as woefully

inadequate. Overwhelmingly, they have focused on technologies that generate more energy efficient and less polluting cars. While she supports this stance, she believes it only scratches the surface of the damage done by the car.

Equally angry about our current commitment to cars, Burton is slightly more optimistic about the long haul. He looks to other parts of the world, especially to Europe, noting the progress being made, and he thinks there is a chance that better social norms will be more broadly adopted in this country. He seems a little more upbeat about the human capacity for reasonableness. Although at present depaving Lake Shore Drive seems quixotic, for example, he is quite serious about it, and he believes firmly that it will come in time. In his view, people eventually will realize the social costs of committing such aesthetically important real estate to cars. But his optimism is guarded. He has no illusions about the power of those whose interests lie in maintaining the status quo.

Since achieving an auto-depleted society is by their own estimations a long shot at best, one might ask why they bother. Clearly, a strong existential streak runs through each of them. Kilgore's statement about taking as much pleasure in the commute as in the destination was written with literal commutes in mind. It might well serve as a metaphor for the life she and Burton have chosen, however. They resist. They refuse to be co-opted. And their lives gain meaning in this struggle against what they see as the larger insanity—keeping "a pinkie in the dam," in Kilgore's phrase; "extending the realm of the possible," in Burton's. As Camus wrote of Sisyphus, whom the gods condemned to an eternity of pushing a stone up a mountain, only to have it roll back of its own weight, "The struggle toward the heights is enough to fill a man's heart. One must imagine Sisyphus happy."

In this process, Kilgore and Burton have become intimately involved in a community of like-minded souls, people who are engaged in an effort to make life a little better—not just for themselves but for others as well. Burton is saddened by people who come home every evening simply to "veg out in front of a TV." He considers them to be damaged. "People miss the sense of working together to get something good done," he says. Kilgore concurs. They are not on the fast track of material acquisition, which is the definition of success propagated by the dominant culture. Nevertheless, she concludes, "Our quality of life is very high."

Jane Healy: Biker Mama

Jane Healy, forty-one, is a vivacious mother of three who grew up in the working-class suburbs on the South Side of Chicago. She went east to attend Sarah Lawrence in New York, majoring in biology. After graduation, she taught school in Connecticut for a couple of years before returning to the south suburbs. We agreed to meet for an interview on a cold December evening at the Exchequer, an iconic Chicago pub in the heart of the Loop. Healy was coming into town to participate in a "do-it-yourself" Messiah performance. She told me she would likely be arriving on her bike. It was cold, it was dark, and it was the Loop, but her arrival at the Exchequer was unmistakable. Ensconced in winter riding gear, she was also bedecked with enough lights to resemble a Christmas tree.

Healy has always been physically active. She competed in multiple sports through high school and participated in intercollegiate athletics. She was a fairly active recreational bike rider into adolescence, although once she turned sixteen the car took over. Her parents ride bikes in retirement, and her husband Mike is an active recreational rider as well. During the seven years she was back east however, Healy did not ride.

When she returned to Chicago at the age of twenty-four, she "rediscovered" the bike. She accepted a job teaching biology at Mother McAuley, a Catholic girls' high school on Chicago's South Side. Since she lived only a couple of miles from the school, she rode her bike there on comfortable fall or spring days—but "never in winter." She locked her bike at a central location on the school grounds and soon gained notoriety as the bike-riding teacher. "The students seemed to enjoy it," she says. Her interests in biology contributed to her decision to start an environmental club at the school. She describes her political orientation as "pretty green," and biking fits easily into that consciousness.

After her marriage, Healy took a teaching job at a public high school. Her new school was some distance from her home in Blue Island, and so she stopped riding her bike to work. She and Mike, a high school history teacher, regularly rode bikes for recreation, until they were stolen from their garage. A child came along, then another, and Healy stopped teaching in order to provide more care for her children. Without a bike for three years, she was feeling increasingly trapped in the house. She had a car, but strapping two young children into car seats was a constant hassle. And she missed not being physically active.

Recognizing his wife's unhappiness, Mike got her the perfect gift for Christmas: a bike with a kids' trailer attached. Healy was elated and on Christmas Day strapped her two young children into the trailer and set off on a ride. That ride was an epiphany. She loved it, and her kids did as well. She realized, "I can do this," and began to ride everywhere with her kids in tow. Because she was not working, most of her trips were around her community—going to the store and taking her kids to various activities, including riding them to and from their preschool, which was an eight-mile round trip.

In her spare time, she began to use the Internet to learn whatever she could about biking in the Chicago area. She found the Chicago Critical Mass Web site, where she began to "listen" to conversations on their list-serve. She listened for months before posting. The people chatting seemed much more into biking than she, and she doubted her ability to complete their rides. She posted an inquiry and was encouraged to join them. She decided to try a ride by herself and was immediately taken by the fun and camaraderie of it all. The next month her husband joined her, and the following month the entire family participated. Critical Mass quickly became a regular event on the Healys' social calendar. Healy estimates that they do about eight of them a year. Their kids love them, as they are always great theater. To the children, it is like riding in a circus parade. The Healy family has grown to five, and the oldest child, Will, has transferred out of the child carrier and can, at eight, do the rides on his own bike.

Building on their experience with Critical Mass, the Healy family has made the bicycle an important means of social interaction. Mike could make extra money by teaching in the summer but chooses not to. The family often uses the bike for summer excursions in the Chicago area, taking picnic lunches along, visiting museums and other points of interest. Bikes are usually carried and used on family vacations as well. The family does lots of night riding, and the parents are concerned and conservative with respect to safety issues. Everyone wears a helmet; bikes and riders are festooned with lights and reflectors.

Healy is convinced that the bike has had a positive impact on the quality of their family life. "In a car, the main parental preoccupation with kids strapped into child seats is trying to keep them content. That is not a problem on the bike." When she feels one of her children may need some special attention, she will sometimes go riding with that child. Coming home from school, she often stops at parks to let them play. While recognizing that this is possible in a car, she believes it is less likely. "On a bike, you're riding through the park. It is just so easy to stop and play for a while." She speaks with great conviction of the valuable lessons the bike imparts to her children: their growing sense of autonomy and mastery; the linking of accomplishment and effort. She also loves the contribution that the bike makes to her children's health and fitness, and she glows with motherly pride at the ease with which eight-year-old Will knocks off twenty-five miles on a bike.

The bike has also changed Healy's connection to her community. She says that riding around her community on her bike affected her perception of it. People and neighborhoods revealed themselves in a way they had not before. She began to think about her community in a new way—what she liked about it, and what she did not. Blue Island is ethnically quite diverse, and as an experienced teacher, Healy knew that this diversity was not represented in school board policy. She decided to become a candidate for the school board. As it turned out, the bike was a major asset in her campaign. People already knew her as the lady who rode around the community with her kids in tow, and they voted her into office.

In addition to the regular concerns of the school board, she is leading the board to consider transportation issues. Blue Island schools have joined the national Safe Routes To School movement, an effort in which districts around the country have promoted biking or walking to school as a way to combat childhood obesity. As part of this program, she leads a "walking school bus" with her bike. Children walk together over a designated route and are "dropped off" along the way. At the end of the route, Healy rides her bike home. Bike racks have been installed at several schools; bike safety week is promoted. At the end of bike safety week, one middle school stages a four-mile "bike parade" through the town. The student council at this school recently purchased two large bike racks as their class gift.

Jane with her son Will "the Animal" Healy (Photo courtesy Michael Healy).

Healy firmly believes the bike can improve her community. Blue Island is actually older than Chicago, and it has a historic downtown. Like many smaller communities, however, it struggles to retain its vitality. Healy has sought to convince city officials of the economic advantages of more bike-friendly policies. "People in cars are not looking at shops," she argues. Slowly, the officials have begun to respond. Additionally, she is actively promoting the construction of a bike path that would connect several south side communities, as well as hook up with other trails in the region. She is cofounder of the Blue Island Bike Club, which organizes biweekly community bike rides. One of her greatest interests is getting more women on bikes—particularly senior women. If they could overcome their fears of road riding, she knows the bike would empower them.

Healy's commitment to the bike seems long term, buttressed by the fact that her parents continue to ride in their seventies. She does not anticipate giving up the automobile entirely, but she expects her "car-lite" lifestyle to continue indefinitely. It fits into her larger, environmentally sensitive worldview. It accords with her fitness concerns for herself and her family. She values the sense of community the bike nurtures. And she still finds riding exhilarating. At our interview, she told me of a school board meeting the previous week that ran late into the night. The weather was frigid that evening, with the temperature in single digits. Yet she described her midnight ride home as "magical." She was prepared for the cold, so that did not bother her. The evening was peaceful, clear, and quiet. She loved being centered in the tranquility and the fact that she was able to make her way home without disturbing the area she was passing through.

Anyone who has biked at all seriously will recognize the kind of moment Healy described, and they will recognize its opposite as well—those times when one is forced unexpectedly to grind through sleet or wind. There is something about a bicycle, however, that makes the best moments of riding far more exhilarating than the worst moments are dreary. Perhaps this is because the worst moments also offer their compensations: Pride in having conquered them.

These sketches of biking eccentrics belie the image that those saturated in the dominant culture have of such people. Being a nerd implies lacking the capacity to function effectively in the larger culture. Whatever one might think of the choices they have made, all of the biking eccentrics profiled here are where they are as a matter of choice. They are far from inept. All have thought quite a bit about what it means to live a good life, and all have chosen not to follow the money/consumption trail that beckons so many. Some grew into their current orientations over a period of time; others experienced an epiphany. Regardless, they share the sense that the bike is much more than a means to move from one place to another. For all of them, the bike is used to frame the world. Indeed, they are united in the conviction that the bike can lead to a better world. This belief comes easily to them because it grows out of their personal experience. That is exactly the way it has worked in their lives.

Eccentrics are vital to any society, for they shed light on uncommon possibilities and thus are the gateways to change. It is not clear that the particular eccentrics profiled here are correct in the perspectives they articulate, but it is understandable that such folks are marginalized and regarded as eccentric. Their ideas are countercultural and therefore dangerous to those whose interests the current culture upholds. But these days, that culture is pressing against the limits of its plausibility. As evidence of its exhaustion mounts, the pressure for an alternative cultural vision increases. These biking eccentrics are interesting because they hold alternative, and to them more compelling, visions of the values they believe ought to bind us.

Time will tell if they are right. But it is worth recalling that the lesson of Napoleon, Pedro, and the forty-year-old virgin, after all, was that the real nerds were not those who were identified as such at the outset of the two films. Rather, they were the many who had given no thought to their lives or to the mindless, stultifying conformity typifying them. To everyone's surprise, Napoleon turned out to be one helluva dancer.

Chapter Five

Building the Case

The Political Advocates

K Street in Washington, D.C., is famous (or infamous) in the lore of American politics. Concentrated along this street in the heart of the city, convenient both to the White House and to the Capitol, are some of the most potent lobbying organizations in the nation. K Street has become a metaphor, and it might be said that K Street is to the business of Washington what Wall Street is to the financial business of the nation. The K Street Project was an effort spurred by former congressman Tom Delay and others to create very close relations between the lions of K Street and the Republican majority in Congress at the turn of the century. Eventually a number of people associated with the project were sent to jail, as payoffs for political favors grew too direct. Corruption emerged as an important issue in the 2006 congressional campaigns in which Democrats gained majorities in both houses of Congress.

But political advocacy is inevitable and, within clearly articulated limits, perfectly reasonable. Since the number of things people might want government to do is virtually limitless, and since resources are not, a struggle over "who gets what" ensues. Sometimes the inherent "rightness" of an action is sufficient to carry the day. More often, political decisions reflect the distribution and assertion of power. Numbers matter in U.S. politics because we are, at least roughly, a democratic society. Democracy comes up against its limits, however, when power, or the ability to achieve an intended result, is unequally distributed. Even in a purely democratic society, broad and diffuse sentiment can often be overcome by organization and discipline. For this reason, those seeking favorable government outcomes enhance their prospects by organizing to press their claims.

Formal bicycle advocacy began almost with the bicycle's invention. The Bicycle Touring Club formed in 1878 with the intent of popularizing the sport.[1] The oldest advocacy group dates to the nineteenth century and is still active. Originally known as the League of American Wheelmen, the name was changed a few years ago to the League of American Bicyclists. In the 1890s, the League was instrumental in the push for improved roads. Bike advocacy was soon eclipsed by the growth of the car culture and was dormant for most of the twentieth century. Over the latter third of the century, however, the political dynamics began to change, and the biking movement revived.

Two developments in the 1970s stimulated the contemporary bicycle advocacy movement. One of these, the rapidly spreading realization of ecological imbalance and environmental erosion, involved a change in consciousness that ultimately sought to affect resource distribution. Many scientists had been concerned about the fate of Earth for some time, and books like Rachel Carson's *Silent Spring* communicated these concerns to large numbers of people. This in turn stimulated the first organized political action around the issue.

The second stimulus to bike advocacy was the sudden and surprising emergence of an erratic energy supply line. The United States had been an oil-rich nation that could, over the first half of the century, easily and inexpensively handle the growing thirst for oil. But that thirst grew exponentially, causing us to look elsewhere for a continuing supply of cheap oil. By 1970, more than 40 percent of the oil consumed came from other nations. Quietly but suddenly, this dependency meant that cheap oil was no longer a matter that was completely within our control.

When anger erupted over U.S. policies that they believed sharply favored Israel, the Organization of Petroleum Exporting Countries, or

OPEC (dominated by Mideast nations), announced a trade embargo against the United States. Whether as a result of the embargo, oil company profiteering, or some mixture of both, within a year the price of gasoline at the pump quadrupled. Motorists, long accustomed to cheap gasoline to power their oversized, gas-guzzling vehicles, became upset. Over the short term, demand for gas is relatively inelastic, so the increased price of gasoline hit many Americans hard. Trapped in an auto-centric society, they had few options. Jittery and unstable markets also created long lines at the pump and even gas rationing in some states. Not only was driving costing Americans more, but the hassle factor grew as well.

This energy "crisis" was yet another jolt to the American psyche that had already been battered by a politically tumultuous decade. Until the "energy crisis," few Americans knew how dependent we had become on foreign oil. Nurtured on limitless consumption, Americans found it daunting to think that concept was in fact limited and flawed. It is hardly surprising that, once the immediate crisis ebbed, most Americans returned to their regular routines. But not all did. The new awareness of finite resources, along with growing environmental consciousness, caused many to rethink how they connected to the planet and even to consider lifestyle changes. A smaller number became politically active around these issues. And within this group, a smaller number still became intrigued by the possibilities of the bicycle. These people began to think of the bike as more than a recreational diversion. Advocacy organizations began to spring up around the nation.

National Organizations

Bicycle advocacy is best conceived as a confederation of interests. By its very nature, bike riding is linked to the communities in which it occurs. This means that the quality of biking environments varies substantially and is significantly affected by the receptivity of local political environments and the skill and imagination of local advocacy groups. The localized nature of biking does not make national organizations irrelevant, however. On the contrary, they play an important role in advancing bike policy. The crucial contribution that national organizations make toward bike friendliness is to broaden the playing field and expand the limits of the possible. By banding local organizations together, they increase the power of these groups at the national level. This matters, because the federal government is an important source of funds for local bike projects. Decisions about "the authoritative allocation" of resources are often made in Washington, D.C., even for something as "local" as biking.

National organizations are also important because they provide a structure for sharing ideas and information. Though they may be separated by thousands of miles, local biking advocacy groups learn from each other through national organizations, borrowing and adapting strategies and tactics that may be applicable to their particular circumstances. Finally, national organizations are a major resource center for those seeking to establish advocacy groups in their communities. These functions have been greatly abetted by the Internet, which not only allows access to an extraordinary amount of information but also is a vehicle for instantaneous, interactive communication.

At first blush, bicycle advocacy work at the national level seems daunting. Our auto-centric society exists both because it resonates with our culture and because auto and allied interests wield substantial political power. Given this apparent power imbalance, it is tempting to conclude that significant change in transportation policy is a pipe dream. On the other hand, the current period of cultural flux may provide more latitude for maneuver than was the case a few years ago, and recent history has taught that power in asymmetric relations can be miscalculated. Power is not irrelevant, but assessing it accurately is a complex business.

In fact, despite the bike's minority—possibly even fringe—status in our society, several things favor bike advocates. First, groups pushing for more bike-friendly policies are widely dispersed geographically, giving the potential to influence an array of congressmen. Second, they are well organized, as substantial effort goes into organizing and expanding local groups and connecting them. Third, by federal standards, they are not asking for much. Biking is so efficient that it does not take huge outlays to increase bike friendliness.

This leads to a fourth advantage: the absence of significant opposition. The kinds of changes bike advocates push for are so tiny that they mostly pass beneath the radar of the auto industry, for example. A bike lane here, bike racks there, kids riding bikes to school—such small things do not rouse the ire of potential opponents. Bike advocates hope that the cumulative effect of these changes will someday lead to significant reductions in auto usage, but each change in itself seems not to matter very much. Finally—and this advantage should not be discounted—is the transparent rightness of the cause. There are other just causes against which advocates must compete for limited dollars, and power can extort support for unrighteous causes, but the collective and individual advantages of biking are such that it is difficult to imagine a legislator opposing increased support for biking based on the merits. The other side of this coin, but equally important, is that a legislator rarely gets into trouble supporting bike growth. This is an important bargaining chip for biking interests.

It is impossible to know the relative contributions of these factors to the federal success of bike advocates, but from 1988, when advocates began to make claims on federal outlays, to 2003, the year of the most recent renewal of the National Transportation Act, federal funding for bike projects increased from $5 million to $423 million. This rise is in one sense a remarkable achievement and seems like a substantial sum to the average citizen. It is, however, a thin sliver of the transportation budget.

The most well-known and oldest national organization, as mentioned earlier, is the League of American Bicyclists. On May 31, 1880, 133 cyclists from 31 clubs met in Newport, Rhode Island, and founded the League of American Wheelmen.[2] It was an immediate success. Within ten years it became a thriving, robust political organization as its membership swelled to more than one hundred thousand, including such luminaries as the Wright brothers, John D. Rockefeller, and Diamond Jim Brady. The League was in the forefront of the Better Roads Movement, and in the 1890s, it submitted a petition to Congress with 160,000 signatures appended on a single, spectacular scroll. The scroll was wrapped around a large wooden spindle much like the ones used for industrial cable today.

Seldom has the proverb "Be careful what you wish for" been more apt. Cars dominated the improved roads and pushed bikes off the political agenda, and the League receded in importance. Since its revival in the 1970s, it has grown to a membership of forty thousand individuals and over six hundred affiliated organizations. When the members of these organizations are counted, the League can claim a national membership of more than 300,000.

The organization's advocacy work runs in two directions.[3] First, with its office in Washington, D.C., the League is a watchdog for federal biking interests. One way it calls attention to federal policy is through the National Bicycle Summit. Each March, the summit gathers bike advocates from across the nation. They come to Washington to receive training, to share information, and to develop strategies relevant to national policy, legislation, and appropriations. They share roundtable discussions with representatives from Congress and key bureaucracies, including the Department of Transportation and the Department of Health and Human Services. Time is given to allow the advocates to descend on Congress to meet with their elected representatives and relevant congressional committee staff. Most congressional offices are visited during the Summit. The hope is to elicit commitments for bike-friendly policies and, if not, to make sure representatives know that their constituents are interested in these matters. The summits are particularly intense during the times when the National Transportation Act comes up for renewal.

The League thus reaches "upward" in its effort to generate favorable decisions from the political structure. It also reaches "outward," stimulating biking and bike advocacy at the grassroots level. One example of this form of advocacy is its annual "Bicycle-Friendly Communities" competition. In this competition, local governments submit detailed applications to the League that are ranked by a panel of experts at one of six points on an ascending scale. The assessment process is quite thorough. It examines education policies, actual on-the-ground developments, the quality of advocacy organizations, the commitment of local governments, and political leadership. The upper levels of the scale are difficult to reach, and the competition serves as a carrot to communities. It is good publicity for local politicians, as positive results are regularly reported by local media. Portland, Oregon, for example, is so interested in obtaining the highest rating of "platinum" (a goal that the city has publicly articulated) that it recently sent a nine-person delegation to Amsterdam to obtain ideas for additional bike policy development.

Another form of outward reach is the League's encouragement of local advocacy group formation. On its Web site are detailed suggestions about forming and growing a bicycle advocacy organization. In hard copy, these run to eight pages and include tips on bylaws, how to obtain nonprofit status, record keeping, and money raising. The site encourages those wishing to form advocacy groups to submit any additional questions they may have directly to the League. When asked to document the growth of the biking movement, Marthea Wilson, the deputy director of the League, pointed to the growing number of bike advocacy organizations at the local level and, more importantly, to their remarkable staying power. "This is not like a cycle, with groups ebbing and flowing," she said. "New groups are forming, while the others are continuing."

Finally, the League serves as a grassroots advocate by directly encouraging individuals to get on bikes. It discusses bike safety and offers guidelines for safe riding. It appeals directly to employers to consider the advantages of biking to their businesses (healthier and happier employees, lower commuting costs, lessened traffic and parking congestion), and it encourages them to make their work places more bike-friendly. This grassroots advocacy extends to children, as the League actively promotes getting kids into riding.

The Thunderhead Alliance is a national coalition of state and local biking and pedestrian organizations. Unlike the League, it has no individual memberships, but its organizational base allows it to draw upon thousands of full-time bike advocates. The immediate impetus to organize was provided by the Intermodal Surface Transportation Efficiency Act (ISTEA—pronounced like the rapper's name). Passed in 1991, the provisions of ISTEA structure government decisions about how to spend federal dollars in the field of transportation. The law is renegotiated every six years, and in 1996 biking advocacy groups met at the Thunderhead Ranch in Wyoming to develop strategies to influence congressional decisions to be made later that year. The Alliance grew out of this meeting.[4]

In the first years of its existence, the Alliance focused largely on procuring national funds, but it quickly expanded its efforts to pressure state and local governments for resources as well. In 2002, the organization moved its offices from Washington, D.C., to Prescott, Arizona. A key distinction between the League and the Alliance is that the latter focuses more on the formation of local advocacy organizations. The cornerstone of the Alliance's vision is to have 15 percent of all trips Americans make to be via bicycle. To achieve this end, an immediate project is to have sustainable bicycle and pedestrian advocacy organizations in all fifty states and in the fifty largest metropolitan regions of the nation.

To support this "50-50 Project,"[5] the Alliance offers manpower and technical assistance to fledgling local organizations. The annual retreats of the organization, held in different parts of the country, provide opportunities for information sharing, inspiration, and strategic planning that accommodates the goals of emerging local groups. Thunderhead training sessions spread information about how to manage campaigns to achieve the specific goals that are important to the locality. Young advocates are taught how to conduct a "power analysis" (figuring out where and who makes relevant decisions), how to achieve effective access to the media, and how to raise money for the campaign.

In March 2005, the Thunderhead Alliance issued its first Complete Streets Report.[6] The idea of "complete streets" is at once visionary and nostalgic, as it refers to streets on which people can safely move, no matter what their mode of transport. A complete street system accommodates bikes and pedestrians, as well as cars. It recalls the multipurpose streets of a century ago and seeks to adapt that norm to contemporary conditions. After years of considering only auto movement, U.S. transportation policy is inching fitfully toward more complete streets. In response to the Transportation Equity Act for the twenty-first century, for example, the U.S. Department of Transportation (DOT) issued a Design Guidance Policy statement titled "Accommodating Bicycle and Pedestrian Travel." It states, "Bicycle and pedestrian ways shall be established in new construction and reconstruction projects in all urbanized areas unless one or more of three conditions are met."

This policy statement was an important step in the complete streets movement. It pertains to new construction, which greatly reduces the costs of the program. The three conditions allowing for exceptions in urban areas are roads on which bikes and pedestrians are prohibited, where the costs for accommodations are excessive, and where there is an absence of need. One might conclude that this means that virtually any case can be considered an exception, and this is true. But there are reasonable standards for excessive costs, and so the key part of the policy pertains to the question of need. This is a classic "bootstrap" problem. When bikes are accommodated, the number of bikers increases. "Need" can sometimes be determined only in retrospect. This is why the Alliance considers the growth of advocacy groups as essential to expanded bike policies, as such groups help articulate the need for better bike accommodation.

The DOT Design Guidance Policy also calls for paving shoulders on rural roads, which is a big issue in many areas. As a graduate student living in a rural area five miles from the campus of the University of North Carolina, I soon learned that the most direct route to campus was very dangerous for bikers. This two-lane road had no shoulder and lots of motorized traffic, including large trucks hauling chickens to slaughterhouses. Keeping a bike on the road as one of these trucks raced by, spraying feathers in its wake, was a challenge. I soon chose an alternative route to campus that was four miles longer but much safer. Others who might have ridden to campus decided not to do so because neither the nine miles nor the chicken truck options were acceptable to them. After I left North Carolina, the state added an apron to the more direct route to campus, and bike traffic increased significantly.

The first Complete Streets Report was a compendium of government authorities that have taken steps to implement the policy. It is a baseline, information-gathering document, and it recommends strategies to advocacy groups for expanding the miles of complete streets. Complete Streets is an ambitious, long-range project, but two things encourage advocates. The first is that the DOT policy statement is itself a weapon useful to complete streets advocates. As noted, there are ways around implementing such a policy, but the policy's existence stimulates interest. The second encouraging thing is that cost is not a major problem in the implementation of complete streets so long as the concept is built into the projects themselves. That is a lesson the Alliance seeks to instill in its member groups. There has been some success in getting state and local governments to accept the idea of complete streets, and more will come as advocacy groups proliferate. In 2001, 45 advocacy groups were part of the Alliance. Five years later, that number had grown to 128.

For a long time the bike industry eschewed politics. This is ironic because it is the industry that stands to gain the most materially from increased bike usage. One bike-advocate member of Congress, who is used to dealing with groups that have a very clear sense of their economic self-interest, told me that the lack of political sophistication in the bike industry in the 1990s was "truly bizarre." But things have changed, and industry groups are now making an impact at the national level and are active in a variety of ways.

Planet Bikes is a bicycle accessories company that, since its inception in 1996, has earmarked 25 percent of its profits to support bike projects and advocacy work. The largest industry group, Bikes Belong, awards $150,000 to $200,000 annually to grassroots projects around the country, including Safe Routes To School.[7] This organization also sponsors the Bike-Friendly Communities Program and provides significant financial support for the annual Bike Summit meetings in Washington. Finally, it supports BikesPAC, the industry's political action committee (PAC). The existence of a PAC that can contribute to electoral campaigns has encouraged politicians to take the bike movement more seriously. By American standards, these contribu-

Bikes Belong has given a big boost to the national Safe Routes To School program (Photo courtesy Bikes Belong Coalition).

tions are not great, but to cash-strapped politicians bound by the current rules of political life, any contribution is appreciated. Most Americans simply want politicians to do "good things." The existence of BikesPAC is tacit recognition that politicians cannot do good things if they are not elected.

The 2007 National Bike Summit illustrated the current strengths and weaknesses of the bike movement nationally. Drawing 450 people, it was the largest bike summit ever held. Industry representation was stronger than it had ever been, and the conference teemed with bright and energetic activists. The new Congress was friendlier than it had been in quite a while. Earl Blumenauer received a rousing reception. At the same time however, Congress was beset with problems, especially the controversial war in Iraq, and huge budget deficits that dominated concern. League executive director Andy Clarke noted that funding for bike projects seemed to have reached a plateau, at least for the moment, and the greatest concern was over recisions—money being returned by states to the federal government to ease the debt—coming disproportionately from programs that fund bike projects.

Local Organizations

Although national advocacy groups have had an important impact on biking policies, the real action is at the local level. Check out an urban area that is bike-friendly; inevitably a strong advocacy group will be there as well. Not only do such groups push for changes where they must happen—in their own local areas—but they are also skilled at accessing vital federal dollars. Sometimes state governments make funds available for biking projects, but more typically funds originate at the federal level and pass through the states. Cities, always strapped for funds, often will form quasi-alliances with strong local advocacy groups to access these funds and implement specific projects and programs. In this section, two of the strongest local advocacy organizations will be discussed: the Chicagoland Bicycle Federation and the Bicycle Transportation Alliance in Oregon.

If one knew nothing about bike politics and simply guessed which U.S. cities have strong biking policies, it is unlikely Chicago would immediately spring to mind. Its size and complexity might be expected to dwarf a simple machine like the bicycle. Negotiating the downtown Loop with its huge buildings and dense traffic is daunting for any first-time rider in that area. Neighborhoods tend to be insular, and insularity breeds suspicion. People regularly offer opinions about how dangerous certain areas are and, for them, riding a bike in such areas would be unthinkable. Winter months can be brutally cold, and while the terrain is quite flat, this advantage must be balanced against the problems posed by frequent stiff breezes. As an older city, Chicago's streets were built for an earlier era. They seem to shrink as cars grow larger, leaving less room for bike riders.

Nevertheless, Chicago does have some biking advantages. Its density makes large swaths of the city accessible to riders. The street system is laid out on a grid that is easily mastered, making it difficult for riders to lose their way. For an American city, it has a good public transportation system that bikers can use to their advantage. It has a bike-friendly political structure that begins with Mayor Richard M. Daley. And it has the Chicagoland Bicycle Federation (CBF).[8]

The CBF is the largest and surely one of the most powerful and most successful bicycle advocacy organizations in the United States. It was formed in 1985 by a small band of starry-eyed riders "to improve the bicycling environment and therefore the quality of life" in greater metropolitan Chicago. From its earliest days, its members considered their organization part of a larger social justice movement. Because a diversified and integrated transportation system is by its nature more inclusive, the founders of the CBF were inspired by the belief that they were working on behalf of social equity.

In politics, as in other realms of life and nature, acts beget other acts in ways that are often unpredictable. The popular designation of this phenomenon is the butterfly effect, drawn from the recognition that the flight of a butterfly in one part of the world can precipitate a string of events leading to a hurricane on the other side of the planet. Follow the flight of one particular butterfly: The first Earth Day was held on April 22, 1971, at which, in response to a growing awareness of environmental decay, people gathered in rallies across the land. These actions, regarded as largely symbolic at the time, nevertheless increased awareness of environmental issues and pushed them onto the agenda of national politics. Shortly thereafter, Republican president Richard Nixon proposed the creation of the Environmental Protec-

Biking organizations have been quite successful in getting access to public transit systems.

tion Agency, and a Democratic Congress quickly complied. In 1978, at President Jimmy Carter's urging, Congress passed the Clean Air Act. Among other things, this act required states to examine transportation alternatives. In response to this, Susan Pinsof, a senior planner at the

Northeastern Illinois Planning Commission, authored a report titled, "Encouraging Bicycle Use in Northeastern Illinois."

Such reports are frequently buried deep in the bowels of bureaucracies and forgotten. But the one undeniable effect they have is to educate those who write them. Recognizing that governments rarely move unless prodded to do so, Pinsof and a few concerned citizens she had met in the course of her research incorporated the CBF as a not-for-profit in 1985. It had seven members, no staff, and no money. Dues were set at $5 a year. A $4,000 grant from the Chicago Area Bicycle Dealers Association enabled the purchase of stationery and the publication of a quarterly newsletter. In 1987, political organizer and "biking eccentric" Randy Neufeld, profiled earlier, applied for a job with the CBF. He was hired, initially without pay, and soon became the first executive director of the organization.

In 1988, the CBF took its first faltering step of direct political action. The Village Board of Winnetka, a wealthy North Shore community, voted to ban bikes from Sheridan Road. This major thoroughfare runs north along Lake Michigan from Chicago to the Wisconsin border. Serious cyclists like using the road because it is beautiful, has some of the few hills in the Chicago area, and contains relatively few stop signs. The Sheridan Road bike ban was instituted because some of the village residents considered the bikers a nuisance. The CBF entered the fray on behalf of the bikers and sought to enjoin the board from instituting the ban.

It was a losing battle. On the one hand, the CBF was a regional organization seeking to put pressure on a local township. Most of the riders who raced along Sheridan were not from that township, greatly reducing their political leverage. And altruistic arguments about "sharing the road" proved unpersuasive as well. Many who live in Winnetka do so for the privacy and protection such a community affords. The idea of "sharing the road" with outsiders did not resonate strongly with them. In the end, CBF gained some small concessions from the board, but they lost the battle; Sheridan remained closed to bike traffic. However, the issue had a powerful galvanizing effect on members of the organization. They had learned something about politics, and the struggle left them with a much greater sense of political purpose.

In the fall of that year, Neufeld attended a national conference on biking in Tucson, Arizona. He made an important discovery at that conference about the nature of biking advocacy that would later prove vital to successful efforts. It was an epiphany, and it reshaped how the CBF went about its business. Policy success, Neufeld learned, is maximized by institutionalizing the idea of biking in the planning process. Wherever possible, it is essential for a bike voice to be heard from the beginning, so that biking is incorporated into the vision of the policy. When biking advocacy enters the process at a later stage, it inevitably creates problems for the planners. Rethinking can occur, but it is more difficult and far more costly than original inclusion. As a consequence, bike advocates are much more likely to be considered a pain.

A corollary to this insight also came from this conference: Make and discover friends in high places. Advocacy organizations must learn with whom they can work—those people at various points in the political structure who might be willing to carry some water for them. Making friends often assured greater success than confrontation. These two ideas—getting in early wherever possible in the policymaking process, and making and using friends in official positions—has been the modus operandi of CBF ever since.

In 1991, Congress passed ISTEA as part of highway legislation that comes around every six years. The highway construction and renewal bill is always huge, with federal funding in the hundreds of billions for highway and highway-related projects. The inclusion of ISTEA as part of the larger bill meant that, for the first time, money was made available to communities for bicycle projects. The CBF was strategically situated to capitalize on the new political reality created by the passage of ISTEA. Public officials love being able to spend money on projects in their districts, especially if the money comes from elsewhere. Such expenditures provide palpable evidence that the officials are productive. The CBF had established positive relationships with regional government officials and were already involved in the transportation planning process. The organization was, moreover, skilled at scrounging for money.

For local leaders, therefore, having the CBF assist them in garnering federal resources distributed to the states for bike projects was a no-brainer. As with interstate highway funds, if local governments put forward a small amount of seed money, they can get grants of much greater value from the federal government. The passage of ISTEA was a landmark because it made federal funds available for bike projects to cash-strapped state and local governments. The symbolic effect of the law was fully as important. The passage of this legislation by the national government in effect sanctioned the idea of more biking and by so doing boosted the legitimacy of the biking movement.

The CBF operates simultaneously at two levels of policy promotion. First, it puts significant energy into "big picture" work such as establishing broad organizational goals, long-range planning, and so forth. The CBF was instrumental in the conception and development of Bike Plan 2015. If the plan is implemented, it would represent a large step forward in bike friendliness. The most ambitious part of the plan calls for establishing a five-hundred-mile, interconnected network of "bikeways" in the city with arteries extending to within a half mile of every resident and neighborhood of the city. (*Bikeways* are streets and trails designed specifically, but not always exclusively, for bike travel.) Included in this expansion would be an upgrading of the entire system with better signage and improved pavement marking. There will also be some experimentation with elevated bike lanes, in the fashion of Amsterdam. Priority destinations, such as schools, transit stations, and the Loop, will be emphasized under the plan. The bike parking system will be enhanced and made more secure. Biker access to public transportation will be expanded by increasing the options for transporting bikes and the security of parking bikes at transit centers.

The second operational level of the CBF is much more visible: It is involved in a wide array of activities that connect in some way to the mission of the organization. The relations between the CBF and local political officials are such that it is not always easy to see where the two entities begin and end. The idea of having friends in the political structure has borne fruit. City biking coordinator Ben Gomberg, for example, has very good relations with the CBF and will contract with the group when he believes it is in the city's interest to do so. "There is a tremendous amount of expertise in the CBF," Gomberg said in an interview. "When the goal is to improve the bike friendliness of Chicago, it makes sense to consider the views of those who have thought most about this, and who actually have the wheels on the ground. We don't always agree, but I have a very high regard for their input."

An example of this collaboration is the City of Chicago bike map, which is updated each year. This map designates all off-road bike trails in the city, all roads with bike lanes, roads where bike lanes are projected, and preferred biking streets without lanes. By inference, it also indicates roads that are not safe. The map also locates all rapid transit stops and all bike shops in the city—both important pieces of information in emergencies. It is quite reliable and a very valuable tool for a rider. Resources of the city are used in its production, and the map is also subsidized by a local bank. It is distributed without charge as a city service. But the legwork for the bike map is done by the CBF, as the group can disperse riders throughout the city to accomplish this task. This legwork is key to the map's accuracy.

The CBF has a number of other successes to which they can point. Its leaders make no claims that they are solely responsible for these accomplishments. On the contrary, they are quick to credit the commitment of public officials to them. Such officials have been sought out, however, and the CBF has been an active, knowledgeable, organized, and consistent voice on behalf of these projects. It also maintains a substantial, highly interested membership base. Public officials who are sympathetic to the goals of the CBF are reassured by the existence and support of this organization; those officials who might not be supportive understand that opposition may be politically costly.

As a result, the Chicagoland area has become substantially more bike-friendly in the past fifteen years. A far from exhaustive list of accomplishments includes the following: The quality and quantity of off-road trails has significantly increased; on-road bike lanes have proliferated; racks for parking and locking bikes have been widely installed; bike-carrying racks have been installed on all Chicago city buses; bikes are allowed on city and regional rapid transit lines during nonrush hours; bike festival days that close portions of the auto transportation grid to motorized traffic are held annually; education programs on bike safety are regularly scheduled in schools and city park offices; the "Walk and Bike to School Day" was established and expanded as part of a Safe Routes To School program; the establishment of secure "bike valet" services were organized at more than twenty public events (in 2005, eight thousand bikes were safely parked through this program); and the completion of a solar powered, state-of-the-art bike parking facility, including a bike shop, lockers, and showers, was built in Chicago's new Millennium Park.

The CBF has evolved into a formidable not-for-profit organization, with a staff of forty and a 2007 budget of $2.2 million. Current executive director Rob Sadowsky has led a process that seeks greater institutionalization; this includes strategic planning for the development of policies and procedures and "evidence-based" work to implement them. The intent is, wherever possible, to measure progress empirically.

One of the CBF's goals is to move more completely into the suburbs that surround the city. The density of the city gives advantages to biking: Distances that many need to travel are not very large; density exacerbates the problems of moving by car. But suburbs also have bike-friendly advantages. Many jobs are now located in the suburban ring, and the wider streets make it easier to establish bike lanes on them. For at least some forward-looking suburbs, Sadowsky believes it is possible to create near ideal biking environments in which the bike is the first transportation option. One of the beauties of the bike, he believes, is that it is so adaptable. It is simply a matter of recognizing the opportunities a particular locale presents and capitalizing on these.

As for the city, one project in particular is generating considerable excitement at the CBF. It illustrates both how the CBF works with others to advance biking policies and also biking's broader relevance to politics. It is an adaptation of a program currently popular in a number of Latin American cities. Basically, it involves closing a substantial number of streets to motorized traffic—buses excepted—for a limited period of time. The CBF has paid the closest attention to the Cycla Via program in Bogotá, Columbia, and to Guadalajara, Mexico, where the program is called Viva La Recreativa. CBF representatives have traveled to Bogotá, and delegates from Guadalajara have come to Chicago to discuss their programs.

In Mexico, when people go out, they will often say, "*Me voy en la calle.*" Though translated "I'm going out," this expression literally means, "I'm going into the street." This phrase recognizes that in much of Latin America, the victory of the automobile is far from complete. Streets are more clearly seen as multipurpose public spaces, not simply for car movement. Throughout the region, people still gather in them. So when Enrique Penalosa, the mayor of Bogotá, made his fateful decision in 1998 to open the streets of the city by closing them on certain days to motorized traffic, it was controversial, but not without a base of support. The original trials of Cycla Via were experimental, but it has proven to be very popular. It has expanded and become a permanent feature of the life of that city. Today, 120 kilometers of roads are closed on 70 different days during the year in Bogotá. On peak days, more than 250,000 have flooded the streets on foot and on bicycle.

Chicago has a boulevard system that connects a number of major parks throughout the city, and the CBF now sponsors an annual "Bike the Boulevard" event. These events are interesting, but they do not close the boulevards to motorized traffic. Drawing from the Latin American model, the federation is pushing to take this next step. They are designing a program that closes several miles of boulevard to motorized traffic on summer Sundays, called Sunday Parkways. Accomplishing this task in a metropolis like Chicago is mind-boggling in its complexity. It requires the cooperation of a number of city departments including the city police, as well as private corporations and neighborhood groups. Relevant city agencies in the areas of public health, the environment, and city parks have bought into the idea of the program, as each considers it central to its mission. The neighborhoods have been more mixed in their reaction. The proposed route passes through several Latino neighborhoods, and many members of these communities were particularly proud to see a program adapted from the Latin American experience. Some local neighborhood associations and aldermen also support the idea. On the other hand, gentrification is an issue in Chicago. Many working-class people are being priced out of their homes and are struggling to keep traditional ethnic neighborhood identities intact. A program that brings large numbers of "outsiders" into these neighborhoods is a cause of concern for these people.

Sunday Parkways would not be solely a biking event. Bikes are a central mode of transport, but foot traffic, roller bladers, and other forms of nonmotorized traffic are also encouraged. The Chicago Park District will make provisions for entertainment and food, much of which will be supported via corporate sponsorship. The idea is to get out, exercise, have fun and enjoy the day. No fees will be charged. Cross streets to the boulevards will not be closed, and participants in the Sunday Parkways program will have to obey the normal traffic signals. It is hoped that this will minimize the irritation to nonparticipating motorists.

It is possible to think of Sunday Parkways as simply a few days of fun, but it is also worth considering the ways in which such a program is political. Most obviously, several government agencies will commit resources to the project, and they will do so because they believe it helps fulfill their missions. Since the route passes through several neighborhoods where gang and territorial issues exist, neighborhood groups see the program as contributing to better feelings and possibly reducing violence. The program will likely draw participants from all parts of the city. If so, it will reduce insularity and contribute to more healthy and nuanced views of the neighborhoods. Bikers and pedestrians have a much greater opportunity for neighborliness; thus, a broader sense of community will be nurtured by Sunday Parkways. Whether this might lead to increased gentrification is an open question. The CBF is particularly interested in the Sunday Parkways project because it revives the notion of streets as multipurpose thoroughfares. In all these ways and more, this event connects to the world of politics. Once it is established, the goal is to expand it until eventually it encompasses the entire boulevard system of the city.

While in general the United States lags behind other economically advanced nations in its accommodations to the bicycle, retrograde biking policies are not uniform. Some excellent biking cities exist here. These include several relatively small cities, such as Boulder, Colorado; Eugene, Oregon; and Davis and Palo Alto, California, where universities exert a strong influence. The popularity of bikes in and around college campuses has given such municipalities a leg up in the struggle for bike friendliness. Among cities large enough so that universities do not exert disproportionate influence, Portland, Oregon, stands out for its excellence. In its assessment of bike-friendly cities, the League of American Bicyclists has awarded Portland a penultimate "gold" rating. Portland is the only city of its size to receive this level of distinction. Unlike Chicago, finding Portland at the top of this list is not surprising.

Many things contribute to Portland's place in the forefront of America's biking cities. It has a long progressive political tradition and an environmentally conscious, limited-growth culture. Those attracted to this ethos are drawn to Portland, which presents the city with the ironic dilemma of keeping the ethos vibrant. (It has been said that all who move to Portland hope to be the last to do so.) Oregonians are unusually exercise- and health-conscious. The state may lead the world in joggers per capita, and the corporate headquarters of Nike is in suburban Beaverton. The city also has a congenial climate and a wonderful biking topography. Its gentle undulations foretell the more challenging Cascade Mountain Range that sits within easy biking distance. By American standards, the bicycle culture in Portland is an old one. In the early 1970s, Oregon passed the nation's first law requiring the regular expenditure of transportation revenues for biking and pedestrian improvements. Commonly known as the "Bicycle Bill," this law mandates that municipalities use 1 percent of the state's general transportation revenues that they receive to support bike and pedestrian traffic. Additionally, the law requires all new or reconstructed roadways to include appropriate bicycle and pedestrian facilities.

The array of natural and cultural advantages that tilt Portland toward favorable biking policies are complemented by the fact that the city is home to the Bicycle Transportation Alliance (BTA), one of the most outstanding bicycle advocacy organizations in the country.[9] It was established in 1991, which is somewhat surprising given Portland's friendly culture and the fact that the Bicycle Bill had passed years earlier. In that year Jim Ferner, a dedicated cyclist, tried to get his bike on a Tri-Met bus. The driver refused to allow him on the bus with his bike, whereupon Ferner and his bicycle lay in protest in front of the bus. That display of civil disobedience did not end matters for Ferner. He printed and distributed fliers that called for a meeting of all who were interested in establishing a bike advocacy group. In a few weeks, nine people, sitting around a kitchen table, formed the Portland Area Bicycle Coalition. Initially, the group was entirely voluntary, but they met with immediate success in pressing their first issue. After gathering more than five thousand signatures on petitions requesting bike racks on Tri-Met buses and presenting these to local authorities, the Coalition carried the day.

The group soon evolved into a not-for-profit, professional organization, and along the way the name was changed to the Bicycle Transportation Alliance. Early BTA members recognized that the Bicycle Bill had largely been ignored, as roads were being built and reworked without any effort to add bike lanes. This was a galvanizing issue for the organization in its early years, but it soon established a broader, more encompassing appeal. The BTA now advocates for the entire state, although Portland remains its most important focus. It has a full-time staff of nine and it can count on hundreds of volunteers from its more than 4,500 members.

The BTA has played a key role in making Portland what is perhaps the leading biking city in the country. As we have seen, Chicago is a very good biking city, especially for its size, but it lags behind Portland. Portland has all the things Chicago has (bike maps, bike lanes, bike trails, bike access to public transportation, etc.) and more. The bike lane and trail system is more elaborate and more integrated than Chicago's, for example. Bikers in Portland can take their bikes on the light rail system at any time including rush hours, thanks to a technology that allows riders to hang their bikes on hooks near car doors. This has sharply reduced complaints from nonbiking commuters about gouging pedals and greasy chains. Both cities respond to bikers' calls that identify roadway maintenance needs, but the Portland system is much better advertised. Contact information is contained in outreach program literature and included on all bike maps. And once contacted, the response time is shorter—usually within twenty-four hours for potholes.

Many advocacy groups throughout the nation sponsor Bike-to-Work Days, or Weeks. For ten years, the BTA has organized a month-long, Bike-to-Work Challenge, and it is outstanding. Bikers employed at various businesses try to get their workplaces to sanction and encourage the event, and similar businesses are often drawn into a kind of friendly competition of the sort that occurs on many municipal softball diamonds. Distinction goes to those who get the highest proportion of employees biking to work over the month. Sometimes single employees have represented their companies; other businesses have become enthusiastic participants. In 2005, 484 local businesses took part, generating a total of 4,000 commuters. Of these, 1,600 had never ridden to work before.

The BTA has a distinguished and elaborate bike education program. It is, for example, deeply involved in the bike education of children, and in 2003 it won the National Bicycle Education Leadership Award from the League of American Bicyclists. This is a hands-on program in which BTA volunteers work directly with middle school children, providing ten hours of on-bike, on-street training. About half the middle schools in the city have participated in the program thus far. An additional aspect of youth safety is the BTA's participation in an exemplary Safe Routes To School program. They have worked intensively with schools and local authorities to identify and reduce those areas where conflict among cars, pedestrians, and bike riders is greatest. Special bike- and walk-to-school events now occur at more than thirty city schools. Grants have been obtained to support these efforts, and the city now earmarks a portion of traffic fine revenue for traffic safety programs, including safe routes to school.

The advantages of youth bike education and safety programs are obvious. The programs make biking safer for kids, which makes parents more willing to allow their kids to ride. The influx of kids on the "safe" routes makes them safer still. Their larger numbers enhance visibility, making them a more routine part of the transportation scene and therefore more fixed in the consciousness of motorists. And young regular riders have a greater probability of becoming adult regular riders with firsthand knowledge of some of the work the BTA does. This eventually will add to its base and augment its political power.

The BTA has a distinctive adult education program as well, and it is one of the few programs that contain a serious focus on nonriders. While not as integrated or extensive as Amsterdam's, this BTA initiative acts on the understanding that drivers need to become more conscious of bike traffic. The city undertakes a significant "share the road" education in targeted areas. Residents of these areas get "share the road" messages in newsletters. Individualized information kits have been delivered to new residents of a target area. The messages dispensed also encourage people to consider bicycle use. Information is provided about free classes that teach adults how to ride a bike and other classes that provide instruction on safe urban riding. In conjunction with these efforts, the BTA runs a public advertising campaign that includes prominent billboards throughout the city urging motorists to share the road with other users. Recognizing that riding will be more extensive if bike owners can handle minor maintenance problems themselves, the BTA sponsors regular, free workshops called Bicycle 101. Such programs not only keep people riding but also impart a sense of mastery that is close to nonexistent among car owners.

Regularly scheduled bicycle clinics are conducted by an experienced "bicycle lawyer." At these clinics riders learn of their rights and their responsibilities under Oregon law, obtain information about insurance, and learn what to do in case of an accident. The

To create a buzz about biking, Louisville has made bike racks works of art (Photos courtesy Louisville Downtown Development District).

organization lists several attorneys who are experienced in cases involving bicycles.

The bicycle movement in this country is growing in part because of the hard work of advocacy organizations such as the ones described in this chapter. As with other work in the not-for-profit sector of society, the remuneration is modest. Despite this, many who are employed in this field are well educated, talented, and enthusiastic about their work. What attracts them is not the pay but the conviction that the work they are doing is important. Karen Frost, the first executive director of the BTA, is fairly typical. Karen worked for AT&T, and after participating in Cycle Oregon '91—a popular cross-Oregon bike ride—she began biking to work. She became active in the BTA from its outset and left her corporate job to take over the leadership of this group. She has since formed her own company, the Westside Transportation Alliance. The mission of this organization is to work with businesses, helping them to do the kinds of things that make it easier for employees to bike to work. She has given up her car completely, using her bike and public transportation for mobility. "The thing that I like most about bike advocacy work," she says, "is that you actually get to do the thing you're advocating."

Catherine Ciarlo, an attorney who succeeded Frost as executive director of the BTA, is cut from the same cloth. "I never expect to have another job as rewarding as that one was," she says. But she also points to another reason for the political success of the BTA. A study in Portland a few years ago sought to figure out the things that correlate with political activity. This was not a bicycle study, because it had a much broader focus. But the study found that membership in the BTA was a very strong predictor of political activity and engagement, stronger than almost any other variable. In short, the study found that to be a member of the BTA was to be interested and engaged in politics. The question of causality cannot be resolved by such a study, but the results are consistent with the idea that bikers tend to have strong connections to their social world.

Other, less formal groups are also relevant to biking and politics. They do little direct advocacy, but they contribute in other ways that matter politically. Such groups are therefore key players in the biking scene. It is to a selection of these that we now turn.

Chapter Six

Pushing the Envelope

Populist Politics

The previous chapter highlights an active mix of biking organizations at the national and local levels whose central mission is to influence allocation and policy decisions made by various governmental authorities. Such groups seek a place at the table where "who gets what" decisions are made, and they are thus integrally involved in politics. But to let the matter rest here would be to miss other essential dimensions of biking politics. Political action flows out of consciousness. In everyday life experience, people sort and share values; and in politics, they act on the basis of those values they deem politically important. Politically relevant values may ebb and flow. A dramatic event can sharply elevate a particular value, as the concern for security was elevated in the post-9/11 world. Values can also become more important because they resonate with changing experience. Interest in national health care policy grows, for example, as private systems of health care become more exclusive and less reliable.

Since biking affects perception in politically relevant ways, it is important to consider the proliferation of other kinds of bike groups beyond those engaged in full-time advocacy work. Such groups typically do not have an explicit political agenda—at least in the narrow sense of that term—but they are a major stimulus to bike riding in this country. As riders increase, the perceptual world generated by riding becomes more broadly shared. Increased riding thus serves to "grow the base" of the biking constituency, and they are politically important in other ways as well. For want of a better term, we have called the groups that pull people into riding without asserting immediate political goals "populist groups." Some are tightly organized, with regular meetings, dues, and the like; others are quite loose, meet-up groups. They are remarkably profuse. What follows is a sampling of these "populist" groups.

Critical Mass

The term *critical mass* has its origins in physics, referring to the minimum amount of substance necessary to sustain a chain reaction. Like many scientific terms, however, it has been adapted and applied to social situations. With respect to biking, the term has been used to describe a pattern American visitors first observed twenty-five years ago while watching Chinese traffic flow. Even though China was the most bike-centric country in the world, individual riders there, as elsewhere, were intimidated by motorized traffic. The imposing nature of the car gave it an inherent advantage. The visitors noticed that, in response to this intimidation, bikers would cede the right of way to drivers. But as they waited for cars to pass, bikers accumulated, gathering more mass. When a certain point was reached, the bikers edged into motorized traffic, reversing the process of intimidation. Overwhelmed by the sheer number of riders, cars would simply come to a standstill until the bike traffic thinned sufficiently for car drivers to regain control of the road. The Chinese lurched about in such ebbs and flows, conducting their daily business.

The idea for a similar "critical mass" experience took hold in San Francisco in the early 1990s. No one is willing to take credit for its genesis. Many early supporters of Critical Mass (CM) shared a strong antihierarchical, quasi-anarchic, and democratic ethos in which people more or less spontaneously take control of their lives. Such sentiment persists among CM partisans, and works against the very idea of "leadership." Some have suggested that Chris Carlsson was the main force behind the first CM, but he strongly demurs.[1] He admits suggesting to the San Francisco Bike Coalition in August 1992 that a regular event be staged, but he claims that this idea had been discussed for several months and had evolved through a number of Coalition meetings.

Whatever the case, on September 27, 1992, the world's first organized and intentional Critical Mass (as distinguished from the Chinese version) was staged by several dozen riders in downtown San Francisco. It was an idea whose time had come, and it spread quickly throughout the country and across the world. A CM information Web site[2] lists more than three hundred regularly scheduled Masses throughout the world. Of these, 175 are held in 43 American states. American primacy may be an indication of how badly this nation trails others in biking policy. I discussed Critical Mass with Natascha Van Bennekom, the head of the cyclists' union in Amsterdam. She noted that this group tried staging a CM in Amsterdam, but they found very little interest. Since so many Amsterdamers ride every day, an event celebrating riding was not seen as serving any particular purpose. (While I was there, however, I did see a Rollerblading mass.)

True both to the philosophical predispositions of those prominent in the CM movement and to the inherently localized nature of these rides, there is no central mechanism to provide direction and lend coherence to Critical Mass. Describing a "typical" CM ride is therefore problematic. It is possible, however, to consider central tendencies—as well as some of the variations—of the CMs. First, the rides are not single-event happenings. They recur, most often monthly, and most often on the last Friday of every month. Riders gather at a designated spot that is constant over time—typically central to the urban area. The rides vary widely in size, from a few dozen participants to several thousand. The routes are rarely spontaneous—it is difficult to keep the group together if they are—but the levels of spontaneity vary. Some rides cover the same route every month; some change them monthly; some vote on alternative proposals at the point of gathering. Some return to their points of origin; others seek out interesting and varied destinations and let riders make their way home on their own.

The aim of Critical Mass is for bikes to take over the streets of the city for two or three hours. An organized ride along some bike path is not a CM, even if it is a regularly scheduled event with several hundred participants. CM offers riders periodic respite from a long-standing grievance: That riding on streets is dangerous and regularly subjects bikers to the indifference, ignorance, and the occasional hostility of drivers. In most urban areas, bikes have not only a right but an obligation to use the streets. As such, they are entitled to the same rights as motorists, including the full right to traffic lanes. For reasons that include safety, comity, and efficiency, riders rarely exercise these rights. Instead, they pedal along at the margins of roads. Most motorists are cooperative in turn, but enough have assimilated a sense that the streets are exclusively for cars to make biking a daunting experience. Some bikers are annoying as well, but the asymmetry of the two vehicles is rarely lost on them.

A CM ride is an affirmation that this asymmetry can be altered. To do so, however, it is essential for the riders to remain a mass. Larger CMs inevitably contain a variety of riders. Some are seasoned road warriors; others are quite inexperienced. Seniors ride next to children. Some do CMs on novelty bikes. The idea is for the riders to bond into a single entity, simulating an organism. To achieve this, those in the first ranks of the ride proceed very slowly—at a pace of seven or eight miles an hour—making sure the group stays "massed up."

The extent to which Massers feel obligated to obey normal traffic laws varies from city to city and, in specific CMs, from rider to rider. Some CMs try to obey all the traffic laws, but most fudge some of them. For example, once a ride starts through an intersection, it will typically continue through that intersection without stopping. For larger CMs, this procedure may involve passing through several signal changes, which commonly provokes motorists. A few of the riders seem to enjoy the provocation, perhaps recalling times when motorists have ignored bikers' rights. Others are sympathetic to the motorists, and shout out their appreciation of the motorists' patience. Often riders will take it upon themselves to become goodwill ambassadors. They stop and chat with motorists, explaining the ride and thanking them as the CM passes by. Patience is not a characteristic virtue of motorists, so it is somewhat surprising that so many of them simply chill and enjoy this moment of street theater.

Although some motorists are upset by such "law breaking," it is probably the right thing to do. Traffic laws are not intended to accommodate a CM, and it is most efficient to allow large urban CMs to move along as expeditiously as possible. Having large rides obey the letter of the law by stopping at all red lights would segment the CM and create an unmanageable traffic nightmare. It is a solution far worse—for motorists, riders, and police officers—than the problem. Many law enforcement agencies recognize this and help keep the CM moving, but not all do.

Things get more controversial when CM routes include areas—such as interstate highways—that normally prohibit bikes. Jumping on interstate highways is much more likely to provoke confrontation with municipal authorities. It is controversial within CM groups as well; many individual Massers oppose potential confrontations of this nature. And taking a CM onto an interstate requires great discipline and coordination. On-ramps, for example, must be shut down while the riders pass. And once on an interstate, there is an almost irresistible urge to crank up one's bike. This means that the CM will thin, which significantly increases the danger for slower riders. Some people do not participate in CM because they think it is too edgy and too confrontational. (The edginess, of course, varies from city to city.) This is a reasonable position. On the other hand, there is an undeniable sense of empowerment that comes from taking over an interstate and enjoying, however briefly, the silky-smooth surfaces that are reserved for motorized traffic. It calls attention to the imbalance between what government does for bikes and what it does for cars.

Given the emphasis on democratic decentering, it is not surprising that motives for participation in CM vary. Interviews taken over several Chicago rides typically found participants offering a number of motivations, the balance of which varied from rider to rider. Going into these interviews, I anticipated most riders would not be particularly aware of the political implications of this event. So many people have such obvious fun on these rides that I assumed fun would be the primary motivation for participation. It was somewhat surprising that the great majority of people queried first mentioned straightforward political or cultural reasons for participating. Perhaps these responses were evoked by the inherently artificial nature of interviewing. Someone running around with a tape recorder might well impose a sense of solemnity. Even if the instrument did structure responses somewhat—and I believe this effect was marginal—it is noteworthy that such thoughts quickly came to the minds of the respondents.

There was substantial endorsement of the bike as a good means of transport (healthy, environmentally benign, pollution-free) that deserves strong community support. Another political dimension frequently mentioned was the sense of empowerment the CM provides. Time and again, riders referred to their first CM and the thrill of riding through a major urban center without constantly worrying about cars. Additionally, riders like the idea of bonding with each other. CMs generate a sense of community among the riders, which is interesting because it is exactly the opposite for cars. For motorized traffic, the fewer on the road, the better. With CMs, it's the more the merrier. What this says is not completely clear, but it certainly says something.

There is no denying, however, that fun is the most pervasive, if not the deepest, motive for CM rides—and the reason people return to them time and again. In cold-weather cities like Chicago, people like seasonal rides for different reasons. The winter rides are smaller, but they also draw more devoted riders and evoke a particular brand of camaraderie. Participants in winter rides get a charge out of an experience that most others think is just a bit crazy. The whoops of riders in the cold winter air seem a little more joyful than they do in other seasons. Riders gladly take on a "That's right—it's frigid! I'm ridin'!" persona. Such exquisite adversity generates a special sense of companionship.

On the other hand, the larger rides of summer are carnivals, sprinkled with assortments of novelty bikes including tandems, recumbents, nineteenth-century high-wheelers, choppers, and homemade two-story bikes. Preadolescent riders pedal alongside octogenarians. Some parents have their children in tow; others tote small pets; still others have boom boxes strapped to rear racks. People often dress for the rides, donning unique ensembles not normally associated with riding. (This is especially true for the October/Halloween rides.) Some riders, such as San Francisco's infamous Dildo Man, assume the same character from month to month. Thus, as a CM snakes its way through urban corridors, it assumes the aura of a Mardi Gras parade, a cornucopia of possibility not generally recognized in everyday life experience. Some riders toss candy to onlookers; others simply shout out, "Happy Friday."

I have never been to a CM without encountering irate motorists. In my hometown, the rides take place on Fridays, departing around

6:00 P.M. from the heart of the Loop. Most drivers, having made it through the work week, are naturally interested in getting out of town as quickly as possible. Any impediments can be irritating, and impediments resulting from the conscious actions of others can exacerbate the irritation. Such situations are usually defused, sometimes by riders talking the drivers down, and sometimes by drivers simply recognizing that there are, after all, hundreds of riders.

On the other hand, the rides are often fun for many of those not participating in them. Pedestrians and neighborhood residents overwhelmingly seem to enjoy this distinctive diversion, as do many motorists—especially those on the opposite side of the street from the CM flow. But a substantial proportion of motorists who are enveloped and ensnarled in CM seem not to mind too much. Perhaps they feel that, although they are being delayed, they are also being entertained. It is at least better than unanticipated road construction.

Apart from the inherently political nature of CM, some rides are specifically organized to address a political issue. In Chicago, for example, the winter ride coinciding with the annual auto show always passes by that event. The intent is to call attention to the social and political problems generated by unbridled enthusiasm for the automobile. Rides in various cities are often calibrated in this way to connect explicitly to political matters. The most notorious of these occurred in August 2004 in New York City. The Manhattan Critical Mass is loosely organized under the auspices of Time's Up!, a city environmental organization. By 2004, it had become one of the nation's larger CMs, regularly drawing several hundred riders. The last Friday of August fell on the eve of the National Republican Convention, which was being held in Madison Square Garden. A route was designed to pass by the Garden and protest the environmental policies of President George W. Bush, as well as his renomination. The chance to protest the policies of the president "grew" the ride, as politicians might say, to more than five thousand riders, making it one of the largest CMs ever.

The CM also occurred the day before a more typical anti-Bush march was scheduled. The increased security concerns for presidents after 9/11 were exacerbated by the unprecedented efforts of President Bush's handlers to shield him from his detractors. The president's political operators wanted to sustain the perception of presidential popularity, which would be undercut by the adverse publicity of large

The August 2004 Manhattan Critical Mass sets out to protest the renomination of President Bush (Photo courtesy Fred Askew).

demonstrations. This increased pressure on New York officials, who, for their own reasons, wanted the convention to run smoothly. The fact that these officials presided over a large constituency that was broadly opposed to the president complicated the matter and increased the volatility of the situation.

New York police, geared up to prevent disturbances to the convention, came down hard on CM. They arrested more than 260 riders, mostly for disorderly conduct and obstructing traffic. The offenders were arrested for parading without a permit, and for violating traffic laws by "corking" intersections to allow for the CM's unimpeded flow. Corking is a practice widely used by CM riders, and it had been allowed in Manhattan during previous rides. Many of those arrested were detained for more than twenty-four hours, which was unusual for such minor infractions of the law. Those arrested felt the detentions were deliberately punitive. Moreover, bikes were kept for more than three weeks, causing hardship for many who regularly used them to get around the city.

Most of the charges against the riders were later dismissed in court, but the controversy continued. Mayor Michael Bloomberg's administration sought an injunction to prevent the next ride, charging that CM needed a parade permit. Members of CM contended that, as regular traffic, they needed no such permit. The injunction was not granted by the courts, but the tensions between the police and the bikers continued. In the ensuing year, 518 additional arrests and bike confiscations were made at CM events. Undercover police officers infiltrated CM rides and have been captured on film provoking incidents. The city sought a second injunction, which was denied by the courts in February 2006. The judge strongly encouraged both sides to cool off and settle their differences.

This admonition did little to ease hard feelings on either side. In an editorial[3] issued on the day of the last ride of 2006, the *New York Times* argued that the continuing hostilities threatened "to create a losing proposition for both sides." It noted that the vast array of police resources used to confront and regulate the CM—scooters, vans, unmarked cars, and helicopters—was not only wasteful but also created a greater danger than the CM itself, as police raced the wrong way and on sidewalks in their zeal to enforce the law. It called for CM leaders to work with police in prearranging a route that would be corked by police officers. All the while, another New York City CM ride had been taking place in the borough of Brooklyn without incident. That ride uses the same corking procedure that had become controversial in Manhattan. Matthew Roth of Transportation Alternatives notes that the rigorous enforcement of the letter of the law has had a corrosive effect on the Manhattan Mass, and it turned bike riding into a civil rights issue there. Many erstwhile Manhattan massers have fled to the Brooklyn Mass to recapture the joy that is traditionally integral to these rides.

Sustained CM confrontations have occurred in other cities, most notably in San Francisco and Portland, Oregon. But in both of these situations tensions have been eased by negotiations between local authorities and CM participants. In San Francisco, a confrontation began when Mayor Willie Brown's limo was caught in a traffic snarl created by a ride. Tensions ran high over several months in 1997 as police cracked down. In the end, Brown seemed as anxious as the CM participants to end the controversy, and accommodations were made. Now radio stations regularly announce Mass rides during traffic updates. In Portland, long-simmering tensions were eased by newly elected, sixty-five-year-old mayor Tom Potter. An avid rider of a recumbent bike, the former Portland police chief campaigned hard for the bike vote. In one of his first acts as mayor, he rode in a CM.

Such confrontations have brought attention to CM, but they are not typical. The great majority of these rides occur without serious incident. But they have generated a broad discussion among those in the biking community who seek friendlier transportation policies. Is Critical Mass politically efficacious, making a contribution to the broader acceptance of biking as integral to our social life? Or is it reactionary, provoking a backlash against riders in the broader community?

This argument has deep historical roots and is in fact common in any movement seeking to alter an imperfect political and social system. As accommodations are sought, how accommodating should the aggrieved be to the system they think is unfair? It is the argument of W. E. B. Dubois and Booker T. Washington, of Martin Luther King Jr. and Malcolm X. One side of the progressive spectrum pushes from within the political system; the other side worries about being "co-opted" into accepting small changes and is therefore more confrontational. Some of the most devoted along this divide are disdainful of those on the other side. Some policy advocates consider CM to be a largely irrelevant spasm; some CM riders think of themselves as actually "living the revolution," while the advocates accept crumbs from the political table.

Perhaps such dichotomies distort the process of social change. A social system is in place because of the underlying power dynamics in that system, which means that change is usually hard. Advocates for change often need all the help they can get, and a variety of approaches may be necessary to overcome inertia. At its most confrontational, when one might conclude that motorists and civic authorities are angriest at Critical Mass—and at bikers in general—attention is called to the needs of bikers in ways that are difficult to match through more acceptable processes of politics. Angry motorists are angry because they do not want to be bothered. They really want bikers to go away and leave the streets to them. But bikers are not going away. This dynamic can spur politicians to figure out ways to reduce the irritation.

Dave Snyder, the former executive director of the San Francisco Bike Coalition, worried about the negative impressions from the rancorous confrontation between the San Francisco Critical Mass and Mayor Brown. Lots of irritation was directed at CM, and Snyder worried that this would be attached to cyclists in general, and therefore create resistance to better biking policies. But he ultimately concluded that the controversy helped to put biking issues on the political agenda, noting, "Taking into account the negatives, Critical Mass, at its most raucous heights, is still great for the bicycling movement."[4] It was "great" in Snyder's view because city officials began to ask, for the first time, "What is it that you folks want?" Although theoretical differences persist between the insiders and the outsiders, the point that Snyder makes seems to be largely recognized at some level. Many policy advocates frequent the CMs in their cities; many CM riders can see that incremental policies have had an important cumulative effect.

Another dimension of the political relevance of Critical Mass deserves to be noted. For many, it rewires consciousness, changing the manner in which participants think about their condition and the condition of the world they inhabit. Chris Carlsson expresses a strong version of this notion:[5]

> Critical Mass is an unparalleled practical experiment in public, collective self-expression, reclaiming our diminishing connectedness, interdependency and mutual responsibility. CM provides encouragement and reinforcement for desertion of the rat wheel of car ownership and its attendant investments. But even more subversively, it does it by gaining active participation in an event of unmediated human creation, outside of economic logic, and offering an exhilarating taste of a life practically forgotten—free, convivial, cooperative, connected, collective.

Carlsson is a visionary, and it is tempting to accuse him of reading the vision into the experience. Is this what Critical Mass means to its participants? Based on the discussions I have had with a number of people who have participated in these rides, I would have to say, "Something like it." I know a number of people for whom Critical Mass has precipitated feelings similar to those Carlsson describes. While this

may define the outer limits of CM's potential for altering consciousness, many others have a lower-level experience that is nevertheless
significant. They recognize that by participating in Critical Mass, they
are crossing a boundary. They love the fun of the ride, but they also
love it because it is not just any kind of fun. It is fun that grows out
of a larger sense of purpose. It is fun that is rooted in the vision of a
healthier and more humane society. It's the difference between the
fun of Jay Leno and that of Jon Stewart.

SHIFT (to Bikes)

Critical Mass is not in the business of direct political advocacy, but its
rides tend to exude a kind of free-form political buoyancy. SHIFT of
Portland, Oregon, is an activist organization of a slightly different sort.
In 2002, Portland sponsored Bike Summer, a month-long festival celebrating the bicycle. It was hugely successful, drawing more than five
thousand participants to a wide variety of activities. Both the strong
response of the community and the feelings of camaraderie among the
primary organizers of the activities led to the formation of SHIFT.

SHIFT works the cultural side of bike consciousness. It is a nonprofit
organization whose mission is "to demonstrate that cycling is fun,
liberating, empowering, sustainable and environmentally friendly."
It is both more structured and more diverse than Critical Mass, with
a central organizing committee of young bike activists. The central
committee plans and advertises a variety of events. At the same time,
it is open to others using the structure of the organization to promote
biking activities. It describes itself as an "informal, loose-knit group of
bicycle folks," who are drawn together by a common enthusiasm for
the potential of the bicycle. Jonathan Maus, a media contact person,
notes the fluidity of SHIFTers. Some folks have been around since
the outset, but people are constantly moving in and out of leadership
roles. Many are inspired to become more active through SHIFT events
they attend. There are no dues and no membership rolls. Since it is
volunteer driven, the organization requires little funding, and the
group ethos promotes doing things without spending money. People
donate talent and other useful things, and one or two fund-raising
events are held. This is sufficient to meet SHIFT's needs.

The SHIFT calendar is a frequently accessed and valuable organizing tool. Anyone who has a bike event may have it placed on the calendar. The calendar for May 2006, for example, listed sixty-seven events. These included a wide variety of rides, classes, tours, meetings, picnics, and swap meets. The activities that SHIFT plans exemplify its central purpose of highlighting the enjoyment of biking. The regular events they organized include Breakfast on the Bridges (free breakfast on three bridges on the last Friday of the month for pedestrians and bikers), Midnight Mystery Rides (regular late-night rides to intriguing destinations), and Pedalpalooza (described later).

There is a certain kind of rider who recoils at the notion that something cannot be done on a bicycle. SHIFT's "Move by Bike" program appeals to just such a person. This program supports household moves using nothing but bicycle power. Some movers have bikes with special trailers that give them the capability of hauling large items. There is no charge for this service. A request is placed on SHIFT's listserv, indicating the date of the move, location, destination, and incentives—typically food and beer. Cyclists wishing to help simply show up at the designated time and place. I told a nonbiking friend of this service, and she immediately asked, "Why do people do this?" A reasonable question, with a complex answer. In its abbreviated form, the answer is "Because they're crazy bikers."

The annual grassroots bicycle festival Pedalpalooza is perhaps the most extraordinary event that SHIFT sponsors. Held each June, Pedalpalooza features over a hundred bicycle-related events, including a county bicycle fair. It has activities for virtually every subcategory of bikers, including tours of the city and surrounding area, BMX trickster exhibitions, mountain biking, races, a minibike steeplechase, tandem and novelty rides, and commuter-oriented rides. There are rides catering to a rich tapestry of social groups, including women, Latinos, gays, seniors, and kids.

Some of the more interesting of these activities include Polo 101 (sponsored by the People's Republic of Polo, in which instruction, gear, and food are provided for "low-impact" bicycle polo), Bike with Your MAMa (a ride through Portland's "cool riverfront paths" designed particularly for singles meeting through bikes and conversation), Malty Beverage Ride (a tour of Portland's renowned microbreweries), a Fathers' Day Ride (in which fathers pull young children

Portland volunteers move entire households by bikes. In this photo, a stove presents no problem (Photo courtesy Jonathan Maus).

in bike trailers behind them), the annual Donut Ride (with the goal of hitting every donut shop in the city, this event stakes a claim to the "highest caloric intake" event of Pedalpalooza), Daytime World Naked Bike Ride (for those who are tired of freezing on midnight naked rides), Bike Trailer Tango (in which participants "learn how you can transport anything on your bike"), the Hob-Nob (for high-occupancy bikes, including tandems, triples, trailers, and cargo bikes), the Summer Solstice Ride (which begins at 10:00 P.M. and goes all night in celebration of the shortest night of the year), and the Bike Kiss-in (in which bikers ride to the most attractive part of the city and stage a kiss-in for the pleasure of homebound commuters—mints are provided, although kissers must bring along their own kissees).

ChiTown Cruisers

Through Alex Wilson, whose community-centered shop is located in a largely Puerto Rican Chicago neighborhood, I was able to contact Jose Martinez, a spokesperson for a biking group called the ChiTown Cruisers. In the course of our initial conversation, it was apparent that there were a number of things that were distinctive about the Cruisers, and so when Jose invited me to come along on one of their Sunday rides, I immediately accepted. Martinez, an earnest and enthusiastic member, called me a couple of times prior to the ride to make sure I understood where the club gathered, and that I knew the 11:00 A.M. starting time. After the second reminder I assured him that I would probably be there a few minutes early to chat with club members. Casa Puertorriqueño, located across the street from Humboldt Park, is a major social hub of the neighborhood and served as the point of departure for the ride. True to my word, I arrived fifteen minutes early. There was lots of activity in the area—including a number of bikers who were hanging out—but no one from the club. Around 11:15 members began gradually to accumulate until about 1:00 P.M. when the ride actually pushed off.

While we were waiting for the ride to begin, we had ample opportunity to discuss the club. Several members described it as "family oriented," with something in excess of a hundred members. Female riders participate only on special occasions such as the Puerto Rican

The ChiTown Cruisers before one of their neighborhood rides (Photo courtesy Jose Martinez).

Pride Parade, however. The family orientation of the club is more evident in multiple generations of males who are regular participants. Club membership is informal. There are no dues or membership rolls, nor are there formal meetings. Jose Garcia is the president, and his main duties seem to be speaking on behalf of the group, leading the discussions about where to ride, and leading the rides themselves. Decisions about where to ride are made while the riders are gathering each Sunday. The rides usually last between two and four hours and are almost always to some other point in the city. The ChiTown Cruisers is a very urban-centered club.

The aura of informality is somewhat deceiving however. Clear rules of association exist. Most importantly, members of the ChiTown Cruisers must ride classic Schwinn bicycles. There is some variation in the kinds of Schwinns that are acceptable, but they cannot be multigeared, thin-tire jobs—those models that reflect Schwinn's "sell-out" response to the European bike invasion of the 1970s. The overwhelming preference of the Cruisers are the single-speed, heavily-chromed models with balloon white-walled tires, pedal brakes, and push button warning buzzers—models that were the Cadillac of bicycles in the days when Cadillac represented nothing if not excess and luxury. As a special guest, I received dispensation from this rule, but another nonmember who tried to park his bike amid the accumulating Schwinns was told that he needed to move it, which he did.

A few bike stores carry these retro models, but most of the Cruisers get them in other ways—at yard sales, tucked away in basements and garages, and at second-hand stores and flea markets. These older bikes are then rebuilt and restored. Some have put bikes together using parts variously gathered. Part of the pleasure of the club comes from building and adapting bikes, an activity that is also a major focus of group discussion. It is like a teenage or vintage car club in this respect, and this probably accounts for the fact that females are not regular members. This kind of activity is not the sort of thing that has piqued the interest of the women in their neighborhood. When women do ride in the larger parades, they ride on bikes male friends or relatives have restored.

Many of the adaptations are quite creative pieces of work. One teen rider showed up with two bikes, the second ridden by a friend, that he had built over the winter. The Schwinn origins were evident if one looked carefully, but his bikes had about the same relationship to the parent bike as an elaborate chopper has to a Harley-Davidson motorcycle. These two bikes in fact had something of the appearance of low riding, frame-extended choppers. And owning and restoring a classic Schwinn is generally not enough. Most of the Cruisers go to some lengths to personalize their bikes, festooning them with streamers, foxtails, Puerto Rican and American flags, mud flaps, license plates, horns, and other gizmos as well.

When I reminded Jose, who showed up at 11:30, that he had made it a point to tell me a couple of times that the starting time for the ride was 11:00, he said simply. "The rides never start on time." I thought immediately that we were running on "Latino time," but this was only partly true. As members of the group arrived, they lined their bikes up in the street and gathered casually behind them. This time of hanging out was also a time to showcase their rides—and they did draw attention. Some members were initially attracted to the club because they first noticed the bikes displayed in this way and they began to ask questions about them.

Members of bike clubs typically have a preference for the classic bike uniform—the array of apparel that increases the efficiency of riding. Not so the Cruisers. No one even wore a helmet. Most had on baseball caps and T-shirts that sported the club logo. There were no biking shorts, and on this surprisingly cool June day no one wore shorts of any kind. The younger members of the group wore baggy jeans. As they stood around chatting, the group decided to take a neighborhood ride, for two reasons: The temperature was in the low sixties with a chill wind, dampening enthusiasm for riding to the lake, and club members wanted to remind residents that the Puerto Rican Pride Parade was coming up the following Saturday. The ride proceeded at a leisurely pace, with the regular sounding of bells, buzzers, and whistles as we rode along. While many biking clubs stress covering distances efficiently and quickly, the Cruisers see their point as interacting with the community. The community, in turn, seems to know them well, frequently responding with supporting honks, waves, and cheers. We stopped at a couple of parks for a few minutes. At these stops, bikes were lined up side by side, and curious park-goers gathered to check out the show and to inquire about the club. Within a couple of hours, we had traversed the main arteries of the neighborhood and returned to Casa Puertorriqueño.

When asked their reasons for joining the ChiTown Cruisers, camaraderie and "good clean fun" topped the list. Getting exercise was also important. Several also mentioned sight-seeing and the pleasure of taking younger riders places they had never been before. There were frequent comments about thumbing noses at the high price of gasoline. Virtually all of the riders agreed that riding in this club stimulated them to ride more at other times. For some in this group, the bike had become the number one daily transportation option.

In a separate conversation with Garcia, I noted that there were some good bike lanes in the area and that these encouraged people to ride. He agreed that the lanes encouraged riding, but he said, "We don't have enough of them. That's something I have to talk to [Mayor] Daley about."

The Rat Patrol

The Rat Patrol is simultaneously the most visible and the most esoteric of the biking groups in the Chicago area. Their visibility connects to the machines they ride and to their appearance. Uniformly, their bikes are personal creations, imaginative amalgamations soldered together from discarded bikes. There is a preference for choppers and for double-decker "tall bikes" whose frames are welded together vertically. But the overriding norm is for originality. Part of the fun (and the Rats have lots of fun) is creating the most improbable sort of pedal-powered machine that actually works. Adding to the visibility are the members themselves. Johnny Payphone, a key member of the group, was quick to point out that the age of members ranged into the sixties, but the group clearly skews young. And while this also varies, there is a marked preference for body piercing, tattoos, interesting hair, and sartorial distinctiveness. One can get a flavor of the Rat Patrol by going to its Web site at www.chicagofreakbikes.org.

Thus, a Rat Patrol ride is hard to miss; inevitably, its members are a mobile form of street theater. When the Rats show up for a Critical Mass, as some occasionally do, they are the riders whom onlookers find most interesting and amusing. Their presence is a balm for irritated motorists, making the CM more bearable. There is something quintessentially American about an odd assortment of self-conscious misfits gamboling down a street on unlikely machines. When they ride the Chicago streets by themselves, the level of hostility almost entirely dissipates. Something primordial in an American soul is stirred— perhaps a flickering recognition that we may be, after all, a nation of infinite possibility. The impulsive panic many feel when they first roll into view is quickly overcome by smiles as they roll by.

For all their visibility, there is something esoteric about the Rat Patrol as well. Their distinctiveness attracts, but it also establishes boundaries. The Rats are saying, after all, "We're not like the rest of you." Most of their rides take place at night, and much of the riding occurs in the alleys of the city. Dumpster diving is integral to the Rats' gestalt as they search for discarded items—clothes, food, household goods, books, bikes—that they can use. As it is associated with the most destitute and failed members of society, Americans tend to find Dumpster diving offensive. The poor are often shooed out of alleys by residents and police officers, and their presence in such darkened places defines their wretchedness. The Rats dive by choice, and this decision reflects a conscious critique of the dominant culture. When a resident encounters twenty people who may look strange but who are obviously not homeless, chattering away gleefully while systematically going through a large Dumpster, it becomes a pretty explicit commentary on the consumer-driven, throw-away culture in which we live. The name "Rat Patrol" is well chosen, as the group gains sustenance through our garbage. On their rides and in Internet communication, rats are mimicked and language morphed to evoke the patron rodent. Actually seeing a rat on a ride is always a high point.

The group projects a strong anarchist tinge, and most Rats are reluctant to discuss any binding ideas, which may suggest coercion. The irony is the Rats are a pretty tight group. They obviously enjoy each others' company. Members of the Rat Patrol tend to have a much more significant commitment to it than is typical for biking clubs. It lists more than two hundred members, forty or fifty of whom seem to be quite active. "Insider" names are often adopted, and special phrases and language idiosyncrasies adapted. Many discuss club membership in terms of a "way of life." And it is a life at variance with the traditional paths of success in the dominant culture. Cultures confer identities, and it is not too much to suggest that the Rat Patrol functions as a counter- or alternative cultural group.

Rather than postulating some overarching philosophy, it is probably better, and closer to the spirit of the group, simply to indicate norms that are visible as they hang out. In the time I spent with them, two were especially apparent: anticonsumerism and personal autonomy. These norms are connected, as there is a fairly widespread conviction among Rats that the real cost of the consumer society is its requirement that autonomy be relinquished. In the minds of Rats, people make it in the larger society because they decide to play along. They believe

The Rat Patrol, Dumpster diving and prepping their unique bikes for a ride (Photos courtesy EEEEE and photographeeeee.com).

people lose control of their lives because they are convinced that the baubles dangled before them are what they need. To get them, they follow prescribed paths.

The Rats are stylish, but it is not the style that leaps off the pages of *Cosmo*; it is self-created style, one largely constructed out of their own inventiveness and of what others, in the ceaseless struggle to be "now," have thrown away. I visited the apartment of one Rat to see the two bikes she had built and of which she was justly proud. While there, she pointed out the things she had gotten to supply her apartment while Dumpster diving. It was an impressive array. The Rats want to be open to outsiders, but they are also somewhat wary of them—especially if they seem to have an agenda. They worry about co-optation. They understand how agents of the consumer society are constantly trolling for some new "thing" to promote consumption and induce conformity. Think of the X Games. Some Rats have experienced this firsthand.

The norm of personal autonomy leads to skills sharing. Anyone can suggest an event, and everyone is encouraged to do so. In a little over a week, various members proposed and staged rides, a brunch, a silkscreen printing, a camping trip to Michigan, a sewing session, a writers' workshop, and a building day. Five different members proposed these seven events. One Rat organizes a sewing session at which others may learn how to create interesting things to wear. Another puts together a writing workshop where projects are shared and discussed by those in attendance. Music and musical ideas are developed and shared at a Rat party. At a silk screening session, whose purpose is to place various Rat designs and symbols on a variety of materials, members take turns working through the process, and thereby learn about it. The results are not perfect, but this is not a problem as the imperfections enhance the authenticity of the products. And of course all make their own bikes, which requires learning skills, including welding. One can be helped, even helped quite a bit, but it is very important for Rats to put their personal imprints on their rides.

Television is seen by the Rats as something that is absolutely harmful, as it re-creates a corporate version of reality and promotes consumerism. And it wastes time, induces passivity, and stifles creativity. Consequently, TV smashing has become an occasional ritual they enjoy. Sets found in alleys are carted to a factory used to build bikes.

At this factory, there is a device that can crush TV sets. One member will plea on the TV's behalf. "Is there nothing redeeming about this set? What about *Judge Judy*?" When nothing is found, the TV is hurled to its doom.

The group's members come from different places. Some have enjoyed success in the business world, found that life unfulfilling, and opted out of it. Others have found niches in that world that provide sustenance but also enough latitude to be a Rat. Still others have never been in that world. A fair number are students. Many hold jobs that allow them to live without significant compromise to their values. Their lower sense of need allows them to accept jobs that others would find paid too little. Additionally, the Rats are very good at making their own entertainment. And so they can get along with such jobs as waiting tables, walking dogs, and delivering things on their bikes. The group includes aspiring writers, musicians, and artists.

It is easy to see why the bike is such a central metaphor for the Rat Patrol. The freakbikes, as they are called, serve to pique interest in the group. Whenever I discussed bikes with Rats, they invariably said that membership in the group caused them to think much more seriously about the machine and to integrate it more completely into their lives. In part, the bike is an explicit rejection of the dominant symbol of the consumer society—the automobile. It is a technology that is built to human scale, one that anyone can master. That mastery nurtures autonomy. But the Rats believe that this machine can also be co-opted by the consumer society, and they are disdainful of people who scurry to get the latest high-end models and the various accoutrements that are marketed as a necessary part of bike riding. This is why it is so important to the Rats that they make their own bikes, and it is why they love them so.

Ratification, an annual "celebration of accomplishment," takes place at the end of each summer. At the one I attended there were contests centered around various club themes and awards for such things as the "rattiest rat bike," the inner tube with the most patches (each patch representing $5 that was not spent on a new tube), and the best fashion statement. There were rat bike races and tall bike jousting. (Injuries are common in this event and tend to be seen as badges of honor.) The celebration was held in a low-income neighborhood, where a number of Rats occupy a good portion of an apartment building. There was no yard space, and much of the party occurred in the street in front of the building. Consequently, this made it something of a public affair. This bothered neither the Rats nor their neighbors, who strolled through the party checking out the bikes and what was cooking on the grill. The grill itself is of interest. It is a converted oil drum that has been mounted on the front of a three-wheeled (adult) tricycle, so as to be portable. People brought things to grill, including vegetables for the numerous vegetarians in the group. But the piece de resistance was a "varmit," the grilling of which had been announced in e-mails leading up to Ratification. It was in fact a rabbit that had been gutted and skinned but was otherwise completely intact. Splayed on the grill, it looked remarkably like a skinned rat on steroids, which they winkingly told wide-eyed neighborhood kids it was. Of such things are urban legends made. Police kept eyeing the party, but no one was complaining, and so there were no hassles.

One Rat called for a midsummer's night ride to celebrate the completion of two new Rat bikes. It was a Dumpster diving ride, and most of these begin at a service station parking lot on the north side of the city. As they gathered, there was a fair amount of banter and experimentation with the various bikes. When unaffiliated riders pedaled by, the Rats would beckon them to join the party. None did, but one or two stopped to check out the scene. Eventually, twenty riders began working their way mostly through alleys in search of booty. It was a playful ride, with lots of joking, mimicking, calling of rats, and self-effacement. "It is truly amazing to see what people throw away," one of the riders assured me. One large Dumpster was relieved of about half of its content, including a bottle of still-cold champagne that was opened and consumed on the spot. Some of the riders had trailers to carry the booty; others found inventive ways to affix it to their bikes.

The Rats were never hostile, and they never left a mess. Nevertheless residents who happened to encounter the group in an alley seemed a little nonplussed. This is understandable. It was dark. It was an alley. It was Chicago. And it was an assortment of odd-looking people interested in garbage. After a few minutes at one Dumpster, a cop car pulled up, causing most of the Rats to scramble off on their bikes. Johnny Payphone lingered to chat with the police officer. "We're the Rat Patrol, just looking for things to help us get by," he said, in a calm voice that might have been describing a Rotary Club meeting. "You haven't heard of us? We've been doing this for seven years." When the officer said that someone had called in to complain about a disturbance, Johnny said, "Yeah, sometimes we do get a little noisy. Sorry." And with that, he rode off to join the others.

When the Rat Patrol ventured onto the streets, the reception was quite different. The direction of any particular ride largely depends on who happens to be at the front of the group at any given moment. As this ride developed, one Rat mentioned a rumor that there was live music at one of the north beaches, and eventually the group began to meander in that direction. This involved riding along a significant stretch of relatively busy streets. Motorists did not object and seemed content to follow along, despite the slow pace. Pedestrians frequently cheered. The rumors of music proved unfounded, and the police were closing the beach because of the 11:00 P.M. curfew. The Rats slinked away into the night.

Bike Clubs

The foregoing provides a taste of the variety of ways people organize around bikes for fun and camaraderie. This should not obscure the continuing profusion of more typical biking clubs that simply organize group rides on a regular basis in their areas. These clubs exist by the thousands, in every state of the country. Some are more formal, with officers, dues, meetings, club rules, and the like. Others are more casual word-of-mouth groups that regularly meet at some designated spot and simply take off. Such groups are generated at the workplace, as adjuncts of other kinds of groups, or by interested riders communicating via the internet through such sites as Yahoo! groups. And bike clubs have proliferated on university campuses, with many having more than one.

The online group Bicycle Clubs in the U.S.A.[6] regularly lists, by state, those clubs that send a data sheet to the site. Since the listings depend on self-reporting, the hundreds of clubs substantially underrepresent even the more formal clubs, while the spontaneous groups are not listed at all. Even with these limitations, perusing this site provides a flavor of the growing popularity of organized biking. There are biking clubs that are designed for specific groups such as women, singles, Christians, gays, scorchers, or tandem enthusiasts, as well as general riding clubs. And there are umbrella organizations that contain subgroups appealing to different interests.

The Spring City Cycling Club of Huntsville, Alabama, is a good example of an umbrella organization. The club has a proud, if intermittent, history. Founded in 1892, it is one of the oldest biking clubs in America. Its purpose is "the promotion and development of bicycling for sport, fitness, recreation, transportation, and safety education." The constitution bans discrimination on the basis of "race, nationality, age, sex, creed, religion, or riding capability" in the admission of members. The club has been growing in recent years, and now has more than 250 members. Mike Bayler, the club president, says that this is an indication of a general growth in biking in northern Alabama and Tennessee. New clubs are coming into existence, and there has been a growth of independent riders as well. Rides are organized on at least a weekly basis throughout the year.

In recognition of the diverse schedules of its members, the club publishes a Riders Directory and encourages members to organize on their own at times that are convenient. It also has racing and mountain biking subdivisions. A monthly newsletter publicizes club activities and spreads information of interest to the membership. An extensive and well-maintained Web site provides lots of useful information to members—including links to five regional weather forecasting services. One of the largest events sponsored by the Spring City club is the annual All-You-Can-Eat Century, which has been held every September since 1984. The riders can choose rides of several lengths up to a hundred miles through the Appalachian foothills. There are several food stops along the way, in addition to the all-you-can-eat meal at the end of the day.

Those driving near Georgetown in the southwest Texas hill country might notice an unusually large number of senior citizens on bicycles. Most likely, these riders are members of the Sun City TX Cyclists. The Cyclists organization, established in 2003, is a recent addition to the biking scene. The home of the club, Sun City, is a retirement community located near Georgetown. The club is open to anyone but, befitting its location, about 90 percent of its more than one hundred members are retired senior citizens. Although the club does serve as a social gathering point—there are regular parties and potlucks that may include nonriding spouses and friends—its primary purpose is to facilitate rides. The rides vary from serious sixty-mile "endurance" rides to more relaxed excursions to nearby sites. In some regions of the country, dogs pose a problem for bikers, and one of the more interesting features of the Cyclists' Web site is a "dog alert," at which the precise locations of unfriendly canines are reported.

One might expect the Cyclists to log fewer miles than clubs composed of younger riders, but this is not the case. Retirement has its advantages, and with regards to biking, one of these is that rides can be more frequently scheduled. The greater availability of club riders and the Hill Country weather allow the Cyclists to schedules rides on an almost daily basis. Club publicist Scorchy Smith says that members are quite goal oriented. Each establishes personal yearly goals varying from 2,500 to 7,500 miles. The miles are accumulated in a variety of ways, including rides sponsored by the club, national and international bike tours and special single-day events in other parts of the Southwest. The term "Scorcher" has a special meaning in the biking community, as it identifies a flat out, high-energy race of relatively short duration, but eighty-three-year-old Smith's nickname does not connect to that. A 1948 graduate of the Naval Academy, Smith notes that the name goes back to his days as a navy pilot. But the sobriquet is still fitting, as Scorchy will log about three thousand miles this year. He does not accept compliments for this feat, however. "My friend Walt Lawrence is a year older than I am, and he rides more," he says.

Calvin College is a private liberal arts school of 4,500 students in suburban Grand Rapids, Michigan. Founded and operated by the Christian Reformed Church, it is part of the evangelical Protestant tradition, and the school enjoys an excellent academic reputation. Calvin's bike club is a little different from the clubs normally found on college and university campuses. In most cases, biking itself, whether touring, racing, or recreational, is the ultimate goal of college clubs. At Calvin, the purpose of the club is framed by the larger mission of the college. Jonathan Seely, the cochair of the club at the time of our interview, says that the club would not have been chartered without this connection, and he fully supports this idea. Its overarching purpose is "to get more people out on bikes," in ways that also reflect Calvin's religious tradition. As a form of service, for example, it sponsors a free bike maintenance and repair day. Seely, who is a part-time mechanic at a local bike shop, estimates that between sixty to one hundred bikes are serviced.

The club also sponsors charity rides in which money pledged to riders goes to support worthy causes. And it is active in "Spokes for Folks," a local effort to refurbish and distribute used bikes to people who could not otherwise afford them. Perhaps the greatest emphasis of the club, however, is to increase awareness of the human responsibility for "environmental stewardship." Evangelicals tend toward biblical literalism, and there is growing alarm in parts of that community about a general failure to be "faithful stewards" in preserving and nurturing God's creation. This responsibility is seen as a clear biblical admonition. Calvin College, which has an Environmental Stewardship Program as part of its curriculum, is in the forefront of this movement. The rides sponsored by the bike club encourage reflection both on the natural environment that exists not too far from the campus and on the urban sprawl that has engulfed Grand Rapids.

The groups discussed in this chapter differ from bike advocacy organizations in that they do not press an explicit political agenda. Thus, in Portland's Bike Friendly City application to the League of American Bicyclists, the authors wrote that SHIFT was "primarily dedicated to creating fun *nonpolitical* events that highlight the enjoyment of bicycling" (emphasis added). Something similar might have been written about each of the groups considered in this chapter. But such statements are sustained only by a very narrow concept of politics. Pushing a political agenda does not identify the limits of political relevance.

The groups discussed here were culled from a vibrant populist movement on the bike front, a movement that penetrates the nation's social demography. At this grassroots level, there is not a great awareness of the scope of this movement, even among the most active members. One thing unifies them, however: Each of these groups has caused its members to expand their views about the possibilities of biking. Participation in any of them characteristically leads to more riding. I asked members from every group discussed in this chapter whether the association increased their use of the bike, and no question received a more consistently affirmative response. Sun City's biking seniors began to ride their bikes to shop after first using them for recreation. ChiTown Cruisers started riding their bikes to work. Some members of the Rat Patrol simply got rid of their cars.

Just getting on a bike begins to alter one's perceptions and one's references in politically relevant ways. One reason riders "grow the base" of advocacy groups is because, whether riding on city streets, country roads, or off-road bike paths, they begin to see the world differently. Indeed, consciousness changing is a primary motivation of Calvin College's biking club. The club has no political agenda, but its leaders recognize that biking through an area, whether it is the relatively "natural" settings that exist a few miles from the campus or the urban sprawl of Grand Rapids, intensifies one's perception of it. No petitions are passed around for members to sign, but when perceptions are altered, so are the things one thinks about when one turns to politics.

This altering of consciousness is most evident with the Rat Patrol, for whom the bike symbolizes a lifestyle choice that rejects the enticements of consumer society for a simpler and more autonomous life. Not only do their Dumpster diving rides serve to remind them of American wastefulness; by extracting useful things from our garbage, they reduce the amount of material going into our municipal waste stream. And this sensibility has led to more explicit political work, although the Rats might not see it as such. Rats regularly volunteer at Workingbikes, a nonprofit agency that retrieves bikes from alleys and municipal dumps. The bikes are restored and the higher-end models are sold at big discounts at a local shop. This money is then used to ship and give the other bikes to nations in Africa, Central America, as well as to our own hurricane-ravaged Gulf Coast. In 2006, Workingbikes distributed more that six thousand bicycles.

Harvard political scientist Robert D. Putnam's study of the decline of civic engagement in the last decades of twentieth-century America illuminates another dimension of the political relevance of groups such as the ones discussed in this chapter.[7] Putnam shows that the decline in political participation in America is related to a decline in face-to-face civic activity not normally considered political, such as

Lion's Clubs, PTA, and Bowling Leagues. The growing social isolation noted in chapter 3 has demonstrable political consequences.[8] The more one participates in the nation's group life, including the groups discussed in this chapter, the more likely one will be politically engaged as well. SHIFT is an extraordinary concatenation of inventiveness. Someone gets an idea from a particular event on the SHIFT calendar and then goes out and makes it happen. In this process, connection to the community is inevitably generated. It is hard to imagine such a person not participating in other forms of community life, including its politics, as well.

Putnam would understand the following episode involving the Sun City TX Cyclists. A plan to convert a road used by some in the group into a four lane highway would have made it much more dangerous for riders. Club members decided to take action and pushed for the addition of an apron broad enough to accommodate bicycles. They called their state assemblyman, who pressed their claim to the Department of Transportation, and the apron was added. The Sun City group is not political. Their club is organized to promote rides and social interaction. But when an issue of concern arose, a structure was in place that allowed them, first to share their common concerns, then to push their claims. If the club had not existed, there would be fewer riders in Sun City, and those who did ride would be more likely to have done so anonymously. One might also assume that the assemblyman was encouraged to see the legitimacy of the request because it came from an organized group, rather than from an isolated constituent. It is doubtful the apron would have been added without the underlying dynamics created by an existing biking club.

Far from the Texas Hill Country, the ChiTown Cruisers patrol their vibrant neighborhood. Along some dimensions, the two clubs seem quite different. The Cruisers share with their Sun City counterparts, however, a purpose that is much more social than explicitly political. Even so, and like them as well, the Cruisers plan to raise a little hell at city hall to get more bike lanes in their neighborhood.

Chapter Seven

Politicians Who Matter

Many prominent politicians have spoken fondly of the bicycle. Looking back on his youth, and before he was stricken with polio, Franklin Roosevelt noted his enthusiasm for biking: "I was brought up on this sort of thing," he said. "From the time I was nine until I was seventeen I spent most of my holidays bicycling on the continent. This was the best education I ever had; far better than schools. The more one circulates in his travels the better citizen he becomes, not only of his own country, but of the world."[1] President Dwight D. Eisenhower's personal physician, Paul Dudley White, was a prominent midcentury cyclist, who ended up living into his nineties—something for which he gave biking considerable credit. After Eisenhower suffered a heart attack in 1957, White prescribed bike riding as part of his recovery program.

While serving as U.S. ambassador to China in the 1970s, George H. W. Bush and his wife Barbara became cycling enthusiasts, regularly riding around Beijing. In a letter to John Dowlin of the Bicycle Network, he wrote:[2]

> The more I think about our U.S. domestic transportation from this vantage point of half way around the world, the more I see an increased

role for the bicycle in American life. Obviously, some terrains make it more difficult, obviously some climates make it more difficult; but I am convinced after riding bikes an enormous amount here in China, that it is a sensible, economical, clean form of transportation that makes enormous good sense.

The younger George Bush inherited this enthusiasm, regularly riding a mountain bike for well-publicized exercise—including stints with Lance Armstrong and with the Chinese cycling team during a state visit to China.

This list could easily be expanded. Many politicians ride bikes with varying degrees of commitment. John Kerry is a serious rider, as is his U.S. Senate colleague Dick Durbin. Tom Ridge, the first director of Homeland Security, successfully campaigned for governor of Pennsylvania on a bike. More than 160 members of Congress are members of the bicycle caucus. If all of them were serious about this membership, American biking would be substantially altered. The four presidents mentioned herein accepted their current worlds as givens for riding. None are noted for policies that would change the environment so as to expand biking possibilities.

Some politicians, however, have had a significant impact on biking policy. Their commitment is not nominal. Such politicians are sprinkled across the nation and exist throughout our federal system. Cycling advocates know them, and they know how much they matter. In this chapter, four such politicians are profiled. We shall consider how their convictions developed and indicate why they have been important to the biking movement.

James Oberstar

The Eighth Congressional District of Minnesota covers the northeastern "iron range" portion of the state. In the east, it shares a border with northern Wisconsin and then continues northward along Lake Superior to the Canadian border. It follows the border 150 miles west through the boundary waters and beyond. International Falls, a city commonly cited in national weather reports to note the severity of winter weather in the northernmost part of the contiguous states, is in the Eighth District. While Duluth, with its population of eighty-seven thousand, is easily the largest city in the district; Hibbing, the boyhood home of Bob Dylan, may be the most famous.

This largely rural district, noted for its long, hard winters, seems like an improbable home for one of the foremost bike advocates in the U.S. Congress. Yet it is, and James Oberstar's constituents seem quite happy with their representative. A Democrat, he was first elected in 1974 and has served continuously since that time. Over more than thirty years, his average margin of victory has been 49 percent. In his closest election, his vote still exceeded that of his opponent by 30 percent. Oberstar's long tenure has allowed him to accumulate significant political power. He is the senior Democrat on the Transportation and Infrastructure Committee, and when the Democrats gained control of the House in the election of 2006, Oberstar became the committee chair.

Congressman Oberstar is widely admired in the biking community. He has won several awards from national biking groups, and the League of American Bicyclists even named an award after him. From a list of three hundred nominees in 2004, the League asked a broad panel of experts to identify the twenty-five most important people in the history of American biking. Lance Armstrong topped the list. Charles Pratt, the founder and first president of the League of American Wheelmen, was there, as was the Schwinn family, and Eisenhower's physician, Dr. White. James Oberstar was one of two politicians who made the final list of twenty-five. (Earl Blumenauer, profiled in the next section, was the other.) The fact that the only two politicians on this list are currently active is one indication that the connections between biking and politics have only recently become apparent.

A visit to Oberstar's office in the Rayburn Building on Capitol Hill immediately suggests his interest in biking. In his outer office, an autographed and framed poster of the U.S. Postal Service Team, which Lance Armstrong captained to his fifth of seven Tour de France titles, is prominently displayed. The congressman and the famous racer are personal friends, and additional pictures of the two hang on the walls as well. Biking magazines, information about the nation's bike trails, and other things of interest to bikers are sprinkled through the literature racks for visitors to peruse. In his inner office is a two-part display of the Paul Bunyan Trail, which runs through the heart

Mayor Jerry Abramson.

Congressman James Oberstar.

Congressman Earl Blumenauer.

State Representative Anne Paulsen with husband Fred.

of his district and is one of the most famous bike trails in the nation. Throughout his office suite, a number of plaques awarded to the congressman hang on the walls, including those honoring his work on behalf of biking.

Oberstar is not a young man. At the time of my interview with him in June 2006, he was seventy-one years old, and his experience with the bicycle was pretty typical for those of his generation. He loved riding as a kid in northeastern Minnesota. As a young child, he remembers riding his bike around the large basement during the long winters, and he enjoyed tinkering with it—taking apart and reassembling the braking mechanism, for example. He recalls his father's belief that a car was not all that necessary, and as a young teen, he got around his town by walking, taking a bus, or riding his bike. But in his latter teen years, as he prepared for adulthood, he put the bike behind him.

That is where matters lay until he was well into middle age, and his biking story might easily have ended as it has for so many of his generation: A youthful flirtation, and then on to the serious tasks of adulthood. In 1983, however, tragedy struck the Oberstars that unexpectedly brought the bicycle back into his life. He and his first wife Jo had four children, and he was well into his congressional career when Jo was diagnosed with breast cancer. She had a mastectomy and subsequent chemotherapy. To combat the debilitating effects of the chemo, the doctor prescribed exercise. The Oberstars bought bikes for themselves and would frequently take rides around the neighborhood with their children. The exercise helped, but the cancer recurred, and Jo Garlick Oberstar died in 1991. After the funeral, as Oberstar was writing responses to condolences the family had received, he noticed his bike hanging on a wall. Thinking it might relieve his depression, he took it down and went on a five mile ride. It helped, so the next day he rode ten miles. He has been riding ever since.

Oberstar's personal connection to the bicycle grows out of his own experience. Regarding it as an important part of a healthy lifestyle, he rides mainly for the psychological and physical benefits. And, befitting his northern Minnesota roots, he is largely a trail rider. Bill Richard, his chief of staff, is an avid cyclist and regularly commutes to the Capitol via bike. Oberstar has done this a couple of times, but commuting is not for him. There are some good bike trails in metropolitan Washington, but part of the ride to the Capitol necessarily involves heavy urban traffic—including large numbers of tourists unfamiliar with the quirky streets of the city. Quite understandably, they are also prone to gawking. "You take your life in your hands on D.C. streets," Oberstar opines. But there is no question that he is serious about his personal use of the bicycle. His bike has an odometer, which allows him to keep track of his mileage, and in the two years prior to our interview he rode 2,800 and 2,700, miles respectively. When he was accused of "slowing down," he chuckled and said that the last year had been a particularly busy time on the Hill.

Committee work is a vital part of the congressional process, and most representatives seek out committee assignments that serve the interests of their constituents. Any representative from the Eighth District of Minnesota would find a seat on the Transportation and Infrastructure Committee attractive. It has jurisdiction over the inland waterway system, including the St. Lawrence Seaway, the port system of the Great Lakes region. Duluth is the westernmost port of the seaway. Although seaway oversight is particularly important to Oberstar and his constituents, this is America, which means that the megalegislation of the committee deals with ground transport of all sorts, especially highway construction and renewal.

As family tragedy got Oberstar back into riding, he began to think more reflectively about the bicycle. He recognized that biking had been good for him and his family and, perhaps aided by his time spent in Europe as a graduate student, that the bike's potential was largely unrecognized in the United States. It was a matter of great serendipity for the biking community that when Oberstar began to think seriously about this potential he was sitting on the committee that provides the greatest chance to do something about it.

In 1991, Oberstar contacted two national biking organizations, the League of American Bicyclists and Rails to Trails—an organization committed to converting unused railroad arteries into bike trails. Two things disturbed him about what he discovered. First, he thought their major policy initiative—a proposal to earmark 3 percent of the highway trust funds for bike-related spending—was unrealistic. (In fact, the proposal, introduced by Congressman Robert Kennedy Jr., never went anywhere.) The second concern was connected to the first: There was a lack of structure in the biking community that would make any proposal offered on their behalf difficult to enact.

"Where's your political action committee (PAC)?" he asked these national organizations when he heard of their 3 percent proposal. When told they had none, he said simply, "Then the contractors and road builders will eat your lunch."

A crafty politician, Oberstar understood that, given the competition for transportation funds, biking initiatives early on needed to "come in under the radar" if they were to be successful. First, he worked on a structure that would eventually provide political support for policy initiatives. He prodded bike organizations to increase their level of political sophistication, and he encouraged the bike industry to establish a PAC that would provide some support for politicians who were working on behalf of bike initiatives. Although the federal government allocates resources, Oberstar knew that individual states decide how highway funds are spent. He introduced seemingly innocuous legislation that allowed states access to the Highway Trust Fund to support the establishment of bike coordinators. These coordinators would create state bike plans to improve the bike friendliness of the state.

Democrats were in the majority in the House through 1994, and as such, they controlled all committees. Oberstar chaired the Transportation subcommittee on Aviation. The chief counsel of this subcommittee was David Heymsfeld, whom Oberstar describes as "one of the finest legislative drafters in the Congress." As it turned out, Heymsfeld was also an avid cyclist, and Oberstar asked him to draft legislation that would allow states to spend money on a wide array of bicycle projects—the legislation that was to become known in biking circles as ISTEA. When the legislation was drafted, Oberstar took it to Robert Roe, the chair of the full Transportation Committee. Although somewhat surprised by Oberstar's unusual interest and commitment, the chair told him, "You keep the planes flying, and we'll get you your biking legislation." Oberstar calls the passage of ISTEA "the beginning of the modern era of biking."

As previously noted, the legislation does not offer a strong national mandate, and it is general enough so that little will be done in a state where interest is low or unarticulated. In other words, the legislation was not an obvious threat to those interests used to gulping down highway funds. On the other hand, in states like Oregon or Wisconsin where the culture is sympathetic and bike organizations are strong, the legislation has been a stimulant to significant action. Moreover, such states become benchmarks for organizations in other states. In a federal system, political analysts have often noted the "race to the bottom" syndrome in which corporations move to nonunion states in order to pay workers lower wages, thus pressuring other states to deunionize. There are occasions—and biking policy appears to be one—where the dynamic is reversed, as biking organizations push to imitate the best practices found elsewhere. The more advanced states also serve as an empirical laboratory that can allay some of the wilder fears politicians in other states may have.

Oberstar looked for other federal programs for which bike projects might be relevant—what he calls "expanding the door of opportunity." Certainly, in his view, bike projects should be eligible to apply for air quality improvement program funds. And when considering transportation safety, bike safety was an area of legitimate concern. The political organization encouraged by Oberstar in 1991 has evolved and found its voice. When representatives of the biking community from around the country gather at the annual bike summit, they now visit the vast majority of congressional offices.

This labor has borne fruit visible in the allocation numbers. In the twenty years prior to the enactment of ISTEA, the states spent a total of $40 million on bike projects. In contrast, since the enactment of ISTEA in 1991 through 2005, the states spent $3.5 billion. After ISTEA was enacted in 1991, 2 percent of the representatives made requests for specific projects in their districts, according to Jim Berard of the Transportation and Infrastructure staff. The legislation was new, and the interests largely unarticulated. Six years later, new transportation legislation prompted 13 percent of all House members to request projects in their districts. With the passage of the most recent transportation bill in 2005, congressional interest exploded as 49 percent made requests for designated projects in their districts. It is impossible to say how much of this increase was the result of the growing political sophistication and structure of the biking movement, but it is undeniable that Oberstar's vision has been important.

In Oberstar's home district in northeast Minnesota, the greatest impact has come with the development and elaboration of bicycle trails. Oberstar takes obvious pride in these. He notes that when the Paul Bunyan Trail opened, it drew 40,000 riders in its first year. In 2005, 650,000 rode on the trail. To the list of positive things associated with biking, Oberstar adds its economic impact on the small towns along its hundred-mile route. Riders of the trail frequent bed and breakfasts, restaurants, and bike shops. They attend fairs and fests and other local attractions. The trail also creates construction and maintenance jobs. "You could not take that trail away from those towns with a team of horses," Oberstar avers. And he likes the idea that these trails invite tourists into this region in a low-impact way that helps sustain the loveliness of the area.

Despite the growing recognition that biking deserves a seat at the table of American politics, Oberstar believes that the "real tidal wave" of change is just getting started. In his view, the greatest barrier to a more bike-friendly nation rests in the fact that most Americans, when thinking about matters of transportation, simply do not think about biking as an important alternative. It is not that Americans are antibiking; it is that biking does not register in their consciousness as a viable solution to people movement. He has become a principal sponsor of the federal Safe Routes To School (SRTS) program, which he hopes will help change that. This program is designed to get children walking and riding bikes to school by eliminating the risks associated with doing so.

The SRTS program follows a familiar pattern. Federal resources are made available to states that hire program coordinators who evaluate and select projects from local school districts wishing to participate. The aims of the program are to improve safety; to encourage a healthy lifestyle in children; and to reduce traffic, fuel consumption, and pollution in the vicinity of K–8 schools. One aspect of the program concerns infrastructure—making changes by adding traffic signals, bike lanes, signage, traffic calming devices, curb alteration, bike racks at the schools, and so forth. A second aspect concerns education—advertising and explaining the project, instruction on bike safety, driver awareness projects, and the like.

Early pilot projects carefully monitoring results have been encouraging, and in the 2005 transportation bill, $612 million was allocated for SRTS for 2005 through 2009. Oberstar is impressed by the immediate results of the program, but he is more excited about its long-range implications. "SRTS not only gets kids on bikes; it also teaches them the personal and social benefits of biking. It is reasonable to assume that many of them will carry these ideas with them into adulthood."

Oberstar's rise to chair the Transportation and Infrastructure Committee that came with the Democratic Party's takeover of Congress in 2007 should be a boon to biking interests. Committee chairs have considerable power to influence the ultimate output of the committee. They control the agenda, schedule, hiring practices, and general operations of their committees. Legislation they prefer has a strong chance of clearing the committee. They have special relations with the House leadership. If Oberstar is chair when the transportation bill comes up for renewal in 2009, that will be very good news for biking advocates.

The dominance of the Democratic voice on this committee is good for bike friendliness as well. Although interparty relations on this committee were less hostile than was typical of committees during the twelve years of Republican control, there are clear partisan differences. In general, Democrats are more supportive of environmental protections and of alternative transportation systems such as mass transit, trains, and the bicycle, while Republicans are more supportive of automobility. One measure of this difference can be seen in the contrasting ratings that an environmental group, the League of Conservation Voters, gave to Oberstar and Republican Don Young, who chaired the committee when Republicans had a majority in the House. The League ranks representatives on a scale of 0 to 100. The higher the number, the better the environmental record, according to the League. For the most recent 107th Congress, Young received a score of 9, while Oberstar scored 83.

Earl Blumenhauer

Earl Blumenauer was born and raised in Portland and has been a lifelong resident of Oregon's Third Congressional District, which he now represents. He is something of a political prodigy. As an undergraduate at Lewis and Clark College, he came to public attention as he led an unsuccessful bid to lower Oregon's voting age. He was elected to the state House of Representatives in 1973 at the age of twenty-three where he served several terms. In 1978, he was elected to the Multnomah County Board of Commissioners and, in 1986, to the Portland City Council. In 1996, he won his first election to the U.S. Congress and has served continuously since that time.

As he led me into his office for an interview, Blumenauer was limping and wearing a walking cast. Noticing his bike leaning against a wall, I asked if he had been in a bike accident. He replied with a tinge of exasperation that, on the contrary, he was injured because he was doing something instead of riding his bike. Blumenauer has a well-known reputation for biking to his office in the Capitol. He jokes about being known as "the bike guy" by his colleagues, but it is a label he clearly enjoys. As with all serious riders, it was clear that being unable to ride while he was recuperating was a minor aggravation. Early in the conversation he claimed that he was not "a hard-core cyclist," but it soon became apparent that, if not, he had pretty stringent criteria for this category.

Blumenauer rode some as a child and in college, but he began to take biking much more seriously at the outset of his political career while working to lower the voting age. Because of this work, he spent quite a bit of time in the state capitol and he witnessed a representative he had previously known and admired, Don Stathos, doggedly engaged in shepherding the Oregon Bicycle Bill through the state legislature. This was the legislation that, in 1971, called for municipalities to spend 1 percent of state highway funds to support bicycle and pedestrian traffic. This visionary piece of legislation was far ahead of its time. It preceded the establishment of significant bike advocacy groups in Oregon, and nothing like it existed in any other state.

The more Blumenauer thought about this bill, the greater sense it made to him. He considered the various positives associated with biking: the pleasure, the utility, the environmental friendliness, and so forth. He supported the bill, and became personally committed to the idea of riding. He biked for pleasure extensively, and he says that some of his most memorable vacations, at home and abroad, have involved cycling. He also began to use the bike for utility, often riding it to work. When he was elected to the state house in 1973, he used the bike to get to his office most of the time.

More important, Blumenauer began to think about the bike politically. His positions in local government gave him the opportunity to work for bike-friendly policies in a direct way. As a county commissioner, he established a program allowing for the use of unclaimed stolen bikes that had been retrieved by the police. The program allowed county employees to use these bikes as an option to the county's motor pool. On the Portland City Council, he gravitated toward planning and transportation issues.

Portlanders, like Americans everywhere, were heavily dependent on a private, car-oriented transportation system. In the individual experience of daily life, a car can seem the essence of rationality. It takes something of a visionary to see that the accumulation of thousands of seemingly rational individual decisions can generate significant problems at the collective level. Blumenauer recognized that the existing transport system carried enormous hidden costs and that ultimately it would be unsustainable.

Consequently, Blumenauer fought for a diversified transit system, especially for light rail mass transit, and for increased bike capacity. In the few years he was on the council, bike paths tripled, an effective glass removal program was established, and bike ridership began to climb. To boost this ridership further, Blumenauer knew that safety issues had to be addressed. He worked to "calm traffic," something that is integral to the more sophisticated and elaborate transportation systems in Europe. Soon the city was installing traffic circles, dubbed "Earl's Islands" by friend and foe alike. Traffic calming had some detractors, particularly among those who wished to sustain a monolithic, auto transport system, but it was encouraging to riders and pedestrians. And safety-conscious parents liked the idea of calming traffic even if they were totally dependent on the car.

This political work was begun before there was a strong advocacy group pushing for change in the biking policies of Portland. Blumenauer recognizes the positive contribution that advocacy groups are currently making toward better biking policies, but he also knows that this was not always the case. When asked to characterize early advocacy efforts, Blumenauer says that such groups initially were far too polite and too narrowly focused. "They were into cycling, and getting on their bikes was their main interest," he said. "In those early days they did not think very much or very well about politics."

Important cultural norms in the Portland area—health consciousness, environmental concern, limited growth, sustainability—did work on his behalf. As a lifelong Portlander, it is hardly surprising that Blumenauer has internalized cultural norms existing there. And while his efforts have detractors, it is obvious that his constituents support him. He is the longest-tenured Oregon politician, and in over thirty

years of electoral political life, he has run for five different offices—
and lost only two elections.

The days of a democratic politician are long and filled with imme-
diacy—demands that must be met or finessed, battles that must be
fought, compromises that must be negotiated, chicken dinners that
must be attended. From the perspective of politicians, it seems like
everyone not only wants, but feels entitled to, a piece of them. Time is
a precious commodity, and distance from constituents, which usually
means not being out pressing the flesh, can be dangerous. Political
life generally does not provide the time and distance that contempla-
tive thought requires. Given these requirements in the everyday life
of politicians, it is the systematic thinker who surprises. When such
are found in political life, their personal philosophical systems usually have been developed prior to entering politics. Perhaps the most
interesting thing about Blumenauer is that he is a systematic thinker
whose big ideas have developed as he has been engaged in politics.

For Blumenauer, the bike is simultaneously part of a larger vision of
the requirements for a livable, decent, sustainable society and a metaphor for that society. He sees the bike as a simple, comprehensible,
low-cost technology that inherently ties people together while giving
them more choices. Biking is a part of what makes a community livable. It calms the rhythm of life, does not threaten the environment,
and invites human contact. Although the bike does this in essence,
Blumenauer knows it is incapable of creating livability in and of itself.
Thus it is a metaphor for a larger idea, the idea of "livable communities" in which people take control of the built environment with an
eye toward amicable association and mutuality.

Livable communities work against the notion of random, unplanned
growth that has led to urban sprawl and its attendant issues, such as increased commuting time, loss of green space, deteriorating air quality,
and ultimately, he believes, dehumanization and alienation. This has
come about because governments have, in the interests of satisfying
narrow demands, avoided the larger questions of public good. There
is a growing recognition that private choices do not necessarily accumulate into the best possible public good, and Blumenauer believes
people are beginning to understand this. As evidence, he points to the
recent surge in the success of "smart growth" ballot initiatives. These
efforts, which seek to address the matter of livability, have popped up

all over the country, and Blumenauer wants the federal government to give them a boost.

A livable community, in Blumenauer's view, is one in which families are safe, healthy, and economically secure. His notion of safety includes environmental safety and safety on the streets, as well as enhancing a general sense of security. Communities must be economically and environmentally sustainable and offer choices in transportation, housing, and employment. While this might seem like an inherently local matter, Blumenauer recognizes that the federal government is inextricably involved with urban development. The federal government's role in generating more bike-friendly policies, for example, is a template for broader things it can do to encourage the development of livable communities and improve the quality of daily life for Americans.

Blumenauer has described his lifelong home of Portland as "ground zero" in the livable cities movement. Washington, D.C., his other place of residence, is another matter. Washington ranks third on the Texas Transportation Institute's list of the nation's most congested cities, and it has other problems of livability as well. Because livable cities are connected not only to the decisions of government but also to the decisions each of us make in our daily lives, Blumenauer decided not to bring a car with him when he came to Congress in 1996. He hopes to alter federal decisions regarding livability by encouraging other representatives to think about daily life in Washington. Blumenauer wants to live the values he espouses. For him, the bike is a symbol of this aspiration. His decision to be carless in Washington was thus partly strategic, partly ethical, and partly symbolic.

Since coming to Washington, Blumenauer has established the bicycle caucus, which he playfully describes as the "bikepartisan" caucus. The receptiveness of his colleagues to this idea surprised him. His prominence as a biker caused him to fall into conversations and he discovered, even for those who did not join the caucus, that "Everyone has a bike story." In its early days, the point of the caucus was not immediately political. It provided an opportunity to meet and have fun; two or three times a year, biking events are staged for members of Congress, their staffs, and families. In 2006, the caucus had 164 members, 45 of whom were Republicans. Blumenauer hoped the caucus would have the immediate political effect of working against the partisan hostility that had emerged in Congress by the time he was elected.

Those who follow politics know that intense partisan ill-will has dominated the Hill in recent years. Given this, a nonbiker might easily conclude either that Blumenauer was naive or that whatever amity might be created by this gesture would be quickly washed away in a broader sea of rancor. Bikers, in contrast, are more likely to understand Blumenauer's point. And something is working on the Transportation and Infrastructure Committee, on which Blumenauer serves with James Oberstar. By contemporary standards, it is an unusually civil committee.

The bike caucus has elevated the general awareness of biking at least among the members of the caucus, and it has likely contributed to the political success of the biking movement in the House. Blumenauer expects the success to grow as more of his colleagues become personally involved in riding. After all, this happened to him, as it had with Oberstar. Blumenauer came to the Transportation and Infrastructure Committee for different reasons than did Oberstar. His prior political work in Portland stimulated his thoughts on livable communities. He saw firsthand how mass transit, light rail, and biking were crucial to such communities, and so he regarded the work of this committee as integral to the broad ideas he was seeking to promote. In our interview, Oberstar had noted that the $3.5 billion allocated to bike-related activities during the twelve years of the first two intermodal transportation bills represented a quantum leap forward. Blumenauer explained that the third bill passed in 2005, while a decent general bill, merited an "A" for biking. In it, $4.5 billion was allocated for biking over the ensuing five years.

Blumenauer expects growing success in the bike movement. He grows impatient at the notion that the United States badly trails other advanced nations in the promotion of bike-friendly communities, preferring to see the glass as half full. "We have come a tremendous distance in a short period of time, and a few American communities are right there," he argues. "For a long period of time automobile interests pretty much got their way when competing for scarce resources. In the last fifteen years, we are seeing cyclists beginning to push back." He credits Congressmen Oberstar, Peter DeFazio, and Joe Kennedy—known as the "chain gang"—for getting the ball rolling in 1991 with the passage of ISTEA. "Now it is like a snowball rolling downhill, gathering speed and mass."

A number of things contribute to this optimism. "There are bicycles in a hundred million American households," he says. "This is a huge latent resource. Many American families today suffer from a double rush hour. First, parents drive kids to school; then they drive themselves to work." Beyond this, parents are often saddled with the time-consuming and inefficient task of driving kids to various after school activities. Once parents start connecting the dots, which he believes the SRTS program will help them do, interest in biking will surge. Indeed, it is surging already. He cites RAGBRAI, or the (Des Moines) *Register*'s Annual Great Bike Ride Across Iowa, possibly the most famous single biking event in the country. The ride has gotten so big that people now must register for it by lottery, as organizers have limited the slots to ten thousand riders. The number of "illegal" riders who bypass the registration and just start pedaling easily doubles its official size. Blumenauer notes that the proliferation of RAGBRAI-type rides in various states is but one barometer of the growing interest in biking.

Blumenauer has traveled widely promoting the idea of livable communities, and he notes that even without this vast latent constituency, there are at present "millions of riders who take this stuff very seriously." He adds that the growing political sophistication of biking groups increases the pressure for bike-friendly policies. In these times of great competition for federal resources, he points out the ironic attractiveness to Congress of biking projects and indicates why funds are increasingly earmarked for things like trail projects, bike bridges, and so forth—each of which gives representatives an opportunity "to cut a ribbon." "Suppose you have a chance to earmark $25 million dollars for one third of an interchange that may be completed ten years down the road," he says. "Or, with 20 percent of that money, you can build five bike paths before the next election, each of which gives you a chance to cut a ribbon and for which people love you." It is the politician's math.

Anne Paulsen

Anne Paulsen has been a Massachusetts state representative since 1992. She serves the Twenty-fourth Middlesex District, which is dominated by her hometown of Belmont, an upper-middle-class community just outside Boston. Paulsen is a longtime resident of Belmont and has a lengthy record of community involvement. She served for a number of years as a town selectman prior to her election to the state house in 1992. She is quite well known and counts it a mixed blessing that she resides with her husband Fred on a fairly busy street in the heart of Belmont. "People are always popping in to tell me what I should be doing or thinking," she says with a smile. Her strong attachment to her community has limited her ambition for higher office, but it stimulates her to effect positive change for that community.

Paulsen, who was sixty-nine at the time of our interview, noted several things that stimulated her interest in biking. "Belmont is on a major access route to Boston, and I have long been concerned with the way traffic flows through our town. Both the rate and the size of this flow have grown tremendously over the years." She also was concerned for the safety of Fred, a lawyer who has biked to his Boston office for forty years on a twenty-mile round trip. Finally, her own biking background has stimulated her interest in biking issues. One month before the birth of her first child, she was given a bike—with a child's seat on the back. She has been a rider ever since, and although they easily could have done so, the Paulsens chose not to give cars to any of their four children. Instead, the kids were encouraged to walk or ride wherever they wished to go. Eventually, one daughter rode the professional mountain biking circuit for several years.

This background no doubt encouraged her to notice, as a Selectman working on education issues, that Belmont was spending $250,000 a year busing kids to school. "Our town is less than four square miles," she says. Over the years, the children of Belmont had stopped walking or riding to school, largely because parents came to feel it was too dangerous to do so. In a better world, she realized, the money spent on the busing program could be put to other uses. (Davis, California, has eliminated busing because so many kids now ride bikes to school.) A further irony was that Paul Dudley White lived in Belmont. Paulsen recalls seeing Dr. White and his wife, both in their seventies, riding their bikes past her house. His national fame meant that his message resonated in his home community more than most. Paulsen feels it is regrettable that sedentary habits have come to dominate even in Dr. White's hometown.

Paulsen strongly believes that biking changes one's relationship to the community and also bestows a greater sense of personal freedom. "There are so many things you could do in a town like ours if people were not afraid to ride." She describes her rides along the Charles River and the things she notices—the rowers, the ducks, the homeless. She feels both relaxed and energized when she arrives at her office. "I notice things when I ride through my district that should be done," she says. "Then when I get to work, I call officials about them." And she firmly believes that biking would benefit children. The health benefits are obvious, but Paulsen also has strong convictions about the importance of autonomy and responsibility, and she believes biking encourages both.

Like Earl Blumenauer, Paulsen came to her current elected position with strong feelings about the importance of a more bike-friendly environment. Primed by her previous bike-related experience, Paulsen arrived at the state house in 1993 prepared to take action. From the beginning, she has frequently biked the ten miles from her suburban home to her office in Boston. So far, she has not convinced any other state legislators to follow suit—"most give the excuse that they live too far away"—but she does believe that she has helped change the opinions of quite a few colleagues about biking. Many of them no longer think of it as "some silly little activity." As we shall see, Paulsen's assessment of her effectiveness is an understatement.

When she began to serve in the legislature, Paulsen gave herself a crash course on what other states had done to improve bikeability. She contacted officials in the most progressive biking states to mull possibilities. Eventually, she introduced legislation requiring bicycle and pedestrian accessibility on road reconstruction projects. The Transportation Committee balked at the legislation and added enough exceptions so that "no community would have to do anything if it did not want to." With these exceptions as part of the legislation, the bill made it to the House floor. Still, the bill was considered something of a long shot to become law. Not especially "dangerous" at this point, it was also considered by most representatives pretty marginal. Charles Flaherty, the House Speaker, told Paulsen, "If you want that bill to get through, just go right down to the microphone and tell us why."

It was a friendly but slightly patronizing gesture. Anne Paulsen is the kind of person one could easily underestimate. She is quite polite, soft-spoken, and congenial, not the sort to look for the limelight. But she is also well centered, smart, and fearless. If she believes in something, she will fight for it. Principles matter much more to her than convention. She was not at all bothered by the fact, for example, that she was the only biker in the House—and a woman at that. If anyone felt she was eccentric, that was their problem, not hers. Eccentric perhaps, she also believed she was right. She made her case to the House members, and the bill passed.

Paulsen began this struggle as something of a maverick legislator. She had no powerful allies, nor was she speaking on behalf of powerful, organized interests. She fought for the legislation because she believed it was the right thing to do. She was not plugged into bike advocacy groups at all. When the bill cleared the House, however, it generated some news, and things began to change. The Senate assistant majority leader, an old friend from her area whom Paulsen calls "my senator," offered help on the Senate side. In addition, the bike community in Massachusetts—represented by a young, fledgling organization, whose attention had been directed elsewhere—was stunned to learn what Paulsen had accomplished, and they immediately threw in with her.

What the bike coalition lacked in political sophistication, it made up for in grassroots contacts. "Bike people tend to be technologically adept," Paulsen observes, and they started contacting riders from all over the state, organizing an email campaign directed at the legislature and, later, the governor. State legislative districts are smaller than their national counterparts, and the legislators are not as widely known. Most constituents have no idea what their state representatives are doing. The volume of mail is less, but, partly for this reason, the response to it is often better, especially when representatives believe an issue is important to a significant number of constituents. In these circumstances, a fairly small number of concerned constituents can be effective—especially if there is no organized opposition. "To my knowledge, it was the first time email was used as an advocacy tool, and it worked. One could feel the ground shift," Paulsen said. The bill passed the Senate and the governor signed it into law.

In political life, passing a law is not always what it seems, and it is clear that some had voted for this legislation because they did not expect much to happen as a result. Moreover, the "wiggle room" in the law encouraged its opponents. The real battle over this legislation was fought in bureaucratic trenches, where support for the status quo ante was considerable. The Highway Department and local municipalities dug in their heels. The former argued that the law required roads to be widened and trees to be destroyed wherever it was implemented, a clearly false claim. Alarmed, municipalities wishing to contract for road reconstruction balked, and with the informal encouragement of the highway bureaucracy, they began to complain directly to Paulsen. She believes the calls were a form of payback from some legislators who had been irritated by all those biker emails. Asked why these bureaucracies would oppose this legislation, Paulsen cited the inertia of habitual thinking. "They were locked into the habit of considering roads to be unipurpose arteries whose sole function was to move cars as rapidly as possible." And multipurpose roads do complicate the job of local police, planners, and engineers.

By this time, however, the probiking forces had become more formidable. In addition to bike advocacy groups, a group of prominent citizens, all of whom were bikers, became very interested in the success of the legislation, and they made their presence felt at various public hearings. Bike committees in many towns strongly supported implementation. The secretary of transportation became an ally, but he recognized that the law would take time to implement. "It is going to be like turning around the *Queen Mary* in Boston Harbor," he said.

An early battleground, not for the first time in our country's history, was Concord. As one of the initial battle sites of the Revolutionary War, Concord is virtually hallowed ground, a place especially loved by Massachusetts citizens. As the town developed plans to resurface their main artery, the Highway Department argued that, because of the new law, the road would have to be widened and many trees cut down. When the dispute could not be resolved, Concord rejected state funds and paid the costs of resurfacing, including the installation of a new bike and pedestrian causeway. Paulsen regards this action as a huge symbolic victory for those who knew that bike usage was far less intrusive than opponents claimed.

The greatest victory came as a result of a decision by the commissioner of the Highway Department in 2004 to rewrite the highway design manual to accommodate the new legislation. The commissioner did not like the new law, but to his credit he appointed a broadly representative task force to update the manual. The Highway Department was of course represented, but so were biking, pedestrian, disabled, and environmental interests. Paulsen served on the task force. Task Force chair Beth Larkin was not identified with any particular interest and was a highly skilled negotiator. "We never left any meeting without a specific action plan, and within a day or two each of us got emails from Larkin reminding us of what we had agreed to and the things we needed to have done before the next meeting," Paulsen says.

Another important member of the Task Force was Luisa Paiewonsky, the leader of the Highway Department representatives. At the time Paiewonsky, who later became highway commissioner, was deputy commissioner. Paulsen frankly believes that one reason the Task Force was ultimately successful was that several of the key players were women. "Women are just better negotiators than men," she argues. "They are more flexible and more willing to think from another's perspective. Everyone made compromises that ultimately led to the successful completion of the work."

This is a claim that has frequently been made by feminists, and there are two reasons it may have been true at least in this case. The first is that the history of automobility in America is larded with images of masculinity. Go to an auto show, a stock car race, or check out the auto ads on TV. Such phenomena ooze testosterone. If driving is disproportionately seen as a "masculine" activity, men may be subconsciously oriented to consider movements away from automobility as forms of emasculation. It may indeed have been more difficult for men to "compromise" on this issue.

A second factor buttresses Paulsen's assertion. As the group struggled over the manual, an agreement to replace the word *motorists* with the phrase "pedestrians, bicyclists, and motorists" wherever appropriate proved a crucial turning point. Paiewonsky convinced the Highway Department of the legitimacy of this suggestion, and to most it seemed harmless enough, but as Paulsen noted, "Words really do matter." This decision changed the tone of the task force discussions and helped to focus on a common goal. There was still much give and take, but decisions became more context centered (e.g., Is this action reasonable in this case?) and less a battle over turf. Ultimately, the decision over phrasing led to a whole new way of looking at roads in Massachusetts. The Highway Department, which had clung to the idea of holding public hearings after a project was 25 percent completed—a point at which modifications would be much more costly and difficult to implement—agreed that various constituents should be represented in the earliest planning stages of road reconstruction. A greater concern for "traffic calming" emerged to reflect the diverse groups using the roads. Throughout the manual, pictures of motorists were replaced with pictures of pedestrians, cyclists, and motorists which served to remind planners of this diversity.

The decision on language turned out to be a significant part of the traffic manual story. It connects to Paulsen's comment about the importance of women on the task force, because for more than thirty years the women's movement has struggled to make discourse more gender-neutral. As a consequence, women are more likely to recognize that language does indeed matter. Ultimately, the result is a highway manual that has won several national awards and has been widely praised as the most progressive in the country.

Paulsen has also facilitated the expansion of bike trails in the state by solving liability problems that faced communities that wanted to convert unused railroad beds into bike and pedestrian trails. The Minuteman Bikeway took seventeen years to complete, but with ten thousand users a day, it is the busiest trail in the United States. One of the biggest problems for communities was that, under Massachusetts law, they had to accept liability for any toxic clean up that might result in the process of conversion. Some of the moribund railroad lines are quite old, and no one is sure what, exactly, lies underneath them. "In all probability nothing serious is there," Paulsen said, but since communities had to accept liability before any digging began, few were willing to take the risk. This logjam was broken when she spearheaded the effort in the House to allow communities to take out insurance policies against the potential liability. Tourism is a major industry in Massachusetts. Older trails such as the Minuteman Bikeway and the Cape Cod Rail Trail have been significant attractions, and Paulsen expects rail conversion trails to boost tourism further.

In recent years, there has been a spike of interest in bike policies among her legislative colleagues. Anne Paulsen is no longer the eccentric bike-riding representative. Today 25 percent of the state legislators are members of the Rails to Trails Bike Caucus.

Jerry Abramsom

Bike-friendly policies are connected to all three levels of the federal structure. We have seen that national politicians make money available for various biking projects and establish program opportunities like Safe Routes To School. As a state legislator, Anne Paulsen helped to contour policies and regulations that encouraged political action. Because biking is an inherently local activity, however, city and regional governments are inevitably focal points of the process. Since it is at the local level where the bike rubber meets the road, having top local leaders on board can make a huge difference. While a number of mayors such as Dave Cieslewicz of Madison, Richard M. Daley of Chicago, and Ron Littlefield of Chattanooga have championed the bicycle, perhaps the most interesting case is that of Louisville mayor Jerry E. Abramson.

Although Louisville has a very good biking program for a U.S. city, it is not the best. According to the standards used by the League of American Bicyclists to measure bike friendliness, Louisville is one of forty cities at the bronze level of accomplishment. Eighteen American cities are ranked above this level. Ten cities have achieved a silver ranking, and seven are gold. Only Davis, California, has risen to the level of platinum. Louisville is interesting, not because it is the best, but because it has exploded on the biking scene, and it is only a slight exaggeration to say that Mayor Abramson has been the detonator.

Abramson was born and raised in Louisville. His father took over the family business, a local grocery store, where Jerry worked while he was growing up. He served in the army for two years and went away to college (Indiana University and Georgetown Law School), but he has otherwise spent his entire life in the city he clearly loves. That affection is returned. He is obviously a very popular politician, serving for three full terms as mayor of the city until he was defeated in 1998—by term limits. In 1993, he served as president of the U.S. Conference of Mayors, an honor indicating the high regard his peers have for him. Additionally, he enjoys an excellent reputation among those who follow the nation's civic affairs, often appearing on lists of the outstanding civic leaders. When Louisville merged with Jefferson County in 2003 to form a new metropolitan government, Louisville became the sixteenth-largest city in the United States. Under the new charter, Abramson once again became eligible to serve as mayor and was elected, and reelected in 2006, by 2-to-1 margins. He has been dubbed "mayor for life" by pundits in that region.

Louisville is something of a "heartland" American city. It is sort of southern, but not really. As a state, Kentucky was probably most ambivalent regarding the Civil War, and if Louisville were on the other side of the Ohio River, it would be considered part of the North. It is well inland, closer to the Midwest than to the East, but not quite midwestern, either. It is a growing metropolis, but it has connections to a more bucolic past. Lovely forested areas still exist within the metro government limits, and Churchill Downs is the nation's most spectacular and nostalgic race track. Louisville is somewhat more progressive than the rest of Kentucky, but not by a lot. It probably is not the most typical U.S. city, whatever that might mean, but it is a place where a pretty large swath of Americans would feel comfortable.

Louisville does have roots that go deep in biking history. In 1896, thirty thousand members of the League of American Wheelmen gathered in Louisville for a convention and celebration, and in those days the city teemed with bike shops along Fourth Street, informally dubbed "Bicycle Row." But the automobile soon crowded the bicycle off the road in Louisville, just as it did in the nation as a whole. The Louisville Bicycle Club, one of the strongest recreational clubs in the nation with more than nine hundred members, traces its roots back to that golden age of biking. A bike advocacy group affiliated with the Thunderhead Alliance, Bicycling for Louisville, is also an active presence. In different ways, each of these groups helps to stimulate consciousness of biking issues in the community and to provide a base for political action.

It is Mayor Abramson, however, who has galvanized the movement and given focus to Louisville's shift toward bike-friendly policies. His biking story differs from the other three politicians profiled in this chapter in that he is not an avid rider. He has fond memories of riding a bike in his youth. In those days he used the bike for more than fun and recreation, as he delivered groceries to patrons of his father's store. But he put the bike away as soon as he was able to drive, and he did not return to riding until 2002, when he, his wife, and his son all got bikes together. The family rides bike trails, but Abramson more often runs them. He has completed the New York City Marathon, and to this day running is his primary form of exercise. He has a continuing wariness about street riding, although he told me, "I'm getting better."

Considering his comparative biking inexperience, Abramson has an extraordinary vision with respect to the bike and a remarkable intuition regarding its potential. Like the program he oversees, he has come very far, very quickly. I asked him how he became interested in bike friendliness. Although casual riding made him more aware of biking, and he knew about the Louisville Bicycle Club and the existence of serious riders in the city, this was not enough to push biking onto his personal political agenda. That switch was flipped by a family vacation trip to Vail, Colorado, in 2003. Riding from the Denver Airport through Aurora and into downtown Denver, he noticed what seemed like a flood of bike riders. "They seemed to have trails all over the place," he said. He liked what he saw, and he began to think about the bike's great potential for recreation and exercise. He is a baby boomer, and he has noticed that many of his running friends were dropping that activity because their bodies could no longer withstand the pounding. He began to think about what the city might do to promote biking.

Abramson likes ideas. One of his favorite words in speeches and conversations is *vision*. Several of his aides discussed his inclination to push for action. "He always wants to know what has been done since yesterday," one told me. But Abramson likes to locate specific actions in a larger context that provides meaning and illuminates their significance. Once the biking idea had germinated, it began to grow. As he continued to think about it, he realized that he was not familiar enough with biking issues to know how to move. A differently oriented mayor might simply have returned from Colorado and put in a bike path somewhere. But that is not Abramson's style. The "vision thing" gnawed at him.

Quite remarkably, Abramson decided to call a local Bike Summit. Blue ribbon panels and white paper conferences are often summoned by governments at various levels. Almost invariably, these are a response to substantial social agitation and discord over seemingly intractable problems—how to end an unpopular war, what to do about deteriorating families, and so forth. Bike advocates are not reluctant to discuss the significance of their work, but there was no widely recognized "bike problem" to which Abramson was responding. The summit was called to think about how and where to move with respect to biking and why. In short, Abramson needed a vision.

He contacted the president of the Bicycle Club, who contacted others. The word spread, and when the summit was held in February 2005, two hundred people filled the facility, including bike enthusiasts, elected officials, city administrators, and community leaders. More would have attended had there been more room. The summit expanded his consciousness further. "I was thinking mainly about recreation," he said. "But there were people at the summit who, quite effectively, pushed the idea of creating an environment in which people could more safely use their bikes for getting around the city as well." The summit created a "buy-in" from the various users of the bike and galvanized pent-up demand. It also generated a broad rationale for the movement, recognizing that bike-friendly policies would improve community health, air quality, and tourism. It established a series of specific goals and a time line for measuring them. Perhaps most important, the Summit laid the groundwork for a structure that would push for continuing action. An Advisory Bicycle Task Force, chaired by Bike Club president Earl Jones, was created to develop a plan to implement the summit's recommendations. The Task Force set to work, and in December 2005, it met with the mayor to discuss specific action plans.

The importance of having a mayor actively committed to bike friendliness is illustrated by the fact that relevant Louisville department heads and cabinet secretaries attended this meeting. This reverses the strategy of bike advocates, who seek early involvement in matters like road renovation. In effect, Abramson recognized the importance of getting administrative buy-in on the overall bike strategy. It made them part of the process, allowing for their input, and it underscored the mayor's overarching interest in the policy. Mohammad Nouri, chief transportation planner for the Louisville metro government, notes that no one in any relevant administrative position doubts Abramson's commitment to the program. In politics, having a clear sense of the boss's commitments is a powerful incentive to action.

What ultimately developed is known as *The Bicycle-Friendly Louisville Plan,* designed to obtain a bike-friendliness rating of bronze by 2008, silver by 2010, and gold by 2014. The strategy is identified in

Louisville as "the 5 E's," The broadest goal, *Encouragement,* inevitably overlaps with the others. Riding is encouraged, for example, as streets are engineered to accommodate bikes. This strategy however, largely focuses on staging specific biking events like the Memorial Day and Labor Day community rides, and an annual bike-to-work day. The first community bike ride, held on Memorial Day 2005, drew one thousand riders, to the exhilaration of both planners and participants. Just two years later that number had doubled.

A private group, the Louisville Downtown Management District, generated the idea to combine bike racks with public art, many of which were created by local artists. While these are too expensive to be installed universally, twenty-two "art racks" have been located throughout the central city to create a buzz about the program while improving security.

Three Bike Stations are part of the plan, and if funding is received for these it will place Louisville at the top in this area. The most novel part of the plan is to locate one at the University of Louisville. Like almost all universities, Louisville is beset by growing outlays and congestion costs to accommodate automobiles. Campus officials hope a bike station will reduce these pressures, while Mayor Abramson hopes it will help integrate students into the city.

Safety programs in intermediate schools, instruction for adult novice riders, as well as a Share the Road campaign comprise the *Educational* component of the program. Additionally, Jonathan Villines, serving in the recently created position of city biking and pedestrian coordinator, maintains a vigorous government Web site, www.louisvilleky.gov/bikelouisville, that assists those considering using a bike more. The site not only underscores the value of riding but also provides useful information to riders pertaining to safety, route selection, winter riding, and new lanes and paths. When I noted that his site was similar to the nongovernment sites bike advocates maintain in other cities, Villines was pleased, saying, "I think of my position as one of bike advocacy."

A crucial part of the program is *Engineering* safe riding space. Commitment to Complete Streets is a major part of this plan, as are the addition of new bike trails and lanes, establishing priority corridors connecting key parts of the city and a visionary hundred-mile urban greenway that will surround the city. The plan also calls for equitable law *Enforcement,* which includes training police officers about bikers' rights and responsibilities, and putting police officers and safety personnel on bikes. Finally, the fifth *E* to the program is a strong *Evaluation* component that provides feedback regarding what is and isn't working.

This is an ambitious program, but if implemented fully, it may well transform the city. Parts of it are expensive, but Abramson is moving ahead, confident that the investments are worth the costs. Prior to the Bicycle Summit, there were fewer than two miles of bike lanes on city streets. By 2007, there were ten miles of lanes, with plans to triple that number by the end of 2008. City buses had already been equipped with bike carrying racks. Over the past several years the use of these racks has grown at the rate of 10 percent a year. In 2006, these racks were used by passengers more than one hundred thousand times.

The hundred-mile urban greenway planned to loop the city deserves special notice. In the nineteenth century, famed landscape architect Frederick Law Olmsted established a series of parks that formed a rough outer belt around Louisville at that time. That system proved crucial to the subsequent development and integration of the city. When the city and county governments merged, it offered opportunities for a new outer ring. The "vision" is to have a twenty-first-century counterpart to those nineteenth-century parks that have served the city so well. It is an expensive idea, requiring both public and private fund-raising. It even includes two bike-pedestrian bridges that would carry travelers across the Ohio River into Indiana. Substantial progress has already been made on this formidable challenge. When asked where things stood, Abramson paused, calculating and revising numbers in his head. "By 2010," he said, "we should have sixty miles of the greenway completed."

It is interesting that the bicycle has helped drive this project, as a bike/pedestrian trail system is central to it. A hundred-mile greenway around the city, fully accessible by Complete Streets, is exactly what Congressman Earl Blumenauer means when he says that the bicycle is a key component to a "livable city." Abramson is a seasoned politician, well aware of the difficulties of financing the vision of a bike-friendly city. At the same time, he is skilled at his craft, with a knack for building consensus around an overarching vision. He has managed to move Louisville very quickly and also to create some excitement about that movement. To bike-friendly advocates around the country, Louisville has become a city worth watching.

As they make decisions, politicians are constantly weighing, assessing, and calculating. Of necessity, prudence weighs heavily on them. The tendency is to be careful. At some times, in some places, on some issues, politicians are also moved by conviction. They may support a policy, not only because it is prudent, but because they believe in it. In the adherent's view, the politicians actually seem to "get it." The four politicians profiled in this chapter are of this latter sort with respect to bike policy. What distinguishes Abramson from the others is that this conviction has not been generated by time in the saddle. Recently, he noted, "For decades, we in Louisville—and cities around the nation—have built roads only for vehicles. That was an urban policy mistake."[3] This simple declaration nails the core issue as bike advocates see it. Having identified the problem, Abramson is seeking to correct it by introducing the notion of Complete Streets to the local planning commission.

Abramson was keynote speaker at the 2007 National Bike Summit. His selection was itself a tribute to his leadership in guiding Louisville to a bronze ranking two years ahead of its bike-friendly plan. In his address, Abramson of course discussed current achievements and future prospects, but what really connected him with the audience was his visceral understanding of the larger meaning of biking. He recalled that on the first Memorial Day bike ride, he realized how the bike connects and binds people and transforms the experience of population movement. That ride put in clear perspective "the passion across my community that people have for bicycling." Later, he noted the intimate connections one feels to neighbors and neighborhoods on a bike. "You don't just smell the roses, and the forsythia; you smell the barbecue [he *is* from Kentucky], see vegetable and flower gardens, and hear music. You make eye contact with folks on front porches, and other people on bikes." Worried about sounding "corny," he nevertheless averred, "there is magic in the way a community feels on a bicycle."[4] Abramson is relatively new to biking, but he is proving to be a very quick study.

Chapter Eight

Metapolitics, Minibikes

This book has argued, not only that there are many reasons to support the expansion of biking in the United States, but also that there are none for not doing so. As Alex Wilson puts it, "There is no bad in biking." But of all the reasons to support biking, one is notable because it connects to a great specter hanging over us—global warming, or climate change. This issue is just emerging on the political scene, and Americans still have little sense of its significance. This chapter will suggest why this is the case, but more important, the issue will be clarified and its implications underscored. Finally, the ways biking connects to this issue will be identified. The intent is neither to exaggerate nor to minimize the contribution the bike can make to reduce this threat.

A Global Warming Primer

Chicagoans glean their identity from adversity. Consequently, in a "bring it on" spirit, we take a perverse pride in surviving grueling winters. January 2007 was one of the warmest in recent memory, however, as daily highs were often fifteen to twenty degrees above normal. On local newscasts, this respite was treated as an unambiguous blessing. The banter leading into and out of weather segments was sprinkled with comments like "You gotta love this weather" and "How long is the weather going to be good to us?" There was no recognition that, although the relatively warm days were more comfortable, they might also be cause for alarm.

This example illustrates several things regarding American attitudes about global warming. The first is our lack of a conversation about it. It evokes little serious discussion, all the more surprising because American scientists have been at the forefront in recognizing this historic development. Second, weather is by definition variable, so our daily experience may contradict global developments. On the same newscasts that welcomed the news of the warm Chicago winter, there were reports that Denver was buried in snow. If it is warmer in Chicago and colder in Denver, a person might reasonably ask, What is the problem? The third thing illustrated in this example is that global warming is often considered not such a big deal. Many Chicagoans could get used to the idea of cranking up air conditioners in summer while not freezing at a bus stop in winter.

Systematic knowledge of global warming grew substantially over the course of the twentieth century. Scientists, conservative by nature, look at evidence, and then they look again. They try to assess things that might confound what they seem to be seeing, setting alternative tests or introducing additional variables to create more certainty. In recent years, however, a strong consensus has emerged: Because of human interventions, Earth is undergoing unprecedented warming that is, in turn, sparking climate change. (*Weather* is what we experience in a single day; *climate* is the sum of all weathers over a period of time.[1]) One study examined more than nine hundred articles in peer-reviewed scientific journals between 1993 and 2003. Not a single article disputed the premise that human-caused global warming is under way.[2] Although humans are causing this change, if unchecked, it will have a dramatic impact on all forms of life. Many species will be eliminated altogether; others will adapt. But if warming continues unabated, life as we know it will be fundamentally altered.

The good news is that we know about global warming. We know its causes, we know how to correct it, and we have the skill to do so. Impediments to change are political and cultural, not scientific and technological. The bad news is that the window of opportunity to change course is rapidly closing. We are approaching a tipping point beyond which averting catastrophe will be impossible. This precise point is a matter of argument in the scientific community. A few reputable scientists say it is virtually at hand; most say we have perhaps six or eight years to get seriously engaged in reversing the process. A few say we have longer than this. Given the uncertainty over time lines and the significance of the effects, the obvious rational path is to address the issue immediately.

In everyday lives, time proceeds in linear, uniform increments. In contrast, geologists think of time as episodic, and they divide the history of our planet into five great eras.[3] These are earmarked by *faunal turnover*, or periods when species suddenly appear or disappear. The last time Earth experienced such a shift was sixty-five million years ago, when dinosaurs roamed the planet. Then, quite suddenly, everything weighing more than seventy-seven pounds, and a vast number of smaller species as well, vanished. For years, geologists attributed this shift to an asteroid colliding with Earth. The collision devastated only a part of the planet, however. Recent scholarship has revealed that the truly devastating aspect of the collision was that it suddenly altered the climate by injecting pollutants, especially carbon dioxide (CO_2), into the atmosphere.

The current phase of our fifth geologic era, the Holocene Epoch (also known as the Long Summer), began about eight thousand years ago. Throughout this epoch, humans have achieved a delicate relationship with "greenhouse" gases, of which CO_2 is the most important. Greenhouse gases are emitted naturally into the environment, but these emissions have been episodic, leading to substantial variability in climate over the long history of this planet. Operating in a manner similar to the glass in a greenhouse, these gases form a shield in our atmosphere. The sun's rays pass through the gas "shield," but as they bounce off Earth in the form of infrared radiation, enough is trapped to keep the planet habitable. Too little of these gases in the environment would create atmospheric conditions similar to our frigid neighbor, Mars. Too much, on the other hand, would create conditions similar to our sweltering neighbor, Venus.

Human-made CO_2 mostly comes from burning fossil fuel, which means increased emissions are largely a function of the Industrial

Revolution. Coal is the "dirtiest" of our fossil fuels. In the earliest days of industrialization, it dominated energy production; today it is heavily involved in generating electricity. Oil is also highly polluting, and with its increased use, oil and coal have become the twin engines driving the injection of CO_2 into the environment. In 2002, coal was the source of 41 percent of carbon emissions, while oil contributed 39 percent. Natural gas, the third source, contributed 20 percent.[4]

Because the Industrial Revolution initially was limited geographically and was concerned largely with manufacturing, it did not generate enough additional CO_2 to create an immediate problem. But throughout the twentieth century, the emissions both broadened and deepened. The Industrial Revolution has spread, and burning fossil fuels is no longer simply a function of manufacturing. It has become much more integrated into the lifestyles of "developed" nations, especially in the United States, whose culture spurs fossil fuel consumption. Now each of us is engaged in global warming, and we are engaged daily.

By extracting samples deep in the permafrost of the Arctic, scientists can assess the relationship between Earth's temperature and the amount of CO_2 in the environment over the past 650,000 years. Through this vast expanse of time, the results have been remarkably consistent: When there is more CO_2 in the environment, Earth is also warmer. Since the 1950s, the concentration of CO_2 has been monitored with unprecedented precision from a laboratory in Hawaii. The results have generated what has been described as "one of the most important series of measurements in the history of science."[5] Called the Keeling Curve, the measurements graph a steady increase in levels of CO_2 in the atmosphere. The levels reached 300 parts per million in 2006. Through the Long Summer until the 1950s, CO_2 levels had not exceeded 250 parts per million.

Think how daily routines involve the use of electricity—turning on lights, taking a shower, making toast, turning on the TV or air conditioner. Seventy percent of our electricity is generated by burning fossil fuels. And of course our commitment to automobility is a major source of environmental CO_2. Elizabeth Kolbert notes, "Every gallon of gasoline consumed produces about five pounds of carbon, meaning that in the course of a 40-mile commute, a vehicle like a Ford Explorer or a GM Yukon throws about a dozen pounds of carbon into the air. On average, every single person in America generates 12,000 pounds of carbon per year."[6] With less than 5 percent of the world's population, we have so far been responsible for 30 percent of the CO_2 emissions produced from fossil fuels. China and Russia, the next-biggest polluters, have each been responsible for less than 8 percent.[7] With a coal-driven economic expansion, however, China caught the United States in CO_2 emissions for 2007.

As a result, predictably, the planet has been warming. The last thousand years has seen several periods of warming, which climate scientists can measure with remarkable accuracy. The warming over the last fifty years dwarfs the variations measured in these earlier times and has no precedent in the Holocene Epoch. Annual world temperatures plotted since 1860 show some variation from year to year, but the trend is very clear, and it is accelerating. The 2007 report of the authoritative Intergovernmental Panel on Climate Change, a group composed of hundreds of scientists and representatives of 113 countries, notes that twelve of the past thirteen years were the warmest worldwide since record keeping began.[8] The winter of 2007, just completed as this is being written, was the warmest winter yet.

The evidence of global warming is quite visible to the naked eye. Throughout the world, glaciers are rapidly melting. Oceans are measurably warmer. The Arctic and Antarctic are losing mass. Huge fissures in Greenland are appearing. The permafrost in Siberia is melting. The "Snows of Kilimanjaro" will soon be no more. Global warming can also be seen where people live, as cities throughout the world are breaking heat records in unprecedented numbers.

"Life" is something we take for granted. A few scientists, philosophers, and theologians may speculate about it. Others may be jarred from routines by a war, or a sudden death or illness, but these are jarring because we have life "expectancies." We assume we are going to be here tomorrow. We rarely consider how improbable life is, the fragile balance that sustains it, or how that balance itself is sustained, so that we accept its existence not as fragile, but as ordinary and even inevitable.

The mathematician James Lovelock has speculated about these matters, and he offered his intriguing ideas in his 1979 book *Gaia*.[9] Lovelock argued that Earth is a single, planet-sized organism, which he named Gaia after the Greek earth goddess. The atmosphere is

Gaia's organism of interconnection and temperature regulation. It is sustained by all species-life working together. Initially, biologists were almost universally skeptical of Lovelock's hypothesis, but with our growing knowledge of how life works together to affect Earth's temperature and chemistry, it has gained some respected adherents. One of these is the internationally acclaimed evolutionary biologist Tim Flannery, who argues not only that Gaia exists but that it is important to recognize its existence.[10]

> Does it really matter whether Gaia exists or not? I think it does, for it influences the very way we see our place in nature. Someone who believes in Gaia sees everything on Earth as being intimately connected to everything else, just as organs in a body. In such a system, pollutants cannot simply be shunted out of sight and forgotten.... A Gaian world-view predisposes its adherents to sustainable ways of living.... A Gaian philosophy inevitably makes for good environmental practice.

Flannery argues that it would be a mistake to assume, as some do, that Gaia will automatically "sort out" agents that disrupt the balance. He quotes Lovelock's argument that "there must be an intricate security system to ensure that exotic outlaw species do not evolve into rampantly criminal syndicates." In the context of global warming, that outlaw species is the human being. We may be "sorted out" through the agency of global warming, but we would take so many species with us that "the repair job on the earth's biodiversity would take tens of millions of years."[11]

Gaia may promote an automatic concern for the environment, but one does not need to accept such a theory to recognize the interdependent world in which we live. Whether it is literally true, Gaia is a useful metaphor. Damage to one part of our world has far reaching implications. Consider the following examples.

- *Melting ice*—As ice melts, sea levels rise. This is in part because of former ice sliding into the water, but mostly because of the diminishing capacity of arctic regions to cool the oceans. As water warms, it expands. Most ominously, fissures have appeared in the most stable arctic regions of east Antarctica and Greenland. Because the vast ice deposits in these regions rest on land and are therefore entirely above water, their melting would be particularly devastating, causing sea levels to rise eighteen feet worldwide. The book *An Inconvenient Truth* has photographs showing how maps of Florida, New York City, San Francisco, the Netherlands, and other locales would have to be redrawn.[12] But these maps, dramatic as they are, reveal too little. Throughout history, humans have always preferred living near oceans. Today, a vastly disproportionate share of the world's population lives within fifty miles of a coastline.[13] The costs of sea levels rising even three or four feet would therefore be incalculable, and they would be most extensive in poorer parts of the world where the ability to resist the encroachment is virtually nonexistent.

• *Weather instability*—As the planet warms, weather patterns become more erratic. A study released by the Massachusetts Institute of Technology in July 2005, one month before Hurricane Katrina, supported the consensus in the scientific community that global warming is making hurricanes more powerful and more destructive.[14] This study was followed by Katrina and Rita, two category 5 hurricanes that caused enormous destruction in the United States. A few weeks later, Hurricane Wilma, which ultimately struck the Yucatán Peninsula in Mexico, became the strongest hurricane ever measured. In the same year, Europe suffered from a disastrous number of floods. These followed a massive continental heat wave in 2003 that killed twenty-five thousand people. In 2005, Mumbai, India, received thirty-seven inches of rain in twenty-four hours, by far the largest amount of rainfall ever recorded in India. But as global warming intensifies rainfall, it also relocates it so that some areas experience draught. In 2005, some provinces in China experienced record flooding, while provinces nearby were parched. In Africa, Lake Chad, once the sixth-largest lake in the world, has virtually disappeared due to the extended draught in that region. The resulting famine has almost certainly intensified the gruesome political situation in Darfur. In January 2007, Australia was into the fifth year of the worst draught in the country's 114-year history of record keeping and, some authorities believe, the worst in a thousand years. Debt-ridden farmers were committing suicide at a rate of four per day nationwide, according to an Australian organization that tracks depression issues. Severe water use restrictions were imposed, such that "just flushing a toilet can feel vaguely scandalous."[15] Weather is inherently unstable, and, as the sports cliché has it, records are made to be broken. The occurrence of one or two such weather outliers would not, therefore, cause alarm. But the massing of such events is a deeply disturbing portent.

- *Ecological systems*—Less immediately noticeable but fully as significant is the damage global warming does to ecological systems—the delicate, self-sustaining interactions of organisms and their environments. Environmentalists concerned about the threat to a species or a wetlands region are often derided as scolds standing in the way of progress, of caring more about "parrots than people." The concern actually stems from the fact that our well-being is tied to creatures and habitats in ways that are not generally recognized. As a believer in Gaia, Flannery is one of the most articulate voices chronicling the damage global warming does to ecological systems and the implications this carries for human life. Global warming stimulates the migration of all kinds of species so they can remain in climates that have nurtured them for millennia. This migration has been systematically monitored by scientists, but it has also been observed by ordinary people: farmers who see armadillos where they have never been before; birdwatchers who observe species entering new and exiting traditional geographic regions; hikers who notice plants blooming at odd times and tree lines moving up mountains. The migration of plants toward the poles and up mountains threatens species unable to migrate, which in turn threatens other species dependent on them for survival. Survival is further threatened by human-made barriers to migration such as giant highways and urban sprawl. Tropical disease-carrying insects move northward threatening populations that have no resistance to them. Jonathan Patz, a professor who has studied the effects of temperature on vector-borne diseases at the Center for Sustainability and the Global Environment at the University of Wisconsin, notes that a "half of a degree in temperature could mean the difference between a mosquito being infectious or not infectious."[16] Summing its broader effects, Patz says, "Global warming may be the largest public health threat we've ever faced."

This list is a far-from-exhaustive description of the hazards global warming poses in the near future. It is easy to see why scientists are so alarmed. Such concern must spread to the rest of us. Hurricane Katrina became a category 5 storm because of the unusually warm waters in the Gulf of Mexico. We are familiar with Katrina's devastation and with the fact that the government has thus far not been able to come up with the funds to repair the damage it caused. Multiply this experience many times; mix in new diseases, draughts, and floods in agricultural areas, and threats to fresh water supplies. Consider how long people will be likely to remain civil under the intensity of this devastation and the inability of the government to respond. Finally, recognize that greater devastation would be occurring simultaneously throughout the world. Such will be the costs of our indifference. The fact that bikes would likely be our only means of mobility is scant consolation.

Can We Respond? Not If ...

Certain aspects of global warming increase the difficulty of timely response. First, the most rapid changes stimulated by the process occur at Earth's extremities: at the North and South poles and on mountaintops. Despite the clear early warning signs, the mass of humanity experiences climate change in daily life as simply being a little warmer. In the winter, as chattering newscasters casually note, this may even be seen as a good thing. And unlike climate, weather is intermittent, making it easier to think unusual climate events are "natural." In the United States, the devastating hurricane season of 2005 was followed by a relatively docile season in 2006, encouraging the sentiment that maybe things are not so bad after all. Such thinking is encouraged by a news cycle oriented toward episodic events, not long-term trends. Thus, public opinion may not be aroused soon enough for timely action.

Another problematic aspect of global warming is that the process is not linear. It gathers speed as it unfolds. As Earth grows warmer, the soil becomes less capable of storing carbon, so more is returned to the environment. More significantly, the dazzling white of our vast Arctic expanses (called the *albedo*) has long served to stabilize Earth's temperatures because it reflects a high proportion of the sun's heat back into the atmosphere. As the ice melts, however, more of the sun's rays are absorbed by the water that was once ice, warming it and creating a feedback loop that escalates the pace of ice melt. Additionally, as the permafrost melts in Siberia, CO_2 that has been stored beneath the ice for eons will be released into the environment.

In short, human-generated CO_2 contains internal magnifier effects that, over time, will accelerate the pace of climate change. By September 2007, even experts were alarmed at the escalating pace of the ice loss in the Arctic. If the increased rate of melting continues, the summertime Arctic could be totally without ice by 2030, a date forty years earlier than previously anticipated.[17]

The long half-life of CO_2 poses another problem. Once it is released in the environment, it stays. Even if it is shut off like a spigot, excess CO_2 will continue to work its effects for generations. Both the escalating nature of atmospheric CO_2 and its staying power raise the question of a tipping point. It is possible that we will glide past that point—a point that is open to scientific dispute but that is clearly out there—where the process simply moves beyond our capacity to do anything meaningful about it. The abrupt changes that will eventually come with global warming will certainly capture the attention of the major media, but by then it will not matter.

The response of the United States to the climate crisis has been, to this point, dismal. A culture that promotes unrelenting consumption, directing people toward a narcissistic inwardness and away from a sense of community, is fertile soil for environmental indifference. The existence of vested interests that reap huge profits under the current energy system exacerbates the problem. This is especially the case because our political system requires politicians to raise ever-growing amounts of private money to enter and remain in public life. Add to this mix a unique media system that is sustained by promoting consumption and that therefore caters to those whose profits expand with consumption. In short, a disinterested public, a self-interested private sector, a hamstrung press, and the importance of political money have led us to the precipice of this disaster.[18]

Let us consider some specifics. Al Gore, who as a student was awakened to the potential disaster looming in global warming, stands as the most prominent U.S. politician who is an exception to the general trends. Through most of his career, he has tried to alert citizens to this increasing threat and to spur public action. His vice presidential nomination in 1992 was derided by President George H. W. Bush at the Republican convention that year. The elder Bush dismissed Gore's concern, telling an approving audience that he would "have us up to our necks in spotted owls.... He's crazy." While the president's comments drew media attention, his close ties to Texas and Saudi oil money did not. Despite Gore's presence, the Clinton administration's environmental record was a weak one. Public opinion revealed some national concern, but it was far down the list of priorities, and therefore little was done about it.

Beyond the sparse coverage, the mass media contribute to public disinterest in climate change in other ways. A study recently released by the Union of Concerned Scientists documents how ExxonMobil alone funneled nearly $16 million between 1998 and 2005 to advocacy organizations whose purpose was to instill doubt about global warming. The report compared this campaign with the efforts used by Big Tobacco to create doubt about the harmful effects of smoking.[19] In February 2007, the Intergovernmental Panel on Climate Change released its strongest report ever on global warming. On the day this report was issued, the American Enterprise Institute, a conservative think tank funded by ExxonMobil, offered $10,000 to scientists who would write articles critiquing the report.[20]

This $10,000 bribe is simply the latest episode in the sordid history of efforts to create uncertainty and buy public indifference. In the interests of "balance," stories on global warming have quoted a few skeptical scientists in great disproportion to their existence in the scientific community. The skeptics, moreover, have often worked for institutes sponsored by energy corporations, although this fact has rarely accompanied their statements. Including these skeptics obviously pleases important advertising clients such as energy and automobile corporations. As a result, a fuzzy picture about global warming has been presented to a public that is already distracted by the glitter of consumption. In politics, doubt is often sufficient to sustain the status quo. Human intervention has caused global warming; human intervention has also caused our indifference to it.

The Kyoto Protocol and Self-Interest

In 1997, under the auspices of the United Nations, representatives from around the world met in Kyoto, Japan, and promulgated the

Kyoto Protocol, a treaty that was the first worldwide effort to reduce global warming. The Protocol calls for signatories to voluntarily reduce CO_2 emissions by varying amounts. Developed nations were given more restrictions than developing nations. The treaty was not perfect, but it was at least a start, and it went into effect in 2006, once half the world's nations signed it. The U.S. Senate had balked at signing the treaty, but in the 2000 campaign the younger George Bush agreed with his opponent Al Gore that the Kyoto Protocol ought to be signed.

When Bush became president, the oil industry was jubilant. Both the president and vice president had worked for oil interests in their private lives, and oil money was vital to the Bush-Cheney ticket. One of Vice President Cheney's first acts was to summon industry leaders to Washington to work on administration energy policy. The Bush administration pushed through special tax cuts for oil interests and also sought to expand drilling off-shore and in the Alaska National Wildlife Refuge. The administration faithfully trumpeted the industry line that the science on global warming was not clear. It also actively suppressed information, generated by career civil servants studying this matter, that might cause alarm. The Government Accountability Project, a nonprofit watchdog group, released a 131-page report in March 2007 that chronicled broad White House efforts to stifle climate research.[21] The year-long study reviewed thousands of e-mails and memos that were obtained through the Freedom of Information Act and government whistle-blowers and it conducted dozens of interviews with public affairs staff and scientists. Administration tactics included the inappropriate editing, delay, and suppression of reports and restricting scientists' rights to be interviewed about their research.

President Bush soon reversed his campaign support for the Kyoto Protocol, making the United States and Australia the only two industrial nations that have not signed. He based this decision on the grounds of scientific ambiguity, also saying that it would hurt the economy and that it was unfair to the United States. He was assisted by key allies in Congress, especially Senate Environmental Committee chair James Inhofe, who called global warming "the greatest hoax that has ever been perpetrated on the American people."[22] Between 2001 and 2006, energy political action committees gave more than $500,000 to Inhofe's campaign war chest. This was more than three times the amount of any other industry.[23] Perhaps Inhofe's faithfulness to the interests of the energy industry is an accident, but it certainly was appreciated.

How well considered are the arguments offered by the opponents of the Kyoto Protocol? Would restrictions on carbon emissions hurt our economy? The answer very much depends on the perspective one has. Making industries more energy efficient might, at least in the short run, impose costs that would mean higher prices. Over a longer period, however, much of these costs could be recouped. Regardless, the "hurting industry" argument is a slippery slope; it has always been made by specific interests opposing efforts to promote a more general public interest. A hundred years ago, the meat-packing industry was "hurt" by government health standards established in that industry. Mining interests are similarly "hurt" because of safety standards for workers. Nuclear energy production is "hurt" by safety rules in production and waste disposal. We have long realized, even in this deeply capitalist country, that the right to profit is not unlimited. Sometimes it is rightfully overridden by the general interest. Arguing that restricting our carbon emissions will "hurt" our economy is therefore insufficient. It must also be shown that such restrictions are frivolous.

The longer view, a perspective that does not come easily in corporate boardrooms where heroes rise and fall based on quarterly earnings statements, brings a very different perspective to economic harm. To put it most forthrightly, the longer view holds that the cessation of life would actually be quite damaging to the economy. Even if we act now, Earth is going to warm some, and the Katrinas to come will exert a significant drain on our economy. The longer we wait, the more substantial the drain.

It is not clear, however, that combating global warming will harm our economy even over the narrow and short run that is President Bush's perspective. There certainly will be economic disruption, as some activities are scaled back and others developed. This will not necessarily provoke an economic contraction. The Apollo Alliance, a labor and environmental coalition seeking to create the next generation of environment-friendly jobs, has been central in presenting this claim, but it has been corroborated by other studies as well.[24] Many good jobs would be created by a shift to a society that is energy sustainable. Jobs in fossil fuel and auto production industries might contract, but jobs in solar and green industries and in home weatherization and mass transit expansion would increase. Our well-being is premised on economic growth, which in turn has assumed expanding material consumption. But human desire is infinite, and economic logic is unconcerned about the things that *ought* to be desired. Reducing global warming, therefore, need not dampen economic growth so long as desires are recalibrated to give primacy to those desires that also sustain life.

Thus, the first objection to Kyoto, that cutbacks in CO_2 emissions will hurt our economy, is not compelling. What about the second objection, that the treaty is unfair to the United States? Kyoto does not treat developing and developed countries in the same way, and the U.S. Senate unanimously passed a resolution in 1997 stating that the United States should not agree to cut emissions unless concomitant obligations were imposed on developing countries as well. At first blush, this may seem fair, but Kolbert reveals its perverse logic:[25]

> Suppose for a moment that the total [human-generated] CO_2 that can be emitted into the atmosphere were a big ice-cream cake. If the aim is to keep global concentrations below five hundred parts per million, then roughly half that cake has already been consumed, and, of that half, the lion's share has been polished off by the industrialized world. To insist now that all nations cut their emissions simultaneously amounts to advocating that industrialized nations be allocated most of the remaining slices, on the ground that they've already gobbled up so much.

Andrew Simms[26] adds a powerful moral point: Since global warming has worldwide effects, each human being ought to be held equally accountable for it. He notes that much of the less developed world suffers under debts imposed by the World Bank but argues, conversely, that the developed world is in deep, if unrecognized, "ecological debt." (Recall that the United States, the greatest debtor nation in this respect, has generated 30 percent of all human-caused CO_2 in the atmosphere.) To the extent that a person consumes more than his or her fair share of finite natural resources or has a lifestyle that pushes the ecosystem beyond its level of sustainability, a person runs up an ecological debt. He notes, for example that a typical American family consumes in a day and a half the fossil fuel that a Somali family consumes in a year. Simms's moral point is deepened when it is recognized that, though the effects of global warming will be worldwide, those suffering the most from it will be those who have done the least to bring it about.

Self-interest requires an additional consideration: World public opinion of the United States, well documented in Pew Charitable Trust international surveys, has plummeted in this young century. This trend is found on every continent, among allies and more hostile nations alike. Much of this has to do with the Iraq war, which most of the world sees as misguided. But there is also resentment of our arrogance, of our attitude that rules accepted by other nations do not apply to us. Global warming is in the forefront of these opinions, and Flannery notes why this is particularly ominous.[27] He observes that we are approaching a time when the human influence on climate will overwhelm all natural factors. At that time we will no longer be able to speak of "acts of God" because everyone will know they could have been averted. Would not renewed anger then be directed toward the United States, and can it be argued that we would not deserve it? Anyone who thinks our military power makes this anger irrelevant seriously misunderstands the world in which we now live.

Pedaling into a Future

The accelerated outflow of CO_2 comes largely from fossil fuel energy consumption. In 2004, 38 percent of energy consumed in the United States was in the transportation sector, 35 percent in industry, 16 percent in homes and residences, and 11 percent in commerce.[28] The transportation sector is a huge problem, as all of the energy consumed in that sector comes from oil. But coal, which is dirtier than oil, is heavily involved in the production of electricity used throughout the other three sectors. Capping emissions at current levels will not curb climate change. To account for industrial development in other parts of the world, the industrialized nations need to cut annual emissions by the year 2050 to 1990 levels, which assumes that the developing world will make "cleaner" decisions than have older industrialized nations.

This goal seems impossible, but it is not. It does require immediate action at all levels of social organization. Individuals must make wiser consumption choices. Global warming must enter into conversations and be in the forefront of voting decisions. Businesses must think long term, recognizing their obligations in the production and sale of goods and the tremendous stakes they have in altering course. Governments at all levels must provide the leadership necessary to avert disaster. Incentives must be provided that will speed the transition to soft energy alternatives, to dramatically increase energy-efficient homes and businesses, to stimulate denser living patterns, to require more efficient automobiles, and to expand transportation alternatives.

Robert Socolow, a professor of engineering at Princeton, is codirector of the Carbon Mitigation Initiative.[29] He became involved in this work because he recognized that climate scientists—those who look at research data every day and are most alarmed about global warming—are not necessarily best equipped to structure alternative paths. Socolow has modeled a path to stabilize the environment. The problem is so massive that he breaks it into more manageable blocks, which he calls "stabilization wedges." He has identified fifteen, more than is required to meet the goal. These include such things as wind electricity, use of photovoltaic (or solar) power, and home weatherization. Two wedges involve the automobile: (1) that cars be driven 50 percent less and (2) that they be twice as efficient.

Getting people out of cars is in the national interest, and this can be accomplished by decreasing the incentive to drive and increasing the attractiveness of alternatives. Increasing taxes on gasoline, as European nations have done, is the most direct way to reduce driving. If gas prices were raised to $5 a gallon, people would not only drive less and carpool more; they would demand energy-efficient cars. It seems equitable to ask those who pollute to pay a price for the general harm they cause. But increasing taxation on gas raises other equity problems. Some driving patterns are difficult to reduce over the short run, and a gas tax is regressive, imposing the greatest hardship on those who don't make much money.

To solve this problem, some environmentalists have proposed making the gas tax "revenue-neutral." Along with paying income taxes, working Americans also pay Federal Insurance Contribution Act (FICA) payroll taxes. Most people think these taxes pay directly for

Social Security and Medicare, but they are actually part of general revenues, and they are also regressive. The proposal is to cut FICA taxes in proportion to the amount that gasoline taxes would increase, so that the net revenue the government received would be the same. This "tax swap" would still provide a huge incentive for people to reduce their driving, but it would not "punish" those who could not. [30]

The shift away from cars will increase as alternatives become more attractive. Mass transit needs to be developed, as it is vastly more energy efficient than the auto system. Since bikes are carbon-free, they are an even better alternative. A well-developed, well-integrated biking/mass transit system is best of all, because it reduces the advantages of convenience that a car offers. A mass transit system cannot take everyone to their doorsteps, but it can take them a short bike ride away. On the other hand, sometimes inclement weather deters riding, but less so if bikes are allowed on an extensive transit system.

The juxtaposition of the words that title this chapter—*metapolitics, minibikes*—is, in part, meant ironically. It seems absurd even to mention such a humble machine in the context of the climate change crisis. There is not, moreover, a single solution to global warming. Anyone who says something like "Biking cannot address global warming because what we really need to do is . . ." underestimates both the nature of the problem and the potential of the bike. Many things must be done in different social spheres.

Getting people out of cars and onto bikes does have some important advantages. It can be done immediately, and, compared with some other wedges discussed by Socolow, it is inexpensive. The basic infrastructure is already there. Millions of bicycles currently sit unused in garages and basements. Suppose a city closed a few streets to motorized traffic and turned them over to pedestrians and bikers. The costs saved in road repairs on those routes would go a long way toward financing the other things—such as safe storage areas, bike stations, and showers—that would entice more riders to get into the saddle.

How much behavior could be changed? Currently less than 1 percent of all trips made in the United States are made by bicycle. We noted that in Amsterdam 40 percent of all trips are made by bike. Forty percent seems like an impossible goal in this country, where sprawl abounds, and perhaps it is, but it is inappropriate to establish an upper limit to the percentage of bike trips. For example, if something like the tax swap proposal went into effect, it would immediately put people onto bikes, but it would also do other things that would eventually increase biking. It would redirect people toward dense living patterns and away from suburban sprawl, and it would stimulate desire for mass transit. Each of these would in turn increase bike riding: Dense living patterns create shorter traveling distances; mass transit and biking are mutually reinforcing. The biking facility at the main terminal in Amsterdam allows thousands of commuters to jump on bikes and take short rides to work places. A full-service bike station at a CalTrain depot in Palo Alto, California, has enjoyed steadily increased use since it opened in 1999.[31]

Even as matters currently stand, there is much more room for biking in the United States than commonly recognized. When people think of biking instead of driving, they usually focus on longer commutes that make such a swap seem unrealistic. But Elizabeth Deakin, director of the Cal-Berkeley Transportation Center, notes that about 40 percent of all trips taken by car are under five miles. Bikes are an ideal mode of transport for these. Such numbers suggest that our low riding rates are connected less to utility than they are to habit. Deakin estimates that if urban areas make some accommodations to the bike—such as installing bike lanes and safe bike routes to major destination points, allowing bikes on mass transit, and establishing convenient and safe bike parking—bike trips could account for at least 20 percent of trips taken in the United States.[32] This alone would have a substantial impact on fuel consumption.

American culture encourages the idea that decisions and acts are usually discrete and isolated. But our world is highly interactive. Changes in one area have consequences that are often surprising, so it is useful to think more broadly about the meaning of significantly expanded bike riding. Each year billions of gallons of fuel are wasted idling in traffic.[33] Increased bike usage can, by relieving congestion, reduce this waste.

There is a less direct effect that increased biking could have on fuel consumption. Much has been written about the obesity epidemic in the United States, including its personal and social costs. Unhealthy diets and sedentary lifestyles are the two main sources for surging obesity. In fact, one of the reasons Congress enacted the Safe Routes

To Schools biking program was to combat obesity by encouraging children to be more physically active. Regular biking also would improve the health of adults and promote weight loss. Improbable as it seems, obesity connects to gasoline consumption. Two computer scientists at the University of Illinois[34] decided to test the relationship between weight gain and fuel consumption. Between 1960 and 2002, Americans became considerably fatter, averaging about a twenty-five-pound gain over that period. When the numbers were plugged into their model, calculating drivers and passengers and the effect that weight has on mileage efficiency, they were astonished by the results. Obesity costs about one billion additional gallons of gasoline annually, enough to fill 1.7 million cars for an entire year.

Thus far, we have focused on the effects that biking might have on one of the transportation "wedges" Socolow has identified. But this is not the upper limit of the bike's potential impact, for biking also changes consciousness, including consciousness about the environment. As noted in chapter 1, on a bicycle one feels the heat, notices the wind, and smells pollution every day. Biking also connects people to each other more immediately, cultivating the sense that the planet is something we share. Increased riding is therefore likely to stimulate more general environmental action. It will increase the chances that we will do things at the personal level beyond biking to combat climate change, and it will make that issue a more important consideration in evaluating politicians. Furthermore, riders are visible anti–climate change actors. Not all who notice them will immediately jump on bikes, but some will, and others will be encouraged to think about climate change and to become engaged in other ways. Such peripheral effects of increased biking are quite diffuse and impossible to measure. This makes them no less real and no less important.

This interactive model in which seemingly insignificant acts combine and recombine to build swifter currents of change is admittedly messy. But surely the model is messy because change is messy. A major venture capitalist firm that backed the developing Web sites Google, Amazon, and Netscape in their start-up days has now begun investing in clean technologies. In part, this company sees these technologies as a wave of the future, but the decision also comes from a desire to make them so. In a recent interview, John Doerr, a partner in the firm, attributed the decision to enter this field to a dinner conversation with

By 2007, even the Chicago Sun-Times had raised an inconvenient question, terrifying these students.

his young daughter about global warming, when she told him, "I'm scared. Your generation got us into this situation and you better get us out of it."[35] Who can say where the ripples caused by that young lady's pebble will end?

This chapter began by noting the five great eras by which geologists measure time. Ours is distinct in one sense: We understand what is happening to the planet, and we have the ability to correct it. The question is, Will we? One regularly encounters those who say things like "You'll never get people to give up their SUVs" or who otherwise think human beings are far too short-sighted to change. The problem with human nature arguments is that people never exist in a "natural" environment. Universally, they are located in socially constructed contexts that vary and evolve. Such contexts construe our assessment of human nature. Perhaps short-sightedness is cultural, not natural. We do know that people are capable of extraordinary responses when dire situations are clearly perceived. In any case, we must act on the assumption that the problem can be addressed. Consider the alternative.

Bill McKibben, who has thought as long and as clearly about the ecological crisis as anyone, makes a powerful argument for transitioning to a more localized economic model—one not based on the unsustainable assumption that more is inevitably better. In response to claims that such thinking is nostalgic, he makes a point that is relevant to our considerations: "What's nostalgic and sentimental is to insist that we keep doing what we're doing now simply because it's familiar. The good life of the high-end American suburb is precisely what's doing us in."[36]

There is movement as this book is being written. While people have long been vaguely concerned about global warming, it is beginning to gain traction in popular consciousness. An obvious indication of this is the rehabilitation of Al Gore in the national psyche. During his 2000 presidential campaign, he was the butt of many late-night jokes that played against his seriousness. In January 2007, however, Gore had a pretty good month. A Conservative and a Socialist Left member of the Norwegian Parliament combined to nominate him for a Nobel Prize, the film version of *An Inconvenient Truth* was nominated for an Academy Award (and went on to win for Best Documentary), and the British government mandated that it be shown in every public school in Britain.

The ubiquity of the climate change threat has also stimulated calls for action from unexpected quarters, including evangelicals and corporations otherwise aligned with the Bush administration.[37] In the absence of federal leadership, many states and cities have leapt ahead with plans for capping emission standards. Most important of these is California, where Republican governor Arnold Schwarzenegger has engaged the battle. These local efforts have stirred energy corporations to push for federal action. Shell's president John Hofmeister has said, "From Shell's point of view, the debate is over. When 98 percent of scientists agree, who is Shell to say, 'Let's debate the science?' … We cannot deal with 50 different policies…. We need a national approach to greenhouse gases."[38]

The impulse to change was also stimulated by the Democratic takeover of Congress in 2007. In the House, new Speaker Nancy Pelosi established a special select committee on climate change and asked for quick legislative action. Bike-friendly James Oberstar became chair of the House Transportation Committee. On the Senate side, Environmental Committee chair James Inhofe, who claims global warming is a great "hoax," was replaced by Barbara Boxer, who calls it "the greatest challenge of our generation." Several bills were immediately introduced, including one by new Vermont senator Bernie Sanders (cosponsored by Boxer) that is actually of sufficient scope to address the problem.

Led by President Bush, modern Republicans have generally resisted federal efforts to stem global warming. Nonetheless, federal efforts to conserve the environment are not inherently anticonservative. Since the days of Prime Minister Margaret Thatcher, British Conservatives have strongly supported state efforts to stem global warming. As the Bush-Cheney fossil fuel regime passes into history, it will open opportunities for conservatives in the United States to revive their conservationist tradition.

Bills are not laws; statements are not action. Vested interest in the status quo and, therefore, for mere cosmetic action, is substantial. Furthermore, in a presidential system like ours, significant achievement without decisive presidential leadership is virtually impossible. For those concerned about climate change, the 2008 election is crucial. The run-up to 2008—the actions taken at other levels, inside and outside government, the "noise" generated around global warming—will therefore likely shape the United States' response to this issue.

Scientists worry that we are approaching a climate change tipping point beyond which it will be impossible to recover. As noted, the situation we face raises basic questions about human nature. Alanna Mitchell, named by the Reuters Foundation in 2000 as "the best environmental reporter in the world,"[39] has begun to ask the prominent scientists she encounters a simple question: "Are humans a suicidal species?" It is an interesting but unanswerable question, and in any case, we will know soon enough. But, like the great changes that mark geologic time, political change also is not linear. Sometimes it leaps forward. It is necessary to push for another tipping point, one with enough mass to propel life on the planet toward sustainability.

An Inconvenient Truth ends by listing things each of us can do to reduce global warming. The bicycle receives only passing notice, which is understandable. Biking is one of many things individuals can do, and with the huge tasks confronting us, it does not seem particularly significant. But, if nurtured, biking will grow, and it immediately engages us in the broader battle. It is an ongoing act of nondestructive living, and in today's world, that is no small thing.

Chapter Nine

Conclusion

"There's Something About a Bike"

The desirability of bike-friendly policies extends far beyond the crisis of global warming and the fact that the bicycle barely leaves an environmental footprint. What is striking about biking is not that it solves any particular problem but, instead, that it is part of the solution to several. The rise of the bicycle is connected to its broad and inherent good sense. Those appearing in this book come from varying places in the social demography, but they share the conviction that the bike has multiple benefits. Bike riding is about much more than nonriders often assume, and this fires the imaginations of bike-friendly folks and inspires them. As I gathered information for this book, many of those interviewed would refer to a third party as an "avid cyclist." While the term obviously references someone who rides a lot, it suggests more than this. It suggests an altered understanding and consciousness that comes with time spent in the saddle.

Aurora city inspector Alan LaFan, introduced in chapter 1, struggled to pin down exactly what integrating the bike into his work life had meant to him. Initially motivated by a desire to lose weight, he found that switching to a bike brought many more changes than he had anticipated. LaFan is an ex-cop and no Pollyanna. He worried some about his enthusiasms and that he was going to sound a little odd mentioning them: his new sense of the environment, his greater contact with people, his more positive mental state, how people saw him differently, and so forth. He did not want to appear sentimental, and he had trouble identifying why a bike should provoke these changes, ending by saying, "There's something about a bike ...." Such sentiments might seem murky or odd to nonbikers, but I knew immediately what he was talking about because I had experienced similar feelings.

In 2000, the World Health Organization published its first report on healthy life expectancies, an index that measures a long life lived in good health.[1] Even though it is the richest nation and has the world's most expensive health care system, the United States was twenty-fourth in these rankings. How might we do better? Establishing a health care system that guarantees timely access to medical care for all is obviously crucial, as are healthy diets and refraining from smoking. But medical experts also recognize that physical inactivity contributes substantially to ill health. Obesity has sharply increased in recent decades, and one recent study now ranks it ahead of both smoking and drinking in its harmful effects on health.[2]

Some Americans get the exercise they need; the vast majority do not. Each January the nation's health clubs are jammed, and then February comes along. Exercise is commodified and stuffed into the corners of lives. Many drive to gyms to work out and stop after a while when such regimens become hard to maintain. It is far better to integrate exercise into daily routines, and bike riding is an excellent way to do so. Because it is so easy on the body, biking is also a form of exercise congenial to all phases of the life cycle. As is the case with global warming, the bicycle will not solve the national health problem, but it is a step in the right direction. Active Living by Design is a nonprofit organization that seeks to increase physical activity through community design, and biking has been integral to its efforts.[3]

The bicycle will not overcome alienation and social isolation in America, but it does work against it. In T. C. Boyle's novel *The Tortilla Curtain,* the world of illegal immigrants collides with that of an upper-middle-class California enclave that enjoys the inexpensive services illegals provide but is threatened by their presence. At several points, Boyle uses the car to reinforce the other-ness of the two groups. In one scene, a low-riding car cruises, aptly named Arroyo Blanco:[4]

> The car pulled slowly alongside him, and he could see that it was some sort of American car, older, a big boat of a thing with mag wheels and an elaborate metal-flake paint job. The windows were smoked and he couldn't see inside. What did they want—directions? No face was visible. No one asked. He cursed under his breath, then picked up his pace, but the car seemed to hover there beside him, the speakers sucking up all available sound and then pumping it back out again, *ka-thump, ka-thump, ka-thump* . . . the car crept past him and finally faded to a pair of taillights. . . . It wasn't until Delaney was inside, and the door locked behind him, that he thought to be afraid.

Nothing develops out of this scene, but in it the car represents a vague but ominous divide between "us" and "them."

The social isolation in our society is not the result of the car, but the car is a mode of travel that reinforces it. The bike is not the solution to social isolation, but it is a mode of travel that works against it. When Mayor Enrique Penalosa closed streets in Bogotá to auto traffic out of a desire to create a more civil society, he knew what he was doing, and people responded with requests for further closings. Biking brings people into contact at a level that encourages civility. Throughout Europe, people are warming to this idea. Earl Blumenauer is right to regard bikes as important components of livable cities. Getting on a bike changes one's perceptions and interests, and it also connects one to a broader community. The larger Critical Mass rides are quite heterogeneous, yet riding together creates a bond that cuts across the differences that exist.

Massachusetts assemblywoman Anne Paulsen is unlikely to "Dumpster dive" with the Rat Patrol, but she and they share common ideas about bikes. One reason Paulsen believes so strongly in children riding bikes is that it nurtures autonomy, which is also an important norm of the Rats. By itself, the bike does not make us autonomous, but it is a simple machine that anyone can understand. Its mysteries are not hidden under a hood, and in transit the bike provides a heightened sense that travel is under one's control. Rush hours, unanticipated road work, slow drivers, and the like, are easily negotiated. Is not road rage generated by a sense of victimization—that one's daily travel life (the car itself, as well as the drive) is beyond one's ability to control?

While riding with the ChiTown Cruisers, a club member told me how, since joining the club, he had begun to ride his bike to work. One of the things he most liked about the switch was the money he was saving and that he no longer felt he was at the mercy of oil companies. That conversation touched on another form of autonomy. The bike can liberate us from what Chris Carlsson has called "the rat wheel of car ownership and its attendant investments." Cars are expensive, and continuously so. According to Bureau of Labor Statistics data, the 2001 average annual household expenditure for car ownership and operation was $7,360, almost as much as families spent on food and health care combined.[5] Depending on where one lives, it is possible to reduce the amount spent on cars substantially or even to eliminate it. Put another way, no matter where one lives, car expenses can be reduced by use of the bike.

There is something else about riding. It puts one in a positive frame of mind. Not always, of course, but the tendencies are clear. LaFan recognized this point, as did Gin Kilgore, who noticed the pleasures in commuting, and Congressman Oberstar, who found biking to be a balm for the grief he felt at his wife's passing. Although the source has escaped me, I remember reading many years ago a claim made by an early biking enthusiast. He described biking as "the joy of moving to one's own glad effort." When Alex Wilson, who has never owned a car, began to print T-shirts to distribute at Critical Mass rides, he put the phrase "One Less Car" on the back. Wilson feels strongly that we need to reduce the number of cars we use, but he also came to feel that this slogan said too little about bikes. Bikes are antidotes to cars, but they are not merely that, so he started printing shirts that said, "Bikes Are Fun." And so they are. Doubters should simply visit the annual Multnomah County Bike Fair in Oregon, Iowa's RAGBRAI, or the nearest Critical Mass.

It is the sum of such things that creates passion for the bike, a passion more powerful because it is less a product of abstract thought than in-the-saddle experience. Karen Frost, the former executive director of Oregon's Bicycle Transportation Alliance, aptly summarized this perspective when she noted that the thing she liked most about her job was that one actually got to do what one was advocating. Similarly, Congressional Bike Caucus chair Earl Blumenauer was a little irritable because a minor injury was keeping him off his bike for a while.

This shared knowledge of the benefits of biking cuts across other differences its adherents have, and it is one of the most powerful factors in the biking movement. It helps to explain its success, but it also makes that success difficult to model. The rise of the bicycle in American political life does not follow an easily predicted causal sequence. It is not simply the result of a groundswell of popular interest, nor is it simply the idea of the political elite. It contains elements of both. The political leaders profiled in chapter 7 are not reacting to pressures that they feel from below. In different ways, each has rallied the biking community to the larger cause. But it is also clear that political advocacy groups have been quite effective in advancing bike friendliness. The rise also grows inadvertently, as more people get on bikes and eventually turn to bikes as a means of association.

In all of this, having bikers in key leadership, bureaucratic, and staff positions has been crucial. When James Oberstar began to think about biking policy, he asked a skilled staff member of his transportation subcommittee to draft bike legislation. He was aware of David Heymsfeld's technical skills, but he was more moved by the fact that Heymsfeld was an "avid biker" and that he could therefore be counted on to do the legwork necessary for this groundbreaking endeavor. The result was ISTEA.

Perceived self-interest is a powerful incentive for action, and it is not surprising that many are turning to the bike because they believe it is in their personal interest to do so. They save money, are physically better off, and so forth. Advocates for bike friendliness might be active in politics simply for such reasons. The intensity and dedication found in so many in this movement, however, rests in the perception that biking is not simply good for one's narrowly conceived self-interest but that it also serves the general interest.

This recognition of the common benefits of biking has stimulated a movement in Europe to makes bikes available to rent at very low cost—often at no cost at all. In a groundbreaking program run by the French company JCDecaux,[6] bikes may be checked out at any of a number of stations sprinkled throughout a city and returned to any station. Users pay an annual registration fee of about $6.50 and guarantee each checkout with a credit card. If bikes are returned to a station within a half hour, as most are, there is no charge. After the first half hour, the fee is one euro per hour. The first city to implement the program was Lyon, France's third-largest. It has since spread to several other cities, including Vienna and Brussels.

In the summer of 2007, the program received perhaps its biggest boost, as 1,450 stations with more than twenty thousand bikes were opened throughout Paris.[7] Paris deputy mayor Jean-Louis Touraine noted, "It has completely transformed the landscape of Lyon." Touraine has a feel for the subtle power of the bike, saying that the program is meant "not just to modify the equilibrium between the modes of transportation and reduce air pollution, but also to modify the image of the city and to have a city where humans occupy a larger space." By midsummer, the program, dubbed "Velib" (a contraction of the French words for *bike* and *freedom*), had clocked its first million rides. Once fully up and running, the deputy mayor for transport says that Velib will be carrying as many people as the Paris tramway. Paris mayor Bertrand Delanoe has already ordered a feasibility study for extending the program to the suburbs.[8] To bike advocates this program lends credence to the famous Paris sobriquet, the City of Light. Rob Sadowsky says the Chicagoland Bicycle Federation is seeking to make Chicago the first American city to have such a program.

Thinking about general well-being is unusual in a culture that encourages the opposite, but, as has been noted, that culture's resonance increasingly sounds off-key. He may not be aware of it, but sixteen-year-old Keegan Heron of Portland, Oregon, has put that culture on notice. Keegan became an avid rider in sixth grade when his school sponsored a bike-to-school week. As a junior at Cleveland High School, he organized a group of students to ride bikes to school every day. They converge at a point a couple of miles from school and then ride together to the campus. Initially, they were mainly motivated by a desire to do their part about cutting fossil fuel consumption, but they soon discovered the fun of biking. They like hanging out with each other on their way to school. An article written about this group by a local paper quoted Heron as follows: "Our culture is all about getting from one destination to the other. We have stopped enjoying the journey. Biking slows us down a bit."[9]

Advocates of bike friendliness face serious political obstacles, the most obvious of which is the concentrated economic power that seeks to sustain the dominance of automobility and siphon government resources to that end. But bike advocacy is buoyed by a confluence of personal and general interest that is likely to give it unusual staying power. Unlike weary motorists, no one I talked with in the bike movement is tired.

Chapter 3 suggested that the car ably serves as a metaphor for a culture that, one way or another, is dying. Perhaps the bike can be seen as a metaphor for a new era. Beyond placing us more centrally in the environment, a bike reminds us of truths that, if learned, will help sustain life. One of these is the virtue of simplicity. Another, dating to our earliest days of riding, is the importance of balance. A third is, as we ride up hills and down, both with winds and against them, there is no such thing as a free lunch.

Notes

Notes for Introduction

1. Harold Lasswell, *Politics: Who Gets What, When, How* (London: Meridian, 1958).
2. David Easton, *The Political System* (New York: Knopf, 1971).
3. Noreen S. Ahmed-Ullah and James Janega, "Don't Drive. Just Bike," *Chicago Tribune,* June 11, 2006, section A, 1.
4. Rachel Gordon, "Cycling Supporters on a Roll in S.F.," *San Francisco Chronicle,* August 21, 2006.
5. David V. Herlihy, *Bicycle: The History* (Taunton, Mass.: Quebecor World, 2004), 75.
6. Mark Twain, *A Connecticut Yankee in King Arthur's Court* (New York: New American Library, 1963), 272.

Notes for Chapter One

1. George Gerbner, Larry Gross, Michael Morgan, and Nancy Signarelli, "Television Violence, Victimization and Power," *American Behavioral Scientist,* May 1980, 705–16.
2. Clay McShane, *Down the Asphalt Path* (New York: Columbia University Press, 1994).
3. Mark Cloud, "Don't Look Back, Mr. Nice Guy Driver," *Chicago Tribune,* November 10, 2006, section I, 17.
4. Abraham Kaplan, *The Conduct of Inquiry* (San Francisco: Chandler, 1964), chap. 10.
5. David Herlihy, *Bicycle: The History* (Taunton, Mass.: Quebecor World, 2004), 344.

6. Herlihy, *Bicycle*, 264.

Notes for Chapter Two

1. Quoted in Ministry of Transport, Public Works and Water Management, *The Dutch Bicycle Master Plan* (Amsterdam: Author, March 1999), 20.

2. Ministry of Transport, Public Works, and Water Management, *The Dutch Bicycle Master Plan*, 31.

3. Ministry of Transport, Public Works, and Water Management, *The Dutch Bicycle Master Plan*, 30.

4. Ministry of Transport, Public Works, and Water Management, *The Dutch Bicycle Master Plan*, 31.

5. Directorate of Infrastructure, Traffic, and Transport, "Mission Statement" (Amsterdam: Author, 2005), 5.

6. John Pucher and Lewis Dijkstra, "Making Walking and Cycling Safer: Lessons from Europe," *Transportation Quarterly*, Summer 2000, 25–50.

7. Michael de Jong's story was reported in "Proselytizer for Pedaling Acts on His Words," *New York Times*, November 8, 2005, A27.

Notes for Chapter Three

This chapter is a distillation and extension of my argument contained in *Sense and Non-Sense: American Culture and Politics* (Upper Saddle River, NJ: Prentice Hall, 2001).

1. Clifford Geertz, *The Interpretation of Cultures* (New York: Basic Books, 1973).

2. Jessica Mitford, *The American Way of Death* (New York: Simon & Schuster, 1963).

3. Jeremy Rifkin, *The European Dream* (Cambridge: Polity, 2004), 284–88.

4. Jared Bernstein, *All Together Now: Common Sense for a Fair Economy* (San Francisco: Berrett-Koehler, 2006).

5. Alexis de Tocqueville, *Democracy in America* (New York: Harper & Row, 1966), esp. Part II.

6. Gordon S. Wood, *The Radicalism of the American Revolution* (New York: Vintage Books, 1991).

7. Garry Wills, *Under God* (New York: Simon & Schuster, 1991).

8. T. J. Jackson Lears, *Fables of Abundance* (New York: Basic Books, 1994), 46–56. The phrase "the other Protestant ethic" was coined by sociologist Colin Campbell.

9. Earl Shorris, *A Nation of Salesmen* (New York: Avon Books, 1994), 66.

10. Juliet B. Schor, *The Overspent American* (New York: Basic Books, 1998).

11. Quoted in David Rieff, *Los Angeles: Capital of the Third World* (New York: Touchstone, 1991), 45.

12. Table Base, the Gale Group Accession #25977612, "Table: Top Ten Ad Spenders, 2001 vs. 2002."

13. See Kenneth T. Jackson, *The Crabgrass Frontier: The Suburbanization of the United States* (London: Oxford University Press, 1985), for a lucid account of the development of suburbia and its social and cultural implications.

14. Clay McShane, *Down the Asphalt Path* (New York: Columbia University Press, 1994); Tom Lewis, *Divided Highways* (New York: Viking, 1997); Jane Holtz Kay, *Asphalt Nation* (New York: Crown Books, 1997).

15. National Public Radio (NPR), *All Things Considered*, "Social Isolation: Americans Have Fewer Close Confidantes," June 24, 2006. The NPR interview was with Smith-Lovin, one of the authors of "Social Isolation in America, 1985–2004," by Miller McPherson, Lynn Smith-Lovin, and Matthew Brashears, *American Sociological Review,* June 2006, 353–75.

16. Shankar Vedantam, "Social Isolation Growing in U.S., Study Says," *Washington Post,* June 23, 2006, A03.

17. Rieff, *Los Angeles,* 55.

18. Kay, *Asphalt Nation.*

19. This account is taken from a major investigative report published by Josh Harkinson, "The Mixmaster," *www.HoustonPress.com,* July 22, 2004.

20. Texas Transportation Institute, "2005 Urban Mobility Report," www.mobility.tamu.edu/ums.

21. Tom Vanderbuilt, "The Advertised Life," in *Commodify Your Dissent* (New York: Norton, 1997), 128.

22. Rifkin, *The European Dream,* chap. 1.

23. Schor, *The Overspent American,* chap. 5.

24. See Cliff Zukin, Scott Keeter, Molly Andolina, Krista Jenkins, and Michael X. DelliCarpini, *A New Engagement?* (New York: Oxford University Press, 2006), chap. 3 and *passim* for an excellent assessment of political activity of young people.

25. Rifkin, *The European Dream,* 358.

Notes for Chapter Five

1. David Herlihy, *Bicycle: The History* (New Haven, Conn.: Yale University Press, 2004), 187.

2. Andy Clarke, "125 Years and Counting," *League of American Bicyclists,* Spring 2005, 16.

3. This group has a very informative Web site at www.bikeleague.org. Much of the information on the League was gathered there. Additional information was gained

from interviews with Marthea Wilson, Anthony Yoder, and Walter Finch, all members of the Bike League's executive staff. The interviews were conducted in June 2006.

4. See "History of the Thunderhead Alliance," www.thunderheadalliance.org.

5. See "The 50-50 Project," www.planetbike.com.

6. Thunderhead Alliance, "Complete Streets Report," March 2005, www.thunderheadalliance.org.

7. See www.bikesbelong.org.

8. Information on the Chicagoland Bicycle Federation was obtained at its Web site, www.biketraffic.org, and in interviews with its current executive director, Rob Sadowsky; past executive director, Randy Neufeld; and the City of Chicago's bike coordinator, Ben Gomberg.

9. Information on the Bicycle Transportation Alliance was obtained at its Web site, www.bta4bikes.org; in Portland's 2005 Bicycle Friendly Community Application to the League of American Bicyclists; and in interviews with its former executive directors Karen Frost and Catherine Ciarlo, current BTA policy director Scott Bricker, and Congressman Earl Blumenauer.

Notes for Chapter Six

1. Chris Carlsson, ed., *Critical Mass: Biking's Defiant Celebration* (San Francisco: AK Press, 2002), 8.

2. See www.critical-mass.info. For those interested, this Web site also contains information about how to start and sustain a Critical Mass.

3. "Cyclists, the Police and the Rest of Us," *New York Times* editorial, December 29, 2006.

4. Carlsson, *Critical Mass*, 112.

5. Carlsson, *Critical Mass*, 78.

6. See www.geocities.com/colosseum/6213. Other useful information can be accessed at this site as well.

7. Robert D. Putnam, *Bowling Alone* (New York: Simon & Schuster, 2000).

8. Miller McPherson, Lynn Smith-Lovin, and Matthew E. Brashears, "Social Isolation in America, 1985–2004," *American Sociological Review,* June 2006, 353–75.

Notes for Chapter Seven

1. David Herlihy, *Bicycle* (Taunton, Mass.: Quebecor World, 2004), 359.

2. Perry, *Bike Cult,* 291.

3. Marcus Green, "Share the Road," *Louisville Courier-Journal,* March 8, 2007.

4. Abramson's National Bike Summit Address is available online at www.louis-villeky.gov/Mayor/Speeches/03-14-07-bikesummit.htm.

Notes for Chapter Eight

1. Tim Flannery, *The Weather Makers* (New York: Atlantic Monthly Press, 2006), 20.

2. Elizabeth Kolbert, *Field Notes from a Catastrophe* (New York: Bloomsbury, 2006), 162.

3. Flannery, *The Weather Makers,* chap. 5.

4. Flannery, *The Weather Makers,* 70–71.

5. Al Gore, *An Inconvenient Truth* (Emmaus, Pa.: Rodale, 2006), 37.

6. Kolbert, *Field Notes,* 133.

7. Jim Hansen, "The Threat to the Planet," *New York Review of Books,* July 13, 2006, 8, www.nybooks.com.

8. Robin McKie, "Global Warming: The Final Verdict," *The Observer,* January 21, 2007.

9. James Lovelock, *Gaia* (Oxford: Oxford University Press, 1979).

10. Flannery, *The Weather Makers,* 17.

11. Gore, *An Inconvenient Truth,* 196.

12. Gore, *An Inconvenient Truth,* 196; Flannery, *The Weather Makers,* 17–18.

13. Flannery, *The Weather Makers,* 142.

14. Gore, *An Inconvenient Truth,* 92.

15. *Chicago Tribune,* January 17, 2007, section I, 7.

16. Quoted in the official newspaper of the American Public Health Association, *The Nation's Health,* "Climate Change Predicted to Have Dire Effects on Health," April 2007, 12.

17. David Adam, "Loss of Arctic Ice Leaves Experts Stunned," *Guardian Unlimited,* www.guardian.co.uk/environment/2007/sep/04/climatechange.

18. For a more detailed discussion of U.S. media and the role money plays in our political life, see my two chapters, "Through a Glass Darkly: Television and American Electoral Politics" and "Politics and Money," in Bruce I. Newman, ed., *The Handbook of Political Marketing* (Thousand Oaks, Calif.: Sage, 1999).

19. Union of Concerned Scientists press release, January 3, 2007.

20. "Scientists Offered Cash to Dispute Climate Study," *Manchester Guardian,* February 2, 2007, www.guardian.co.uk.

21. "GAP Report Details Climate Science Politicization," March 27, 2007, www.whistleblower.org.

22.   James Inhofe, Senate floor speech, July 28, 2003.

23.   View contributions to Inhofe and other politicians at www.opensecrets.org.

24.   See www.apolloalliance.org. See also Carrie Sonnenborn, "Generating Jobs," *Perspectives on Society and Environment,* Spring 2000, 30.

25.   Kolbert, *Field Notes,* 155.

26.   Andrew Sims, *Ecological Debt* (London: Pluto, 2005), 98–99.

27.   Flannery, *The Weather Makers,* 284–89.

28.   "Annual Energy Outlook," released by the Energy Information Administration, December 12, 2005, www.eia.doe.gov.

29.   Kolbert, *Field Notes,* chap. 7.

30.   This particular proposal was made by Al Gore in an interview on *The Charlie Rose Show,* June 19, 2006.

31.   Active Living by Design Case Study, "Bikestation Makes Bicycling Convenient in Palo Alto CA," August 8, 2006, www.activelivingbydesign.org.

32.   Deakin made these projections, based on her research, in personal correspondence with me July 13, 2006.

33.   The Apollo Alliance estimates seven billion gallons of gas are wasted idling in traffic; see "Energy and Economy: The Facts," www.apolloalliance.org. The U.S. Department of Transportation puts the number at 2.3 billion; see www.fightgrid locknow.gov.

34.   Jon Hilkevitch, "Americans' Spare Tires Take Toll at Gas Pump, Study Says," *Chicago Tribune,* December 13, 2006, section I, 7.

35.   National Public Radio, *Weekend Edition,* Andrea Seabrook, reporter, December 18, 2006.

36.   Bill McKibben, *Deep Economy* (New York: Times Books, 2007), 122.

37.   Jane Lampman, "New Sermon from the Evangelical Pulpit: Global Warming," *Christian Science Monitor,* November 9, 2006; "US Corporations Call for Global Warming Action," dpa German Press Agency, January 22, 2007.

38.   Steven Mufson and Juliet Eilperin, "Energy Firms Come to Terms with Climate Change, *Washington Post,* November 25, 2006.

39.   Bill McKibben, "The Coming Meltdown," *New York Review of Books,* January 12, 2005, 7 (online version).

Notes for Chapter Nine

1.   World Health Organization press release, "WHO Issues New Healthy Life Expectancy Ranking," June 4, 2000, www.who.int.

2.   R. Sturm, "The Effects of Obesity, Smoking and Drinking on Medical Problems and Costs: Obesity Outranks Both Smoking and Drinking in Its Deleterious Effects on Health and Health Costs," *Health Affairs* 21 (2002): 245–53.

3. See www.activelivingbydesign.org.

4. T. Coraghessan Boyle, *The Tortilla Curtain* (New York: Penguin Books, 1995), 64.

5. The data from the Bureau of Labor Statistics were compiled by Bikes at Work, Inc., "The Real Costs of Car Ownership," February 16, 2007, www.bikesatwork.com.

6. "Paris Rolls Out Free Bikes in Bid to Cut Smog," MSNBC News Services, January 30, 2007, www.msnbc.com.

7. John Ward Anderson, "Paris Embraces Plan to Become City of Bikes," *Washington Post,* March 24, 2007, A10.

8. See rawstory.com/news/afp/Paris_bike_scheme_clocks_up_one_mil_08022007.html.

9. Noelle Crombie, "Cleveland Students Get Pumped on Way to School," *Portland Oregonian,* March 5, 2007, B1.

Index

About the Author

J. Harry Wray is a bike enthusiast and professor of political science at DePaul University in Chicago, one of the bike-friendliest cities in the nation. He received his B.A. from Whittier College and his Ph.D. from the University of North Carolina–Chapel Hill, where the country roads sparked his interest in biking. Now he teaches courses in which students bike through every side of the city of Chicago—from the South Side to the lakeside—and shows them how politics, economics, and the environment combine to affect culture and be affected by it. Wray's previous books include *Sense and Non-Sense: American Culture and Politics* (2000), and, with Robert D. Holsworth, *American Politics and Everyday Life* (1986).